THE GREEN CAPITALISTS

JOHN ELKINGTON is co-author of the No. 1 bestseller, *The Green Consumer Guide*, and one of Europe's leading environmental writers. His books include *Sun Traps*: The Renewable Energy Forecast; *The Gene Factory*: Inside the Biotechnology Business; *The Poisoned Womb*: Human Reproduction in a Polluted World and, with Tom Burke and Julia Hailes, *Green Pages*: The Business of Saving the World. He is a Director of SustainAbility Ltd, an environment communications company which aims to promote environmentally sustainable economic growth. He has visited nearly 300 companies worldwide and his clients have included BP, the Design Council, Glaxo, ICI, Lever, Procter & Gamble and the World Resources Institute. John Elkington also sits on the advisory panels at the Central Electricity Generating Board, the Merlin Ecology Fund and the Nature Conservancy Council. SustainAbility is currently developing a Green Consumer Marketing joint venture with Brand New Product Development and PA Consulting Services. In 1989 John Elkington was elected to the United Nations' Environment Programme's Global 500 Roll of Honour.

TOM BURKE is Director of The Green Alliance and Policy Advisor to the European Environment Bureau. He was a member of the UK National Committee for European Year of the Environment and served on the Environment Panel of Industry Year 1986. He is a member of the Executive Committee of the National Council of Voluntary Organisations and of the Board of Directors of Earth Resources Research. Tom Burke has contributed to and co-authored numerous publications including *The Gaia Atlas of Planet Management* and *Green Pages*: The Business of Saving the World.

THE GREEN CAPITALISTS

How to Make Money—and Protect the Environment

by

JOHN ELKINGTON

AND TOM BURKE

LONDON
VICTOR GOLLANCZ LTD
1989

First published in Great Britain 1987
by Victor Gollancz Ltd,
14 Henrietta Street, London WC2E 8QJ

First published in Gollancz Paperbacks 1989

British Library Cataloguing in Publication Data
Elkington, John, *1949–*
    The green capitalists: how to make money—and protect
    the environment
    1. Environment. Conservation. Role of industries
    I. Title   II. Burke, Tom
    333.7'2
    ISBN 0-575-04583-3

To Max Nicholson, always ten years ahead of the field and
one of the architects of the Environmental Revolution.

Photoset in Great Britain by
Rowland Phototypesetting Ltd, Bury St Edmunds, Suffolk
Printed in Finland by Werner Söderström Oy

CONTENTS

ACKNOWLEDGEMENTS

Given the breadth of its subject, *The Green Capitalists* inevitably draws on a wide range of sources. Some of the more important published sources are listed in the recommended reading section on page 255. Addresses are also given on page 253 for some of the organizations which can provide follow-up information. But most of the information presented here came in other ways, through consultancy projects, company visits, conferences, continuous reading of a wide range of publications, and personal contacts. In these circumstances, a full acknowledgement of all those who have contributed to the shaping of the book is out of the question, but there were certain contributions without which the book would probably never have come together.

Tom Burke, Director of the Green Alliance, has had a very considerable influence on the book, commenting on drafts, contributing directly to Chapter 2 and writing Chapter 11.

I should also like to thank Stan Hope, executive secretary of the International Petroleum Industry Environmental Conservation Association (IPIECA), for his help in interesting both Shell International Petroleum and British Petroleum (BP) in underwriting some of the research and travel involved. The World Wide Fund for Nature (UK) and the J. Paul Getty Jr. Trust assisted with a grant towards the research phase of the project.

A good deal of the information contained in these pages was produced during projects which I undertook as a consultant for industrial clients (such as BP, Glaxo, ICI, the Institute of Petroleum and Monsanto), for government clients (such as the Department of the Environment, the Nature Conservancy Council, OECD and the United Nations Environment Programme), and for clients from the ranks of the non-governmental organizations interested in sustainable development, including the Centre for Economic and Environmental Development (CEED), the International Institute for

Environment and Development (IIED), and the World Resources Institute (WRI). Again, I should like to thank them all for their support, with a particular mention for Stan Parkinson of the Institute of Petroleum, who died before this book was completed.

As far as individuals go, many people have helped in a variety of ways. Pamela Norris, and David Burnett and Liz Knights at Victor Gollancz helped shape the manuscript, although neither they nor anyone else mentioned here is in any way responsible for the remaining defects.

I should also like to recognize the support given by Dr Janet Brown and Gus Speth of WRI; Peter Bunyard and Dr Dhira Phantumvanit (then at the United Nations Environment Programme's Industry & Environment Office in Paris), with whom I worked during and after the World Industry Conference on Environmental Management (WICEM); Timothy Cantell, Helen Holdaway and Nancy Pace of the Royal Society of Arts and the Pollution Abatement Technology Awards; Ian Allan, Editor of the *ICI Magazine*; John Boswell, Editor of *Glaxo World*; Andrew Harper, Editor of the *BP Shield*; and Tim Radford, Editor of the Futures pages of *The Guardian*. All provided fascinating commissions which helped shape the content of *The Green Capitalists*.

Throughout the 1980s, I have drawn heavily on the resources of Environmental Data Services, publishers of the *ENDS Report* which I quote on a number of occasions through the book. Georgina McAughtry and Marek Mayer have been a constant support. Indeed without ENDS, and the backing given to the company over the years by David Layton and Max Nicholson, this book would have been impossible.

I have gathered a great deal of information on the environmental aspects of biotechnology while acting as Editor of *Biotechnology Bulletin* and am very grateful to Catherine O'Keefe, Anita Urquhart, Nicky Purkiss and, most particularly, Nick Coles for their support over the years. *The Green Capitalists* also synthesizes work I did while writing previous books, most particularly *The Ecology of Tomorrow's World*, *Sun Traps*, *The Poisoned Womb* and *The Gene Factory*. In places I have drawn on all four, and should like to thank Penguin, Viking and Century Hutchinson for their permission to do so.

My thinking on the role of the environmental entrepreneur has benefited enormously from the work I was involved in at Earthlife and Bioresources Ltd. I have also greatly enjoyed working with Brian Johnson and am grateful to him for providing me with an early draft of his study focusing on the extent to which IBM has embraced sustainable development principles (see page 217). Additionally, a project I carried out for Groundwork, which involved visiting Groundwork Trusts around Britain, helped me further develop my thoughts on the environmental entrepreneur —indeed, my report was entitled *Groundwork: The Environmental Entrepreneurs*. My thanks here go to John Davidson and John Iles of the Groundwork Foundation and to the Trust directors, who took me around many of Groundwork's environmental rehabilitation projects in the North West of England.

But my greatest debt reflects the fact that the bulk of the book was written in time that should have been my family's, so I should like to conclude by thanking Elaine, Gaia and Hania for their unflagging support and Julia Hailes, Nancy Pace and Jonathan Shopley at John Elkington Associates and SustainAbility Ltd for helping me bring other challenging projects through to successful completion while *The Green Capitalists* took shape. Anyone who is interested in receiving further information on our next generation of projects, including *Green Pages* and *The Green Consumer Guide*, can contact us at the address given on page 254.

John Elkington
London, June 1987

FOREWORD TO 1989 EDITION

The events of two years since *The Green Capitalists* first went to press have seen extraordinary developments. The environment has gone straight to the top of the international political agenda, with speeches by politicians such as Mikhail Gorbachev, Margaret Thatcher and George Bush. At the same time, concerns raised by such issues as the Antarctic 'ozone hole', the Greenhouse Effect, toxic waste shipments and the deaths of North Sea seals and dolphins on the East Coast of the United States have convinced ordinary people that to wait for new regulations may be to wait too long.

The emergence of the Green Consumer in Britain was one of the most striking phenomena of 1988/9—and the trend continues to build with the approach of the Single European Market in 1992. *The Green Consumer Guide*, which I wrote with Julia Hailes, became a No. 1 best-seller. The business reaction was prompt: major supermarket chains like Tesco announced that they were 'going green' and the screws began to tighten sharply on manufacturing industry. The 1990s will see many environmental problems brought into sharper focus, but the late 1980s have shown that environmentalists can use the market to force industry to provide products that 'don't cost the earth'.

John Elkington

INTRODUCTION

There was something distinctly odd about the photographs, recalled Charles Brookes, a senior vice president at W. R. Grace & Co, the US chemical company. Someone had suggested that he decorate his office with a set of aerial photographs of the chemical company's Curtis Bay plant, in Maryland. To his dismay, he and his staff found a 'two-square-mile red blotch staring at us,' produced by a chemical Grace had been dumping into Chesapeake Bay. When Mr Brookes asked a subordinate to 'do something about the pollution,' the man repaired to his office. He returned later with a new set of photographs in which the red areas had been neatly airbrushed out. 'That was his solution,' Mr Brookes explained. 'That was 1970,' he added. 'We didn't think about these things.'

The intervening years have seen a relentless intensification of the environmental pressures operating on industry. Indeed leading industrialists expect no let-up in the environmental pressures on their operations. 'Most political commentators seem to agree that concern for the environment is one of the growth issues of the future,' as BP Oil International chairman, Peter Cazalet, summed up the prospect. Worse, from the industrialist's point of view, what one might call the "green agenda" has shown an alarming tendency to proliferate.

'One consequence of economic growth and technological advance,' Cazalet noted, 'is that there seems to be an ever increasing list of environmental concerns. Despite the enormous improvements that have been made in the environmental sphere, there is almost no limit to the number of environmental issues which claim the attention of interest groups.'

Strikingly, though, when Thomas Peters and Robert Waterman published their best-selling book *In Search of Excellence: Lessons from America's Best-Run Companies*, the green agenda did not rate even a single paragraph. But, as *The Green Capitalists* shows, many of the 'excellent' companies highlighted by Peters and Waterman have also built up a reputation for environmental excellence. For, while environmental excellence may not be a sufficient condition for business success in today's world, it is certainly now a necessary one.

Increasingly, major industrial projects are being halted because they are environmentally unacceptable. Even the World Bank, which has long championed free market forces, suspended a $256 million loan to Brazil, on the grounds that the Polonoroeste project in Amazonia would be environmentally devastating. Other projects, into which Western donors had planned to inject a total of $900 million, have also been abandoned or delayed. Meanwhile, the number of industrial products which have come under environmental scrutiny is constantly growing. Many have had to be reformulated or redesigned, while others have been banned outright.

In fact, despite the occasional claim that the 'environmental crisis is over,' there is growing international concern about a number of pressing environmental issues. These may focus on specific industries, like the nuclear power industry in the wake of Three Mile Island or Chernobyl, the toxic waste disposal industry in the wake of Love Canal and Times Beach, or the chemical industry in the wake of Bhopal or the pollution of the Rhine by Sandoz; on specific types of pollution, such as groundwater pollution, 'acid rain' or the build-up of carbon-dioxide in the atmosphere; or on the erosion of biological diversity, with the impending destruction of the world's tropical rainforests seen as a particular concern.

Most western environmentalists have been inclined to blame such problems on capitalism, which they see as little more than institutionalized greed. The scandals which have plagued Wall Street and London's City have done nothing to change their minds. Ivan Boesky, who pleaded guilty to 'insider trading' on the grand scale, had once bragged that 'greed is healthy. You can be greedy and still feel good about yourself.' Short-sighted greed, however, is an enemy both of the environment and of sustainable economic growth.

There certainly is no denying that market pressures have encouraged many businesses to 'externalize' a significant proportion of their production costs by imposing them on their workforces (with, for example, unsafe working conditions), on local communities (for example, high noise levels), on consumers (for example, defective products based on inadequate research or quality control) and on the environment (for example, pollution).

From an environmental perspective, it is fair to say, there are some fundamental flaws in today's economic rationality. The Greens, who espouse the 'politics of ecology' (see page 60), have challenged many key economic concepts, including the inevitability (and desirability) of exponential economic growth, the conventional definitions of 'wealth' and the methods currently used to calculate Gross National Product (GNP).

Admittedly, even today, the 'profitability' of a given business very much depends on where those who run the business choose to draw their 'bottom line', with costs above the line and profits below. Some of the basic approaches used by contemporary economists, are hardly conducive to sound long-term thinking about environmental problems. Economists, in short, tend to 'discount' the future, using interest rates to make tomorrow comparable with today. Just to show what happens, if you assume a ten-per-cent annual discount rate, $1 million in 100 years is worth just $73 today. This sort of thinking can be very helpful in planning a five-year business programme, for example, but it can lead to some highly undesirable outcomes if the business is involved in the exploitation of 'free' natural resources such as tropical rainforest timber, ocean resources or the absorptive capacity of the atmosphere. Many projects thus look attractive simply because the benefits arrive soon and are therefore discounted less, whilst the costs, only appearing in the distant future, are so discounted as to appear small.

However, *The Green Capitalists* is not a tract on environmental economics, nor does it argue that economics is an environmentally unsound discipline. Like any tool, economics can be used constructively or destructively. All too often, it is true, economic arguments are used to buttress environmentally unsound or 'unsustainable' industrial practices. But later chapters show that the environmental concerns and controls which have emerged in recent years have helped to reshape the markets within which industry operates and will continue to do so, forcing it to develop new practices, new technologies and new product ranges which are more environment-friendly.

Green to the core?

One characteristic marked out the 'excellent' companies analysed by *In Search of Excellence*. They were, and generally still are, highly innovative. Such companies, Peters and Waterman concluded, 'are especially adroit at continually responding to change of any sort in their environments.' In fact they defined eight main criteria of excellence. These were: a bias for action; a willingness to listen and respond to customers; an emphasis on autonomy and entrepreneurship, with risk taking seen as an essential feature of innovation; a focus on achieving high quality and productivity by tapping the skills and enthusiasm of everyone working for the company; an aversion to branching out into unknown businesses; an elegantly simple and lean organization; and a combination of 'simultaneous loose-tight properties,' coupling decentralization and autonomy with a strong emphasis from the centre on a few core values.

As later chapters show, most 'excellent' companies now include environmental quality objectives among their core values. But companies run on exactly these lines can still be hit hard by environmental issues. In the service sector, for example, Peters and Waterman highlighted McDonald's as an 'excellent' company, yet McDonald's has found it hard to shake off persistent—but erroneous—claims that it has been involved in tropical forest destruction. Part of the problem was that the company relied on libel law to pursue those who attacked its record, rather than producing and publicising a clear written environmental policy statement. It has maintained that unwritten policies had been in place all along. However, McDonald's switched its tactics in mid-1989, producing its first written policy statement focusing on the tropical forest issue.

'Excellent' companies may have a profound impact on the natural environment, whether through the production of raw materials and energy, manufacturing and distribution, or through the impact of their products in use. General Motors, for example, was another of the companies endorsed by Peters and Waterman, but think of the pollution caused during the lifetime of the millions of cars made by the world's largest auto manufacturer and of the millions of acres of agricultural land which have been paved over to accommodate them.

Even the most environmentally committed industrialists stress that new laws and standards are essential if the market is to produce the desired results. The difficult balancing act now facing the world's environmental regulators requires them to set standards which ensure that the green agenda is not wiped off the slate by other pressing priorities in an increasingly competitive world market, while simultaneously ensuring that the controls imposed do not knock the wind out of the private enterprise system. Increasingly, there is agreement that much of the primary legislation needed to prevent the most obvious environmental harm is in place, at least in the industrial countries, where the regulatory effort now needs to be concentrated on ensuring the effective enforcement of this legislation.

There is no reason why private enterprise should be any more environmentally damaging than public or state enterprise. The United States may have given us Three Mile Island, but the Soviet Union topped that with Chernobyl. Early estimates put the cost of the Chernobyl disaster, which had spread radioactivity across Europe, at around £4 billion—and the figure has continued to climb. Indeed, some of today's worst examples of conventional, non-nuclear pollution are also to be found in such communist bloc countries as Poland, Czechoslovakia and the Soviet Union. The evidence suggests that once capitalists and entrepreneurs are convinced that environmental regulations are here to stay and that they will be enforced, they respond much more rapidly to the challenge than do highly bureaucratic societies.

Interestingly, when Mikhail Gorbachev visited Britain shortly after taking power, he indicated that he felt that a degree of privatization might help his country tackle its deep-seated economic problems. 'We want decentralization and market forces in industry,' he said, 'and the kind of technical innovation that exists in your ICI.' Mr Gorbachev may not have been aware of the fact, but ICI has been one of the pioneers of environmental excellence in British industry, as Chapter 5 explains. Such companies are responding to the environmental challenge by developing new technologies which are cleaner, quieter, less resource-intensive and increasingly energy efficient.

Enterprise may still be part of the problem, in short, but it is increasingly being invited to ensure that it is part of the solution. For example, at the same time that the World Bank was suspending funding for the Polonoroeste project, its president was calling on governments to harness the skills and resources of the private sector to help the developing countries achieve environmentally sustainable economic development. 'There is an urgent need,' he stressed, 'to reduce, if not finally eliminate, the chronic lack of mutual confidence between developing country governments and business, and to expand and release the energies of the private sector. Its participation in the development process is not an option; it is an essential.'

This view had also been heard a couple of years earlier at the World Industry Conference on Environmental Management (WICEM), held in Versailles late in 1984. The conference attracted more than 500 top-level delegates from 71 countries and proved to be one of the most significant environmental milestones since the 1972 Stockholm Conference, which first placed environmental protection on the world agenda.

Sponsored by the United Nations Environment Programme (UNEP), itself set up as a direct result of the Stockholm Conference, and the International Chamber of Commerce, WICEM highlighted some exciting and highly innovative approaches to environmental management now being pioneered by major industrial companies. Launching the conference, the French Prime Minister, Laurent Fabius, asked whether such an event 'could have been held 20 years ago, or even 10?' He thought not, stressing that WICEM showed 'a dawning awareness on the part of industrialists that they must participate actively in managing the ecological problems engendered by their activities.'

A creative contribution

Many industrialists had originally accepted the invitation to come because they sensed a new mood in the air and the several hundred industrialists who actually attended WICEM found a new appreciation of the key role which they can, indeed must, play in achieving environmentally sound economic development, or, to use the jargon, *sustainable development*.

'Industry's vast experience in the hands-on solving of environmental problems means that industrialists are practical experts in a field in which we (professional environmentalists) are often still theorists,' admitted UNEP executive director, Dr Mostafa Tolba.

But perhaps the most telling comment on industry's uncomfortable position in recent years came from Mrs Gro Harlem Brundtland, former (and subsequently re-elected) Prime Minister of Norway and chairman of the World Commission on Environment and Development.

'You, as industrialists, are often regarded as the prime source of environmental problems, especially pollution,' she began. 'However, you are also seen as the source of comforts, convenient machines, clothes, cars and many basic ingredients of a good life. You are also the source of development and of jobs. You are thus both reviled and appreciated, very often by the same people, although at different times.'

This paradox was all-too-familiar to the industrialists present. They were able to recognize the world which was being discussed as the one in which they, too, operated, with all its day-to-day problems, many of them having nothing to do with the environmental debate and the emerging green agenda. This proved enormously reassuring. The additional fact that they were not having to devote every last ounce of their energy to defending the industrial ethos meant that they could focus much more effectively on their potential contribution to an environmentally sustainable future.

This contribution, as Dr Otto Koch, a director of Bayer, the West German chemical company, put it, 'must be seen as a creative task'. Increasingly, environmentalists are not asking industrialists to put themselves out of business, but to recognize that the worldwide drive for sustainable development will mean new economic opportunities for those companies which are quickest on their feet. Industrialists must recognize, as Dr Koch stressed, that 'the aim of environmental protection consists neither in restoring the past nor in maintaining the *status quo*, but in creating a contribution to the future.'

Even so, if any one word summed up the initial reactions of the journalists attending the WICEM press briefings, it was disbelief. Many simply could not take in what they were hearing. Informed that leading industrialists from all over the world had come to Versailles to report how they were beginning to achieve economic growth and environmental conservation simultaneously, the press clearly had its doubts.

'What our readers will ask themselves,' insisted the man from Associated Press, 'is what does it all mean? Do these industrialists really mean what they say? Will WICEM really change industrial priorities? Do all industrialists, or even many of them, operate—or even think—like those who have spoken here?'

Then, just a few weeks after WICEM had concluded, came one of life's hideous coincidences. In India, over 2,000 people were killed and tens of thousands of others severely gassed in the world's worst industrial disaster to date. Union Carbide joined such companies as Amoco, General Public Utilities and Hoffmann-La Roche in the ever expanding environmental rogues' gallery.

Catastrophe or cornucopia?

Seasoned public interest campaigners, like America's Ralph Nader or Jeremy Rifkin, or Des Wilson in Britain, who continue to challenge the might of the corporate giants with the slenderest of resources will never be convinced that the free market could work in a way which was environmentally acceptable. Indeed, their unyielding suspicion and willingness to undertake long and arduous campaigns have been key factors in forcing major companies to clean up their operations. The importance of the environmental pressure groups is unlikely to fade, although the agenda they address —and the ways in which they do so—will certainly continue to evolve.

Major government reports like *The Global 2000 Report to the President*, prepared for President Carter, have argued that by the end of the century the world 'will be more crowded, more polluted, less stable, and more vulnerable to disruption than the world we live in now. Serious stresses involving population, resources and environment are clearly visible ahead.' The answer, the Global 2000 team implied, is more government intervention, particularly at the international level, and the introduction of government controls on the allocation of scarce natural resources.

The counter-arguments were soon laid out by Julian Simon and the late Hermann Kahn in *The Resourceful Earth: A Response to Global 2000*. 'If the present trends continue,' they argued, 'the world in 2000 will be less crowded (though more populated), less polluted, more stable ecologically and less vulnerable to resource-supply disruption than the world we live in now.' Their central argument was that the longer term balance between supply and demand can always be achieved by means of the price mechanism, with the free market responding to such crises as the OPEC energy crises by encouraging the development of alternative resources and more resource-efficient technologies.

As usual, there is truth on both sides. Private enterprise certainly has a critical role to play in the drive for sustainable development, but will need to ensure that it achieves environmental excellence in its investments and operations. Environmentally unsound activities are ultimately economically unsound. At the same time, even industrialists who are relatively optimistic about the environmental outlook accept that their companies have a great deal to do if their operations are to remain environmentally sustainable.

These themes were developed in depth in *Our Common Future*, the report of the World Commission on Environment and Development. The Commission, also known as the Brundtland Commission, produced a report which was much more pro-industry than previous reports in this field had been. Industry, it concluded, is 'an indispensable motor of growth'. But economic activity, the Commission pointed out, must enter a new era of 'growth that is forceful and at the same time socially and environmentally sustainable'.

The implications of all this for industry are tremendous. 'If the scenario is that we continue our current development without too many shock effects in the world,' as Shell managing director Jan Choufoer had told his staff, 'you will see a lot of things implemented —for instance, catalytic converters in motor car exhausts; further increased desulphurization of fuels, both coal and oil; and flue gas clean-up at power stations and large industrial plants. You will find that waste disposal from factories is no longer tolerated as part of industrial activity. You will have to swallow your own waste.'

But shocks, of course, are guaranteed. Shortly after Mr Choufoer made these comments, the price of oil began to plummet on world markets, leaving companies like Shell hard hit, while many of the smaller independent companies were forced to slash their staffs and exploration programmes. But the basic principle of what he said is eminently sound. Indeed, one of the most important factors now driving us forward is the emergence of a new generation of top industrialists drawn from the ranks of what might be called the 'environmental generation', if not actually from the ranks of 'Nader's Raiders'.

The younger people now moving into management and research

posts, as Choufoer pointed out, 'bring their ideas and ideals with them, and they often have somewhat different values from the older generation.' While increasing numbers of industrialists are being seconded to environmental organizations, to help them manage growth, so a number of environmentalists have moved across to work in industry. George Pritchard of Greenpeace, for years a leading campaigner against Britain's nuclear industry joined forces with entrepreneur Alex Copson to develop new ways of disposing of nuclear wastes under the sea-bed. Graham Searle, who played a leading role in establishing Friends of the Earth in Britain, became a consultant to Rechem, a waste incineration company which had been the subject of considerable controversy. These moves were themselves highly controversial, with environmentalists like Jonathon Porritt talking in terms of 'watchdogs' becoming 'lapdogs,' but they also may represent a significant milestone on industry's road to environmental acceptability.

Women, meanwhile, have often been at the forefront of the emerging trend towards environmental enterprise. One of America's most sought-after management consultants, Rosabeth Moss Kantner, lived in a rural commune in Vermont during the 1960s. As *Business Week* reported, she had 'successfully transformed the exuberant "can-do" philosophy of the Kennedy years, with its echoes of optimism, individualism and social engineering, into a message of corporate rejuvenation.' As Kantner herself put it: 'A lot of Sixties phenomena—the collectives, the alternative institutions, the small enterprises—were entrepreneurial activities.'

The financial world, meanwhile, had been nonplussed by the astounding growth and profitability of The Body Shop chain in country after country. The most striking feature of The Body Shop's corporate culture has been its focus on such 'green' issues as conservation, animal experiments, youth employment and Third World development. Even in today's world, it is unusual for the *Financial Times* to mention the word 'ecology' when talking about a successful business, except where a company has run into environmental opposition. But the word popped up a number of times when The Body Shop was profiled in the pink pages. 'There is something magical about small companies run by people whose thinking was forged in the Sixties,' commented Anita Roddick, the group's founder and managing director. 'You sit down and ask not only how the business should be run, but also what should be done with the profits.'

The emergence of a new breed of 'green' capitalist and of what one might call 'environmental entrepreneurs' is an enormously hopeful trend. They are bringing new perspectives to bear on the future. Indeed, the time has come to identify and develop the industrial constituency for sustainable development. As Continental Group chairman Bruce Smart put it, 'the needs of future generations must rank equally with those now on earth. Yet the unborn do not vote, invest or demonstrate. Someone must speak for them.'

The Green Capitalists shows how environmentalists are moving from reaction to action, from analysis to response. In taking a more positive stance on some issues they are not replacing conflict with co-operation, but adding more constructive roles to their existing campaigning activities. They recognize that no government, or collection of governments, can cope with the environmental agenda in isolation. The role of the non-governmental sector, and increasingly of the new breed of environmental entrepreneur, is likely to be an essential ingredient in the transformation which is beginning to take place in the economies of most major industrial nations.

The book also reveals that the world's environmentalists no longer have a monopoly on environmental thinking. Indeed, later chapters explore the ways in which leading companies in the oil industry, the chemical industry, the engineering industry and the biotechnology industry, to take just a few examples, have adapted to environmental constraints and are beginning, in many cases, to exploit environmental opportunities.

Technologies, like organisms, evolve. Like organisms, too, they are subject to natural selection pressures. Technologies, indeed entire industries, which continue to damage the environment will be judged unfit for survival. Meanwhile, new technologies are emerging which promise to power a 'green sunrise,' as Chapter 8 explains. But if companies are to adapt to, and benefit from, such changes in their business environment, they will need to take the *Ten Steps to Environmental Excellence* outlined in Chapter 10, as have the environmentally excellent companies described in Chapter 9. The final chapter, Chapter 11, provides some pointers for the future.

I

CONFLICT

The Green Battlefront

Chapter 1

THE CUTTING EDGE

Successive industrial revolutions have unleashed
successive waves of environmental degradation. We are
currently in the midst of a new industrial revolution
which will produce its own unique pattern of
environmental impacts. The 'smokestack' industries of
yesterday may be giving way to the 'sunrise'
technologies of tomorrow, but even gleaming Silicon
Valley has its darker, polluted side.

We are looking over the shoulders of two people, one stark naked, the other wearing a white laboratory coat. Each is examining a small chip of material held in the palm of the hand. The first of the two is crouching, over 2.5 million years ago, near what we now know as Lake Turkana, Kenya. He is feeling the sharp edges of a small flake of stone chipped from a rock he has been fashioning into what today's archaeologists would call a pebble chopper. The second, an electronics engineer working in California's Silicon Valley, cups in her hand a tiny fragment of silicon, no bigger than a newborn baby's thumbnail. She is about to run a battery of tests on a microprocessor, a 'computer on a chip'.

These two individuals are operating at the cutting edge of the technology of the day, separated by 2.5 million years. It took over two million of those years for that elementary pebble chopper to evolve into the hand held flint axes which our ancestors in the Pleistocene used to skin and dismember their kills, whereas the Silicon Valley chip, through which information coded as electric signals travels at nearly the speed of light, has, in the space of just twenty years, moved from abstract possibility to everyday reality.

A dramatic illustration of the pace of today's technological evolution is the difference in performance between ENIAC, a computer which, in human terms, would only now be entering early middle age, and one of today's newborn silicon miracles. The world's first electronic digital computer, ENIAC was dedicated in 1946 and weighed 30 tonnes. Our silicon chip, by contrast, is almost weightless, is around 30,000 times cheaper than ENIAC, needs less power than a night-light (instead of enough power to run a hundred light houses), and performs a million calculations a second—which is some 200 times better than anything ENIAC could achieve. Even so, some scientists are now predicting that the Silicon Age may already be on its way out. They are working on superlattices, materials built up almost atom by atom in the laboratory, which could prove 100 times faster than silicon. At giant AT&T and a growing number of smaller companies, scientists are working on 'neural computers', modelled on the mechanisms of the human brain.

It would be hard to think of two more different technologies but, inevitably, they share some important characteristics. Most importantly in the present context, every new tool which spins off from the cutting edge of technology, however simple, however complex, helps change our relationship with the natural world.

Stone tools helped us along the first stretch of our transformation of Eden. Silicon technology, whether in the hands of capitalist, socialist or communist, will once again turn the familiar features of today's world inside out. However, before we begin to consider the ways in which modern forms of industry, and particularly modern capitalism, have affected the environment, it is worth recalling that our assault on our natural environment began a long time before what we now describe as the 'Industrial Revolution'.

Stone Age impacts

While it may seem primitive today, Stone Age technology, including the use of fire, profoundly altered the balance between humans and their environment. New developments such as spear-throwers and bows brought larger, faster animals within range. More successful hunts meant more food, and more food generally meant more people. A growing human population, in turn, meant more hunters. Even as hunter-gatherers, we were responsible for reshaping some important elements of our environment and for helping drive many species into extinction.

The Neolithic Period, or New Stone Age, lasted from about 4,000 to 2,400 BC in Europe and was a period of fairly rapid technological innovation. Just as new materials are assuming an increasing importance in today's high technology industries (see Chapter 8), so the Neolithic Period saw the increasing use of such new materials as jadeite, diorite, or schist, all of them tougher than flint. Many of the tools made from such materials were carefully polished, which meant that they were less likely to jam in a tree-trunk as it was cut down.

Soon the Neolithic farmers of northern Europe were widely using polished axes to clear virgin woodland for cultivation. When local supplies of suitable stone ran out, the Neolithic traders met demand with stone from far-flung flint mines or 'factories', where flint axe heads were roughly shaped before being traded. Neolithic axe 'factories' are now being revealed in Britain's Lake District, for example, whose mass-produced axes began the process of deforestation some 4,500 years ago.

How serious an environmental threat was this Stone Age technology? In a fascinating experiment, scientists at the Danish National Museum bound 4,000 year-old polished axe heads to modern ash handles. Once they had learned how to use this Stone Age technology, three men cleared an eighth of an acre of silver birch forest in four hours. A single axe head, with no extra sharpening, cut down 100 trees. The environmental implications are clear.

The impact of this burgeoning flint industry is nowhere clearer, however, than at the great flint mining complex at Grimes Caves in Norfolk. Viewed from the air, this 34-acre site looks like a shell-pocked battlefield from the First World War. There are around 400 circular craters, the filled-in pits from which the flint was extracted. By the time these shafts were dug, about 2,000 BC, bronze was already beginning to replace stone.

As more pottery was made and the Copper Age gave way first to the Bronze Age and then to the Iron Age, the demand for fuel accelerated the process of deforestation. Metal axes were also very much more effective in felling the trees that were needed for fuel and timber, or which simply stood in the way of the plough. The

Celtic plough, and the many hundreds of different plough types which followed it, helped move cultivation onto less tractable types of soil, while growing herds of cattle and pigs helped slow the regeneration of cleared woodland.

When the Romans came to Britain, largely in pursuit of the country's mineral wealth, they simply accelerated a process of environmental change which was already well under way, although it is probably fair to say that their impact was still relatively small as far as the natural environment of the British Isles as a whole were concerned. Since the Industrial Revolution took root first in the British Isles, we shall focus first on developments there, pulling back later on to look at the way in which country after country began to follow in Britain's footsteps—many of them ultimately overtaking the first industrializer.

A growing timber crisis
The Dark Ages, which are generally held to have lasted from the late fifth century AD to 1000 AD, saw relatively little in the way of technological innovation, although the water-mill was introduced into Britain during the eighth century, or re-introduced, if one considers that the Romans made occasional use of early, relatively inefficient water-wheels. By the time of the Domesday Book, the survey work for which was done in 1086, the country had some 6,000 water-powered corn mills. Then, towards the end of the twelfth century, the windmill also began to be used for grinding corn and the applications of water-power were extended to include a major industrial process. This was the 'fulling-mill', used to compact yarn and cloth through shrinking, beating and pressing.

These developments have led some historians to talk of a *thirteenth* century industrial revolution. However, while increasing quantities of metal were being mined, with bronze and iron used in cannon, copper and iron in domestic utensils and lead in roofing, medieval technology's impact on the wider environment was once again largely confined to deforestation. Indeed, in some parts of Europe the rate of deforestation was such that local industry was beginning to face a real timber crisis. While this problem developed at a much more leisurely pace than the energy crises with which we are now so familiar, it was particularly pronounced in Britain, which was accordingly forced to innovate its way around the developing timber shortages.

Water-power continued to be a key energy source for many centuries and, indeed, was used to run many of the early textile factories, to drain mines and to crush the ore extracted from them. But there were important limitations to the renewable energy provided by wind, water and wood, which encouraged the search for 'alternatives'. Fossil fuel had often been used where it was readily available. Coal, for example, was used for salt-boiling along the shores of the Firth of Forth and was the cause of some local air pollution. Following the dissolution of the monasteries by Henry VIII, considerable coal resources passed into the hands of men who were both interested in exploiting them and had the resources to do so. In 1640 alone, half a million tons of 'sea coal' were shipped from the Tyne to London. By 1700, some 1,600 vessels were busy carrying coal from Wear to London, where its use caused increasingly severe pollution problems.

An early example of pollution caused by the burning of coal dates from the year 1257, when the English queen, Eleanor, was forced to leave Nottingham because of the smoke. In 1273, the first smoke abatement law was passed in England, while by 1306, in the reign of Edward I, the use of coal in London was already so great that the nobility, strongly backed by the townsfolk, successfully agitated against its use. A royal proclamation banned coal-burning, but this early example of environmental legislation proved impossible to enforce, even though at least one man was executed that year for burning coal.

Mining and land drainage schemes also produced severe local effects on Europe's environment. The sixteenth century saw the publication of the world's first mining textbook and it gives an invaluable insight into some of the most pressing environmental problems of the day. Written by Georgius Agricola, the latinised name of Georg Bauer, and published in 1556, *De Re Metallica* provided a damning indictment of many mining operations.

The 'strongest argument of the detractors,' Agricola argued, 'is that the fields are devastated by mining operations.' He also noted that in many cases 'the woods and groves are cut down, for there is need of an endless amount of wood for timbers, machines and the smelting of metals. And when the woods and groves are felled, then are exterminated the beasts and birds, very many of which furnish a pleasant and agreeable food for man. Further, when the ores are washed, the water which has been used poisons the brooks and streams, and either destroys the fish or drives them away.' As a result, he concluded, 'it is clear to all that there is greater detriment from mining than the value of the metals which the mining produces.'

Deforestation, meanwhile, proceeded at such a pace that by the early years of the eighteenth century the British iron industry was facing imminent extinction because the pace of industrial development was exhausting supplies of the traditional fuel, charcoal, which was made from wood. The government was refusing to permit further inroads on the country's timber resources, for fear that it would have none left for building ships of the line. In the seventeenth century, a 1,500-ton man-of-war needed the wood of some 2,000 oak trees. To put it another way, fifty acres of woodland had to be felled to build one ship.

Around the country, meanwhile, growing numbers of inventors, innovators and entrepreneurs, often embodied in the same individual, were struggling to develop ways of replacing charcoal with coal. The key initial problem was to work out ways of dealing with the high sulphur content of much of the coal that was easily available. Whether you were a brewer or iron-master, this could lead to significant contamination problems. By 1650, however, malt was being dried with coke, while a few years later lead, copper and tin were being smelted with coke, not wood.

The iron industry had even greater problems making the transition to coal, but in 1709 Abraham Darby succeeded in smelting iron ore with coke, which he called 'charked coal'. By treating coal in the same way that the charcoal burners treated wood, Darby found that most of the sulphur which had made coal so difficult to use was driven off. By 1800, the old-style charcoal smelting had largely been abandoned. What Darby and others had done, in effect, was to give industry a new set of keys to Nature's energy deposit account, the fossil fuels. By consuming this energy capital, our industrial societies have enjoyed a new lease of life and the subsequent Coal Age and major oil discoveries have fuelled unparalleled economic growth. We are now involved in another transition, towards a more mixed energy economy drawing on nuclear and, increasingly, renewable energy sources—with a growing emphasis on energy efficiency.

Unlike renewable energy, however, coal came in concentrated reserves. Towards the end of the Carboniferous era, a period which lasted for 65 million years some 345 to 280 million years ago, coal 'measures' were laid down in vast quantities. These seams of 'black gold' account for perhaps 80 per cent of the world's known coal reserves and laid the energy foundations for the Industrial Revolution both in Europe and elsewhere.

In what might be called the planet's 'black belt', a great band of coal was laid down in what is now central and eastern North America, Scotland south of the Highlands, England, Wales, France, the Low Countries, Germany and Poland and thence eastwards across the USSR and China. Among later coal measures, perhaps the most important developed in what were to become eastern Australia, India, Antarctica and South Africa, which were all part of the same continent 250 to 200 million years ago. Even more recently, coal began to form in such widely dispersed places as the foothills of the Canadian Rockies, in New Mexico, along the Rhine Valley and in south east Europe.

Once they knew how to exploit coal, instead of scouring the watersheds of local rivers for an as yet unexploited head of water, manufacturers began to move towards the coalfields. In Britain, those who could not move, such as the Cornish mine-owners, still helped fuel the concentration of industry in the coal-rich areas. They sent their copper and tin ores for smelting in Neath and Swansea, for example, which would soon become massive industrial conglomerations and the scene of some of the worst environmental dereliction in the world.

Many different factors conspired to ensure that the Industrial Revolution happened in Britain rather than elsewhere. These included geographical factors. The fact that Britain is an island, of modest size and with a highly indented coastline put most areas within reasonable access of waterborne transport and of foreign markets and suppliers. Then there were demographical and political factors. Although its population was only some six million at the beginning of the eighteenth century, for example, less than a third of France's population, Britain represented the world's biggest single market, because of its relative lack of internal barriers to trade.

However, deforestation coupled with the country's considerable coal reserves, was probably the key factor which forced Britain to become the first country to make the transition to modern forms of industry and modern rates of economic growth and also gave it the less attractive distinction of being the first country to suffer the full ravages of industrial pollution.

Full steam ahead

As the demand for metals and coal soared, miners needed to dig deeper, many of them hitting severe flooding problems as they did so. Mine-owners used considerable ingenuity to harness renewable energy to pump water. A early as 1550, in Bohemia, mine shafts were sunk to a depth of 1,300 feet (400 metres) using water-powered pumps. In one English colliery the records show that a total of 500 horses were involved in hauling out the water, bucket by laborious bucket. Even the earliest steam engines were often seen as a considerable improvement on these more traditional sources of renewable horsepower.

The steam engine may not have evolved as rapidly as the microchip, but the cutting edge of technology certainly moved very much faster in the Steam Age than in the Stone Age. It took only seven years from 1698, when Thomas Savery introduced his engine for 'raising water by the help of fire' (patented in 1693 as 'The Miner's Friend'), for Thomas Newcomen to come up with his improved steam engine. This was both simple and sturdy, but its poor energy efficiency meant that it was confined to the coalfields, where fuel was plentiful. It was not until 1769 that James Watt patented his separate condenser. This found its first commercial application in 1776, eventually cutting the fuel consumption of the typical steam engine by a useful 75 per cent.

Much of Watt's later work on the steam engine was financed by Matthew Boulton, whose Soho 'manufactory', near Birmingham, turned out small metal articles such as silver buttons and buckles. Boulton used steam engines for manufacturing coins for the East India Company and supplied machinery to the Royal Mint. Ultimately, however, the steam engine found even more important applications. It was destined to become the thumping heart of the industrial city. In 1825, for example, it was used to power coal-hauling locomotives on the Stockton and Darlington Railway and in the process launched the Railway Age. The railway industry exploited many environmental engineering techniques already developed during the canal-building era, but it did so on a much larger scale and, more importantly, its growing demands for iron, coal, wood, brick and other materials spurred the growth of other major industries.

Indeed, the railway industry was destined to become a more important economic influence than even these facts might suggest. Before long, it was the most important single influence on the overall level of business activity and, while the major works carried out by the 'navigators', or 'navvies', have long since blended into the landscape, the human and environmental toll involved in building them was tremendous.

By the time the railway boom peaked in the 1840s, the industry was employing well over 200,000 men just on the construction side of its activities, more than were then being employed in the entire textile industry. New approaches to industrial management had to be developed to cope with the pressures of dealing with large, often unruly gangs of navvies working on the roadbed, tunnels and viaducts.

Strikingly, the railways also soaked up about half of the investment funds available in the country at the time, or around five to seven per cent of national income. The astonishing sums of money needed to underwrite all this activity meant that new ways had to be found to mobilize capital, with the result that Britain also pioneered in the field of large-scale corporate capitalism, with a growing emphasis on limited liability companies. These meant that entrepreneurs were no longer held liable for any losses down 'to the last shilling and acre.'

Capital ideas

The main characteristics of capitalism are the private ownership of the means of production, distribution and exchange, with capitalists relatively free to operate or manage their property for profit in competitive conditions. But where did capitalism itself come from? Like industrial technology, capitalism did not suddenly spring into existence during the early years of the Industrial Revolution. The roots of capitalism may not be quite as long as the roots of industrial technology, but the great capitalists of the Industrial Revolution were not a totally new phenomenon: they did what others had done before them, but they operated on a considerably larger scale. The continuous development of capitalism as we know it dates from the sixteenth century, although some precursors of capitalist institutions can be traced back to ancient times, with pockets of capitalism also known to have flourished during the later Middle Ages.

The seed beds for new technology during the couple of centuries before the Industrial Revolution had included north Italy, the Low Countries, and south Germany, but the development of capitalism was also led during the sixteenth, seventeenth and eighteenth centuries by the growing English cloth industry. Often, an urban capitalist would take control of the entire sequence of wool processing activities, from the sorting, carding or combing, through the spinning, weaving and fulling, to the dyeing and finishing. In return, he would provide credit, pay wages, set the standards and designs to be followed and seek out markets for the resulting products.

What really made capitalism different from what had gone before? A key part of the answer must be that capitalists tended to use any profit they made, representing the excess of product income over production costs, to enlarge and improve their productive capacity.

The most influential early writer on capitalism was undoubtedly Adam Smith. Often held up as a champion of modern capitalism, he actually wrote *An Inquiry into the nature and causes of the Wealth of Nations*, published in 1776, before the great age of industrial capitalism. In fact he seems not to have suspected the imminence of the Industrial Revolution, although early symptoms of that impending revolution would have been visible at the time, in the shape of some very considerable iron works just down the road from Edinburgh, where he did much of his writing and was to spend his final days.

Smith, it is true, enthusiastically promoted capitalism as an engine for growth, but he was never a believer in unending growth. Interestingly, too, he was fairly disparaging about the future prospects of the joint-stock company, or corporation, which in the event proved to be one of the key ingredients in the complicated recipe which produced the Industrial Revolution.

The considerable size and complexity of many industrial processes, together with the increasing use of capital-intensive equipment, whether in the form of water wheels or spinning jennies, called for novel forms of industrial organization and new breeds of entrepreneur. Prior to the Industrial Revolution, the most highly capitalized industry was almost certainly brewing. Many brewers in countries such as England, Holland, and Germany ranked as the major capitalists of their day, and their breweries, and to a lesser extent some of the great English glassworks of London and the Midlands, bore many of the hallmarks of the modern industrial factory.

However, the real early proving ground for the joint-stock company had been the voyages of discovery. These, particularly in the fourteenth and fifteenth centuries, had begun to open up the world to trade. Portuguese, Spanish, Italian and English navigators vied with each other to find and exploit new lands and new markets.

At the beginning, many set out as individual adventurers, or operated in loose partnerships with other merchants and investors. As the competition between rival nations intensified, however, so the need to provide heavily armed ships and shore installations grew and with it the capital cost, taking such ventures beyond the means of any but the very wealthiest individuals. At the same time, too, larger cargoes and larger crews were at risk. The joint-stock company, which had occasionally been used in the Middle Ages, evolved fairly rapidly as a means of financing such expeditions.

To be sure, individual London capitalists jointly funded Sir John Hawkins' slaving voyages, Sir Martin Frobisher's search for the Northwest Passage, Sir Francis Drake's raids on the Spaniards in South America, Sir Walter Raleigh's colonization of North America and assorted trade enterprises to Russia and the Levant. If the expedition succeeded, then the investor liquidated the operation, took his profits and that was that. But the Dutch set a new pattern for the future when they launched a company with a *permanent* capital fund in 1602, the Dutch East India Company. It took the British East India Company, founded only two years previously in 1600, over 50 years to catch up and emulate this approach.

Although the Dutch East India Company became flabby and

corrupt by the end of the eighteenth century, the early Dutch ventures appear to have been much more profitable than most of their English counterparts. Where such ventures did not actually make a loss, as did many early French enterprises, they often helped build up the capital which would eventually be ploughed into the Industrial Revolution.

'A nightmare rate of growth'

As this money started to pour into the new technologies and new industries, with one area of activity stimulating others, so rates of economic growth began to take off. Whereas industrial output had been growing at a rate of around one per cent a year, the Industrial Revolution lifted Britain into what was then a new international super-league, with growth rates running at between three and five per cent a year for upwards of 100 years. As a result, within just 50 years, the map of Britain was transformed beyond recognition.

The Black Country was a prime example. Stretching west from Birmingham, this area got its name because of its pollution-coated landscape. Clusters of industrial towns literally erupted around the south Staffordshire coalfield, with collieries, blast furnaces and foundries all belching forth smoke and grime. Although some species adapted remarkably quickly to their highly polluted surroundings, for instance the once pale moths which evolved into darker strains able to blend in with the sootiest background, most did not. The resulting environmental dereliction is still visible in many places.

This was a period, as one writer put it, which saw 'a nightmare growth rate producing nightmare towns'. As W. H. Hoskins recalled in *The Making of the English Landscape*, in areas such as south Lancashire, around St Helens, in the Potteries and the Black Country, 'the landscape of Hell was foreshadowed'.

The coal-iron complex was undoubtedly the most important polluter overall, but there were others. Just as the environmentally disruptive railway industry catalysed growth in other sectors, so the textile industry helped spur the evolution of the heavy chemical industry. As Archie Clow of Britain's Open University noted, 'we must bear in mind that where it did operate, the unfettered early chemical industry could cause devastation unequalled by any other industry, with the possible exception of the Potteries.'

The Potteries, in fact, represented one of the leading 'high tech' industries of the day. Just as Matthew Boulton led the way in applying the latest scientific knowledge to commercial metallurgy, so Josiah Wedgwood's name is inextricably linked with the commercial success of scientific potting in the eighteenth century. His new pottery at Etruria, alongside the Trent-Mersey canal, was the first factory to install a steam engine.

This investment resulted from the advice of Josiah Wedgwood's good friend, the eminent scientist Erasmus Darwin. In one of those intriguing links between the great industrial families and the development of the natural and environmental sciences which were ultimately to spark widespread resistance to further untramelled industrial growth in the twentieth century, Wedgwood's daughter, Susannah, was to become the mother of Britain's greatest naturalist, Charles Darwin.

As far as Wedgwood's patrons were concerned, the products from the Etruria works were in a class of their own, but then so was the pollution produced in the process. As the social novels of the day show, the relatively primitive firing methods then in use, together with the techniques used to produce salt-glazed ware, turned the Potteries into a noisome conglomeration of 'nightmare towns'.

Meanwhile, the roots of the chemical industry can be traced back to two 'vitriol', or sulphuric acid, works built by Dr John Roebuck and his partner. The first, built in 1746, was near Birmingham and supplied the metal-refining industry, while the second was built in 1749 at Prestonpans, on the Firth of Forth, to supply linen bleachers and cotton finishers. Any pollution problems produced by the Prestonpans operation were felt to be more than outweighed by the fact that the use of sulphuric acid in bleaching replaced the earlier use of sour milk and buttermilk. The original process took a great deal of time and involved spreading the cloth out across many acres of potentially productive farmland. The acid process meant that the land went back to the farmer and the buttermilk, perhaps, to the hungry.

However, the environmental equation was very much less satisfactory in the case of the later Leblanc process for alkali production.

Deforestation had also begun to starve industrialists of such materials as potash, which they had previously derived from wood ash, forcing them to look for ways of synthesizing alkali from such commonly available minerals as salt. The Leblanc soda process, originally developed in France, was imported into Britain by James Muspratt, who built an alkali works in Liverpool in 1820. The process, which involved the treatment of salt with sulphuric acid, released clouds of highly corrosive hydrogen chloride.

'Although he operated in Liverpool,' as Archie Clow recalled, 'it is reported that Muspratt's activities blighted the vegetation on the Birkenhead side of the Mersey. What it did locally can be imagined. Even in the pollution-permissive society of the early nineteenth century this could not last and Muspratt was told to leave.' He left for the Cheshire saltfields, which soon developed into one of the largest, and most polluting, chemical production centres in Europe.

Even at this early stage there were industrialists who recognized that some of the pollutants they were emitting represented lost raw materials. Hydrogen chloride, for example, was later used to make chlorine. Charles Tennant set up the St Rollox Chemical Works near Glasgow to make bleaching powder from chlorine. This interest in reclaiming potentially valuable materials from waste, coupled with the desire to avoid law suits from nearby land owners, proved a powerful incentive for innovation in the developing chemical industry. However, further incentives were also desperately needed, and the first of Britain's Alkali Acts, designed to control highly polluting industrial processes, was passed during the 1860s.

Exporting the revolution

By 1851, with the Great Exhibition, Britain was advertising itself as the Workshop of the World, but the country's hold on the leading edge of the Industrial Revolution was slipping. The period from 1815 to 1850 had seen several other European countries beginning to initiate their own industrial revolutions. Belgium came first, in the 1820s and 1830s, with a pronounced emphasis on coal mining and metal-based industries. France was next, although its poor position in coal led it to stress textiles and other light industries. From the 1830s, the Swiss took the same route, while Prussia developed more along the Belgian lines from the 1840s.

During the 1850s and 1860s, there was rapid innovation in the chemical industry, with the development of the first synthetic dyes. Although the first breakthroughs were achieved in Britain, Germany soon joined in the race. By 1870, the more advanced industrial nations were in a position to compete with Britain on increasingly equal terms and were beginning to generate innovations of their own.

Soon Britain found itself overtaken in key industries: in the 1890s Germany surpassed Britain in iron and steel manufacture, but the main challenge came from the other side of the Atlantic. The United States overtook Britain in steel output in 1890, in coal output in 1898 and in raw cotton consumption by the end of the century. On the other side of the Pacific, too, Japan was convinced that the only way it could maintain its independence was to absorb Western technology. In fact the Japanese at this time adopted industrial strategies which are strongly reminiscent of those they are using today: they protected their industries with selective tariffs and strongly supported key sectors which would be slow to generate a profit.

As the original Industrial Revolution technologies spread to new industrial nations, so improvements were made: spindles, for example, span faster and industrial designers achieved taller furnaces. At the same time, larger and larger chimneys were built to disperse the resulting air pollution. Some, like the 400-foot chimney at Charles Tennant's St Rollox works, became wonders of the industrial world. But the pace of technological development was slowing down.

Then came what some call the second Industrial Revolution. Whereas the previous phases of industrialization had been powered by textiles, iron, coal and the steam engine, and later by the railways, a new cluster of innovations began to emerge towards the end of the nineteenth century. This time, again, the key breakthroughs came in the field of energy conversion and distribution. They centred around electricity generation and the internal combustion engine. Electricity has been a critical element in many subsequent technical developments, while the internal combustion engine rapidly began to replace the steam engine in many of its applications. The 'cutting edge' of technology was now to be found largely in the United States.

In 1908, Henry Ford introduced his Model T, heralding the Automobile Age. Like the railways before it, the automobile industry rapidly became the most important single sector of manufacturing, affecting the output of other sectors producing petroleum products, steel, glass, rubber, asphalt, cement and textiles. To begin with, the industry's most significant environmental impacts were probably indirect, reflecting the sheer volume of materials consumed, for example, and the road-building programmes which country after country initiated. However, the motor car was eventually to become one of the leading sources of air pollution in the United States, in Europe and then in Japan.

At the same time, there were major advances in the organic chemistry chemicals sector, and in the manufacture of a growing number of synthetic chemicals. New man-made fibres and plastics, including artificial silk and rayon, bakelite, cellophane and celluloid, were beginning to appear at an increasing pace. The electronics industry was embryonic during the early years of the twentieth century, but its potential was unmistakable. Synthetic chemicals and electronics really began to take off during the 1930s and 1940s. Indeed, their full emergence following 1945, together with the growing use of atomic energy and of computers, is now advanced as evidence of a *third* Industrial Revolution. This time, the 'leading edge' is to be found right around the Pacific Rim, from the West Coast of the United States through Japan and down into South-East Asia.

Big is beautiful

But long before the outbreak of the Second World War, there had been a number of significant changes in the nature of international capitalism which have had a bearing on its subsequent environmental performance. Most notably, all these shifts in technology had once again produced new patterns of industrial organization. The trend towards larger-scale operations was boosted by the growing cost of production equipment, raising the cost of entry into the new markets.

There was also a less attractive motive in this increasing concentration of industrial power: many capitalists wanted to drive out their competitors and increase their profits, either by establishing monopolies or by organizing cartels, trusts and other obstacles to competition. In the United States, tycoons such as John D. Rockefeller and Andrew Carnegie pushed this trend to its outer limits.

Although there were increasing attempts from the 1890s to break up the largest trusts, the First World War actually encouraged the further concentration of industrial production into large units. War-time pressures not only encouraged mechanization, rational-ization and standardization, but also accelerated the search for new synthetic materials. Ultimately, though, the 1914–18 war helped drive the United States economy into an increasingly commanding position, mainly at the expense of Europe.

The inter war years were a period of considerable economic turbulence, culminating in the Great Depression. Heralded by the Wall Street crash of 1929, the Depression took a number of years to take hold. Ultimately, it hit every capitalist country and was a traumatic experience in many ways, not least because it challenged deeply held beliefs about the prospect for unlimited economic expansion.

World capitalism was profoundly shaken by the events of the Depression. Until the 1930s, most economists had tended to argue for minimal government interference in the economy, on the grounds that it could unbalance the natural workings of the 'invisible hand' of the market, perhaps aggravating any market disequilibrium. Increasingly, however, government intervention was seen as a way of smoothing out the wild fluctuations which otherwise threatened to shake the settled world order apart.

In the wake of the Second World War, perhaps because of these government counter cyclical measures, economic cycles tended to become somewhat less pronounced. The recessions were milder, while the upswings appeared rather more restrained. Overall, how-ever, the period from 1949 through to the early 1970s saw remark-able economic growth, the environmental effects of which are discussed in later chapters. Then, with the successive energy crises of the 1970s, the world economy lurched into recession, recovered, then slipped backwards again. By the early 1980s, many analysts were predicting the imminent onset of another full-scale depression.

The next industrial revolution

Buffeted by the resulting turbulence in their business environment, many companies began to ask themselves whether there might not be something in the old theory of long-wave business cycles. Although rarely even mentioned in today's economic textbooks, on the grounds that his theories are unproven, the man who did most to promote the idea of long-wave business cycles was the Russian economist, Nikolai D. Kondratieff. Tragically, he was to die in a Siberian concentration camp because the Communist Party, and Stalin in particular, considered his ideas to be heresy.

In simple terms, what Kondratieff said was that there are some cycles in the world economy which political and economic measures can do little to control. The implication of these Kondratieff cycles, too, was that, while capitalism might run into a world slump for considerable periods of time, it would almost certainly recover.

By studying economic data such as price trends, Kondratieff plotted three previous long-wave cycles. 'The upswing in the first long wave,' he noted, 'embraces the period from 1789 to 1814, i.e. 25 years; its decline begins in 1814 and ends in 1849, a period of 35 years. The cycle is therefore completed in 60 years. The rise in the second wave begins in 1849 and ends in 1873, lasting 24 years. The decline of the second wave begins in 1873 and ends in 1896, a period of 23 years. The length of the second wave is 47 years. The upward movement of the third wave begins in 1896 and ends in 1920, its duration 24 years. The decline of the wave, according to all data, begins in 1920.'

Kondratieff, in fact, died before he could see his theory borne out by the events of the 1930s and 1940s. The downwave which began in 1920, and included the Great Depression, lasted 20 years, giving a cycle of 44 years. The fourth wave, which started in 1940, is now on the downswing, with some analysts predicting that, on past form, the next upswing is unlikely before the early years of the 21st century.

Although there have been attempts to plan for continuous economic growth, in the belief that any such economic cycles are a 'disease' of the market economy, there are good grounds for believing that such cycles are a prerequisite for sustained economic growth. The slump of the 1930s, for example, prepared the way for recovery in the fourth long-wave cycle, which is now on its way out. After a few years during which investment fell sharply, existing commercial stocks were used up and industrial equipment either wore out or became obsolescent. As the slump conditions drove down prices, so the economic incentives for investing in replacement production capacity became increasingly attractive. Weak companies were shaken out of the economy, while the new investment tended to go into the emerging growth sectors of the future.

The same sequence of events has been repeating itself since around 1973. While there have been recoveries and even short periods of relative stability, the process of de-industrialization has been seen in many countries. European countries in general, and Britain in particular, have been hard hit. The environmental implications of this process, as later chapters show, are profound. The downwave has knocked out some significant polluters, for example, including many companies in the metal-processing sector of the economy. In the West Midlands region, the metal content of effluents passed on to the regional water authority were falling by ten per cent a year during the early 1980s, mainly due to the closure of firms.

At the same time, many of the new technologies which are now being developed and deployed are much cleaner and more resource-efficient than those they are replacing. We are living through a new Industrial Revolution. Often, the problem is that these cleaner, more resource-efficient technologies are not replacing the older technology fast enough, because of the constraints on investment. However, as we shall see, some of the emerging technologies are bringing new environmental problems in their wake, even as they solve some of the most pressing problems identified during the last business cycle.

Since we began this chapter with one foot in Silicon Valley, it is worth recalling some of the environmental issues which have been thrown up by the mushroom growth of the microchip industry. As if building over once fertile orchards and hazing the blue Californian skies with air pollution from their car exhausts were not enough, some of the microchip companies have also been accused of polluting the underground water which many Californians rely on for their tapwater. 'The industry that can mount an electronic brain on a pinhead,' the regional press acidly noted, 'cannot stop its tanks from leaking.'

Once—if they were so inclined—industrialists could ride rough-shod over local communities and their environment. Today the situation is very different, with a growing need to take into account both social and ecological feedback in industrial planning and decision-making. Industry (and the financial institutions which underwrite its activities) is increasingly locked into a system where the environmental feedback is very rapid indeed. The 'greening' of national and international politics has seen to that. As a result, industry after industry, company after company, has run into major political and regulatory bottlenecks.

Chapter 2

GREEN BOTTLENECKS

The rapid evolution of environmentalism has been one
of the most dramatic phenomena of a dramatic century.
The 'Environmental Revolution' triggered shock
waves which are still reverberating around the world.
Despite attempts to downplay the importance of
environmental issues, and to cut back on the regulations
and bureaucracy which resulted through the 1970s,
environmental concerns show no sign of abating—
while the environmental agenda continues to evolve.

If the number of enemies you make is any measure of your impact, Greenpeace can claim to have been outstandingly effective. Although France was eventually to admit that its secret agents had planted the magnetic mines which sank the Greenpeace flagship, the *Rainbow Warrior*, the original news of the sinking prompted speculation that the sabotage was the work of a bewildering array of suspect organizations, companies and individuals.

Like many of the environmental and 'green' campaigning organizations that emerged in the 1960s and 1970s, Greenpeace had managed to antagonize an impressive cast of vested interests. As the *Financial Times* commented shortly after the ship hit the bottom of Auckland Harbour, Greenpeace had made enemies 'of the US Government, the Soviet Union, the French, Britain, countless multinationals, the fur industry and British Nuclear Fuels, to name but a few.'

What was soon dubbed 'France's Watergate' or, more simply, '*Under*watergate,' blew up like a succession of mines around the French ship of state. President Mitterrand and Prime Minister Laurent Fabius struggled to plug the leaks, while growing media pressure forced the resignation of the country's Defence Minister,

M. Charles Hernu, and the dismissal of secret service chief, Admiral Lacoste. Hernu, it was later alleged, had 'exploded with fury' when he first heard that Greenpeace intended to protest against France's impending test of a neutron bomb at its Mururoa atoll testing ground.

Paradoxically, France proved to have performed a public relations miracle for Greenpeace. Like England's Henry II, roaring 'Who will free me from this turbulent priest?' and thereupon finding the assassinated Thomas à Becket a far greater nuisance dead than alive, the French saboteurs learned that it rarely pays to make martyrs. For months afterwards, the story dominated the news media, with continual updates and 'exclusives'. Greenpeace's worldwide membership jumped in short order from 1.1 million to 1.5 million. The mass media, in short, had transmuted a rusty, battered ex-trawler into a powerful symbol of the resilience and determination of the world's growing environmental lobby.

Greening the Global Village

The power of that lobby to bottleneck an ever widening range of activities which it holds suspect owes a great deal to the emergence of what Marshall McLuhan dubbed the Global Village. McLuhan, who immortalized the phrase 'the medium is the message' in the early 1960s, was so preoccupied with the social implications of the mass media that he overlooked the environmental implications of the burgeoning web of electronic communication technologies.

Perhaps it is fairer to say that the greening of the Global Village was a special case of the general trend which he had identified. The spread of mass communications technology, he had argued, 'establishes a global network that has much of the character of our central nervous system.' McLuhan's conviction that this developing global network represented, in effect, 'a single unified field of experience,' led him to conclude that the all-embracing reach of communications technology was shrinking the world into a *Global Village*. Today, in fact, the world increasingly is stitched together with electronic signals, streaking through hair-thin optical fibres or bouncing off orbiting satellites. Ethiopians starve in our living rooms, terrorist victims bleed 'live' minutes after the bomb explodes, and the roar of bulldozers moving into virgin rainforest rattles the ornaments on televisions several continents away. Even small numbers of suitably skilled activists can have a totally dispro-portionate impact in the Global Village, so long as they understand, as Greenpeace certainly does, how to use the leverage afforded by the mass media.

It is worth recalling that in the early days of Greenpeace the image the group was able to project had little to do with its actual resources. 'We were probably one of the hardest organizations in town to get hold of,' co-founder Robert Hunter recalled, 'despite the fact that we were also, at the international level, the most famous organization in town. There were millions of people around the world who had never heard of the Province of British Columbia but who had definitely heard of Greenpeace. Somewhere out there, foreign admirals and commanders fumed with rage whenever they heard mention of us. The Japanese whaling industry was already summoning its chiefs into boardrooms to begin planning a counter-offensive against the attack they had heard we were prepared to launch against them.' Yet, had the truth been known, the individ-uals who made up Greenpeace at that time could hardly agree among themselves to make a long-distance telephone call, let alone afford to pay for it.

The developing web of communications technology projected such groups onto the world stage, onto the world's screens, but it also spurred the greening of the Global Village in a rather more subtle way. Whatever the validity of his central thesis, McLuhan hit the nail on its head when he argued that mechanization, as embodied in the Industrial Revolution, had extended the reach and power of the human body without a corresponding adjustment in the reach and sensitivity of the human nervous system. This compensatory adjustment has only recently begun to take place, with the development of electronic sensing technologies.

Whereas the initial environmental reaction to the Industrial Revolution was stimulated by what the nose could smell, the eye see and the ear hear, our 'high technology' nervous system is now extending into outer space and into the depths of the world ocean, and it is signalling the presence of environmental issues which had previously not even been suspected. These range from the discovery that such chemicals as DDT and polychlorinated biphenyls (PCBs) are becoming broadly disseminated through the environment, to evidence that we are affecting the chemistry of the atmosphere, whether through carbon dioxide build-up or the chemical disruption of the planet's protective ozone layer.

Today, we have equipment that can detect the presence of potentially harmful substances in parts per million, or even parts per billion. Consider what one part per million (ppm) actually means: one part per million equals one milligram per kilogram, or, to put it another way, one ppm is roughly equivalent to one drop of water out of 16.5 gallons. It is equivalent to one minute in two years. Some of the latest equipment can detect substances at the level of parts per billion, trillion or even *quadrillion*. Some pollutants are thought to be potentially harmful even at the parts per billion level, which is equivalent to one drop of water in a swimming pool measuring 3m x 3m x 6m, or to just one minute in 2,000 years.

'We must now assume that life today takes place in a minefield of risks from hundreds, perhaps thousands of substances,' said William Ruckelshaus, who was responsible for steering the US Environmental Protection Agency through its early days, and came back later, as we shall see, to rescue it from its darker days under President Reagan's administration. 'Many communities are gripped by something approaching panic,' he admitted.

Thus the advance of technology is constantly increasing our awareness of the number of potential hazards to which we are exposing ourselves. At the same time, too, the technology which took the first astronauts into space also helped transform the way we think about our relationship with our environment and it did so at a fundamental, almost mystical level.

'You might suspect that in such a situation the observer would dismiss the Earth as relatively unimportant,' said Neil Armstrong, shortly after leaving the first set of human footprints on the moon. 'Paradoxically,' he continued, 'the opposite is true. We have been struck by the simile to an oasis or island. More importantly, it is the only island we know that is a suitable home for man. The need to save that home has never been more strongly felt.'

The images brought back by the Apollo crews became a potent symbol for environmentalists. 'Here is the Earth,' an early Friends of the Earth poster version of the full face of the planet was captioned. 'Don't spend it all at once.' The term environmentalists began to use was *Spaceship Earth*, a phrase coined by Adlai Stevenson and subsequently the title of two books, published independently in 1966, by Professor Kenneth Boulding and by Barbara Ward. The basic problem, as the architect and inventor Buckminster Fuller put it at around the same time, is that nobody issued the crew of Spaceship Earth with an operating manual.

The computer that cried WOLF?

Since the outbreak of what Max Nicholson, one of Britain's leading conservationists, dubbed the 'Environmental Revolution,' the world's political leaders and industrialists have been showered with warnings about the hazards which lie along their present course. Some of these warnings, like the Club of Rome's controversial report *The Limits to Growth*, have proved extraordinarily influential. The report's central message was that indefinite exponential economic growth is a physical impossibility in a world whose natural resources, including the absorptive capacity of the natural environment, are limited.

Although the report's conclusions were soon under attack, with one reviewer attributing them to 'the computer that printed out WOLF', it caught the public's attention in a way that the original scientific work on which it was based had signally failed to do.

Clearly, some dramatization of environmental issues is indispensable if they are to compete successfully for society's attention and scarce resources. If Rachel Carson had not written *Silent Spring*, public apathy about the ecological and health implications of the rapidly accelerating rate of use of synthetic pesticides might have extended for another decade. If Dennis Meadows and the Club of Rome had not published the computer runs on their various suggested relationships between economic growth and environmental resources, this area of research would not have attracted the level of funding which it enjoyed following the publication of *The Limits to Growth*.

Soon, however, from *A Blueprint for Survival* (also published in 1972) through to *North–South: A Programme for Survival* (the report of the Brandt Commission), the *Global 2000 Report to the President* (by the US Department of State and the Council on Environmental Quality), and the *World Conservation Strategy* (all published in 1980), environmentalists and their allies were hard at work trying to assemble that missing planet management manual.

'Humanity's relationship with the biosphere, the thin covering of the planet that contains and sustains life,' the *World Conservation Strategy* concluded, 'will continue to deteriorate until a new economic order is achieved, a new environmental ethic is adopted, human populations stabilize, and sustainable development becomes the rule rather than the exception.' This argument was carried forward in the report of the World Commission on Environment and Development, *Our Common Future*, published in 1987. 'The world manufactures seven times more goods today than it did as recently as 1950,' the Commission noted. 'Given population growth rates, a five- to ten-fold increase in manufacturing output will be needed just to raise developing-world consumption of manufactured goods to industrialized world levels by the time population growth levels off next century.'

The Commission was somewhat less concerned than the authors of *The Limits to Growth* about the prospect of running out of raw materials, however. 'Experience in the industrialized nations has proved that anti-pollution technology has been cost-effective in terms of health, property, and environmental damage avoided, and that it has made many industries more profitable by making them more resource-efficient,' it pointed out. 'While economic growth has continued, the consumption of raw materials has held steady or even declined, and new technologies offer further efficiencies.'

All a far cry from the prevailing mood fifteen years earlier. As far as world industry was concerned, the 1970s were a period of intense activity on the environmental battlefront. Few companies were represented at the United Nations' Stockholm Conference on the Human Environment, held in 1972, but industry after industry was soon caught up in the political aftermath. Indeed, anyone who tabulates the number of new pieces of environmental legislation in the industrial nations, cannot fail to notice the unparalleled level of regulatory activity during the period from 1972 to 1976.

This growth in environmental regulation was followed (and then spurred) by a secondary growth cycle in the body politic. Soon every industrial nation had at least an embryonic institutional framework for dealing with environmental problems. The United States had its Environmental Protection Agency, Japan its Environment Agency, West Germany its Federal Environment Agency, Britain its Department of the Environment and so on.

Setting up such an agency is one thing; setting up an effective one is quite another. In the case of Japan, the country's Environment Agency was set up in 1971, the year before the Stockholm Conference, and was originally intended to be a single organization covering all aspects of pollution control and environmental protection. Unfortunately, but perhaps predictably, the existing ministries, including the Ministry for International Trade and Industry (MITI), were unwilling to relinquish their powers in the area. As a result, the Environment Agency was called 'a watchdog without teeth'. Like many such agencies, it could plan and co-ordinate policies, but, with the exception of wildlife protection, it could not enforce them. And when it came to international issues, like Japan's role in the destruction of the world's tropical rainforests, the Environment Agency was almost powerless.

Around the world, however, these new agencies and regulations certainly had a major impact on the business environment. Industry faced a series of unexpected bottlenecks in its attempts to bring new products to market or to capitalize on existing technologies. As later chapters show, an extraordinary spectrum of industrial technologies and products have come under attack in recent years, from aerosols to jet aircraft, from motor cars to microchips.

A growing number of these problems and issues have had to be addressed at the international level. The Stockholm Conference saw the birth of the United Nations Environment Programme, one of the three organizations later involved in producing the *World Conservation Strategy*, while the following years saw the international aid and finance community, represented by such organizations as the World Bank and the United Nations Development Programme, attempting to incorporate an environmental dimension into their investment programmes and decision-making. It was rarely an easy task and it is a task which is still a long way from completion.

Meanwhile, the Organization for Economic Co-operation and Development (OECD) set up its 'Interfutures' team, which produced a report called *Facing the Future: Mastering the Probable and Managing the Unpredictable*. All these activities, together with the successive environmental action programmes launched by the

European Community, were symptoms of a rapidly changing, increasingly environment-conscious world.

It is also an increasingly interdependent world. The OECD, originally established to promote international economic co-operation and development, began the 1980s by announcing its conviction that this interdependence covers 'not only population, migration, energy, food, financial transfers and technology, but also the environment and, increasingly, the ecological basis for development: renewable and non-renewable resources, the oceans, the atmosphere and climate, space, and mankind's genetic resources and heritage.' These may have been mere words, of course, but they showed how far national and international government thinking had evolved.

Yes, but is it cost-effective?

Government thinking, however, is subject to a range of, often conflicting, interests. The worldwide economic recession which marked the period from 1973, punctuated with some short periods of resumed growth, soon led many governments to cut back on their environmental budgets. New legislation was implemented more slowly than originally planned or not implemented at all. Now a key concern among legislators was that environmental protection measures should be *cost-effective*.

The Chairman of the US National Academy of Sciences' environmental studies board summarized the lessons of the late 1970s as follows: 'I do not think that all the census work that I have seen indicated that people are willing to give up clean air or clean water. But they are more willing than before to ask the question whether the cost-effectiveness of certain regulations is defensible.'

Certainly, the evolution of environmental laws had been so rapid that even environmental legislators sometimes found it hard to keep track of developments. Inevitably, too, some of this legislation proved unworkable or misconceived. Part of the problem was that much of it was drafted at breakneck speed in an attempt to close the stable door after a succession of bolted horses.

Sometimes, one set of controls simply triggered the next set of environmental problems. The US Clean Air Act, for example, aggravated Canada's acid rain problems as industrialists built ever-taller chimneys, dispersing their emissions over ever larger areas. At the same time, too, such air pollution controls also forced industry to impound growing volumes of toxic waste in pits, ponds and lagoons, from which they could percolate down to contaminate underground water resources.

The American approach to pollution control, based as it was as much on the opinions of lawyers as on the research results produced by environmental scientists, was bound to provoke a reaction from those who had to foot the bill for the laundering of the national environment. This reaction, in turn, forced scientists and regulators to consider different control options.

Two new approaches formulated during the late 1970s were the 'bubble concept' and the 'emission offset policy', both designed to cut the cost to industry of environmental clean-up operations. The emission offset policy meant that new industry could move into areas with very restrictive pollution controls, provided that existing industrial polluters could be persuaded (usually with cash) to make a compensating reduction in the pollution *they* generated. The second cost-cutting innovation, the bubble concept, may have sounded like common sense, but represented a radical departure from normal practice at the Environmental Protection Agency (EPA). The standard EPA approach to controlling emissions or effluents from a factory or other industrial plant had involved specifying a pollution emission standard for each smokestack, vent or other pollution source on a given site. The new approach, by contrast, involved dealing with pollution in relation to the plant's emissions as a whole, by enclosing it in an imaginary bubble, which was then taken as the pollution source to be controlled.

Under the previous set-up, a large steel mill, oil refinery or chemical plant would have had to meet 40 or 50 different pollution standards, representing a major financial burden on the affected company. The new policy meant that a refinery which was paying, say, $50 a tonne to control smog-promoting hydrocarbons evaporating from storage tanks, compared to an outlay of thousands of dollars per tonne spent on the control of pollution coming from leaks, defective equipment or other 'fugitive emissions', was permitted to save money by concentrating on meeting the overall standard by the cheapest route. The basic idea was to find ways in which industry could be encouraged to be an eager partner in efforts to control pollution, generally by appealing to the profit motive.

However, such advances were often overshadowed by the political over-reactions of some of those appointed by President Reagan to reduce the burden of government regulations on industry. Some of them tried to go too far too fast, while others went off at a complete tangent. They encouraged companies to carry out superficial, essentially cosmetic, clean-ups at problem toxic waste dumps rather than requiring a thoroughly professional operation. Some were perhaps too closely identified with industrial interests to do an effective environmental job. The EPA's budget was halved at a time when its responsibilities had been doubled. Staff morale slumped and, as one senior EPA official put it, 'loyal, hardworking employees are even ashamed to admit to their friends or neighbours they work at the agency.'

Eventually, after a series of court cases, resignations and sackings, the EPA was resurrected by its original Administrator—William Ruckelshaus. He resigned a $220,000-a-year job with the timber products company Weyerhaeuser to take up the $70,000 EPA post. Taking over the EPA for the second time, he announced that there would be 'no hit lists, no political decisions and no sweetheart deals.' The reference to 'hit lists' was effectively a promise to drop a practice which had been rampant under his predecessor, Anne Burford: any scientist who sat on an EPA advisory panel and offended right-wing sensibilities was branded 'a menace' or 'pure ecology type'—and dropped.

Paradoxically, all these changes have resulted in a situation which, if anything, has hit industry harder. A new breed of grass-root activist emerged in the United States and succeeded in forcing numerous laws through state and local governments to replace the laws which were being dismantled at the federal level. As *Business Week* reported, 'these laws tend to be tougher and costlier for business than those previously enacted at the federal level.'

The US experience demonstrates that it is rarely possible to drive a straight line from A to B in environmental politics. Moreover, from the environmentalist's point of view, no victory can be considered final. The achievements of one administration or decade have to be protected during the following administrations and decades. In fact, many battles are ultimately lost. Like any resistance movement, the Green lobby has to be prepared to lose, or at least not to win, skirmish after skirmish, battle after battle, all in the hope that the tide will eventually turn in its favour.

Increasingly, however, the international environmental lobby has been trying to remove the bottlenecks restricting its own freedom of action. No longer does it reject economic growth out of hand. Instead, as the *World Conservation Strategy* illustrated, it has argued for sustainable development, or development which does not undermine its own ecological foundations. This line of thought was taken a stage further in *Our Common Future*, the report of the World Commission on Environment and Development.

There have been signs of a significant and, indeed, accelerating convergence between the thinking of those concerned to promote economic development and those concerned about the conservation of natural resources. Environmentalists have been shifting from essentially negative prescriptions (e.g. stop pollution, stop exhausting non-renewable resources and stop using renewable resources faster than they can regenerate) to a much more constructive approach based, for example, on the promotion of cleaner, quieter and more resource-efficient technologies.

The rise of the NGO

Industrialists often think of pressure groups and other voluntary organizations either as politically inspired ('you Greens are really Reds') or as well meaning, 'do-gooding' amateurs. What they may not be aware of is just how much of a contribution the voluntary sector now makes to the economy.

In Britain, for example, the turnover of the voluntary sector as a whole is estimated to be about £10 billion a year. Its output may be worth in the order of £100 billion a year in Britain. Voluntary organizations employ directly some 300,000 people and deploy assets worth around £20 billion. This is a large industry in anyone's terms, and it is often an extremely cost-effective industry in terms of services delivered.

Non-governmental organizations, or NGOs as they are often styled, have played a key role in driving forward the environmental debate, both nationally and internationally. Many factors have conspired to bring the NGOs to the fore in this way. Whatever else may be said about its successes and failures, the creation of the Welfare State in Britain did release civic energies—with the state taking over areas previously occupied by voluntary organizations. The 1944 Education Act also made secondary education widely available, creating a larger pool of people with the necessary skills for participation in political life. Interestingly, if you look around the voluntary bodies and pressure groups, particularly at the grass-roots level, and check who are the most active members, highly educated professionals are in the minority. Very often it is the lab technician, the library assistant, the senior clerk or the low level tax inspector —people who have been over-educated in terms of their everyday economic role and are satisfying their wider potential by joining in the political process.

Coupled with the growing scale of development projects and the centralization of so much decision-making, these trends made it almost inevitable that there would be an explosion of activity in the NGO sector. Now, whether you want to build a motorway, an airport, a nuclear power station or a facility to exploit onshore oil, a considerable proportion of those who are likely to be affected (and some who are not) will want to have their say in the matter. They, and the pressure groups of which they are members, have been greatly aided by the phenomenal growth in the amount of information in the public domain. The first thing any self-respecting pressure group ever does is to buy itself a Gestetner machine or photocopier and start rolling off its own print product, with computers now opening up whole new horizons of rapid response publishing and direct mail fund-raising.

A long period of relative peace and prosperity, coupled with a considerable unease among key elements of the population about the values of materialism and consumerism, has fuelled the growth of the NGO movement. Entrepreneurial people who would normally have gone into industry have been siphoned off into this movement, ensuring that many NGOs achieve a level of productivity which would be the envy of most mainstream companies.

Environmental NGOs play many different roles in society, with some of the larger organisations combining many different campaigns or even different styles of operation under the same roof. The classic role for a pressure group is that of the 'whistle blower', pointing out something that should not be going on. One of the most dramatic examples in Britain was the Conservation Society's success, in 1973, in highlighting the fact that it was perfectly legal for people to dump cyanide waste on open tip sites to which children had access. A closely related role is that of the 'ferret', winkling out information which others either want to conceal or do not consider suitable for publication. The classic case here was the CLEAR campaign against lead in petrol, which discovered by ferreting around that the chief medical officer advising the British government had changed his mind about the medical effects of lead in the atmosphere. One year later, the government had still not informed the public of the fact that this rather influential person had shifted his position. CLEAR made sure that the facts of the matter were widely known, gaining considerable political advantage in the process.

NGOs also carry out a less dramatic (but just as important) role when continuously monitoring the performance of governments or businesses against the yardsticks laid down either by law or by their own statements of policy. In human rights, for example, one thinks immediately of Amnesty, which monitors the behaviour of governments in terms of their commitments to honour the UN Charter of Human Rights. In the environmental field, groups like Friends of the Earth and the World Wide Fund for Nature have monitored the frequent failures of Customs and Excise and police officers to enforce legislation on the import and export of endangered species—and products derived from them.

A tremendous amount of significant information is also effectively buried in the background 'noise' of information which is now made available from every quarter. The environmental NGOs are past masters at screening this information for significant items, and have also become effective brokers of information, making sure that it gets to where it is likely to be most effective. They often show extraordinary skill in using the media and the educational system to amplify their efforts.

This is not simply a question of pulling off extraordinary stunts. Often, indeed, environmental NGOs will flag up social, economic or political issues which have much broader repercussions well beyond the environmental arena. During the Windscale inquiry, for example, it was left to Friends of the Earth to point out that there might be worrying implications for civil liberties if a country became heavily dependent on nuclear power. They asked whether it would be possible to permit unions operating in the nuclear industry to strike? Whether it might be necessary to have an armed police force to protect nuclear facilities? (It is, it turned out.) And whether the proliferation issue, with growing numbers of countries developing or acquiring a nuclear weapons capability, made nuclear power simply too dangerous to contemplate? Even where the ultimate decisions went against them, such NGOs have done a great deal to open out the debate, ensuring that over-the-horizon problems are at least recognized and discussed in public.

The growing professionalization of environmental NGOs has been another important trend in recent years. Increasingly, too, environmental NGOs act as innovators and as demonstrators of alternatives. Britain's largest utility, the Central Electricity Generating Board, is now testing windmills—but the first machines were erected by environmental pressure groups. Indeed, the debate is beginning to shift in the environmental movement, from discussions of the limits to growth to growing interest in how Britain, Europe and, indeed, the world can achieve 'green growth'. And it turns out that we are not just talking about organic foods and alternative health products here: we are also talking, as later chapters show, about high technology products, such as the Rolls-Royce wide chord turbofan blades which help power some of today's quietest and most fuel-efficient commercial aircraft.

The future role of NGOs, meanwhile, is assured. The voluntary sector increasingly is being seen as another way of providing services, whether as an alternative to state-owned enterprises and local authorities or as a complementary delivery mechanism. In overseas development, for example, NGOs are increasingly seen as an effective means for transferring expertise, funding and other resources. As governments draw them in as partners, so their overall influence can be expected to grow considerably—even more so if the present greening of politics continues to spread and deepen.

The greening of Europe

Green is the new political colour in Europe. Greens have taken their seats in the Bundestag and both houses of the Belgian Parliament. Even in Eastern Europe, ecological groups are to be found associated with both Solidarity and the Czech Chartists.

As orthodox politics throughout Europe responds by hastily sewing a green stripe into the red or blue flag, it is worth enquiring why this phenomenon should be occurring now. Historically, a period of high unemployment, economic uncertainty and intensifying international tension signals the onset of political conservatism. The radical normally flourishes in affluence and wilts in adversity. The greening of Europe is thus doubly curious: it is curious because it is taking place at all and because it has been taking place when Europe's fortunes have been at something of a low ebb.

Europeans, it must be said, have come to doubt their place in the world. After centuries of expansionary self-confidence, a deep anxiety about the future has become Europe's dominant mood. Poised between the grumbling giants of East and West, frozen into the brittle and unnatural posture imposed by Yalta, an insidious weariness has permeated, and frequently paralysed, European policy-making.

The listlessness which characterizes European responses to the dynamic change now occurring in the world is itself dispiriting. Perhaps a shrinking away from global responsibilities was to have been expected from a generation of decision-makers excluded from the centres of power to which they were accustomed and preoccupied anyway with the aftermath of defeat and the retreat from Empire.

In Western Europe, France, Holland, Belgium, Portugal and Britain have all dismantled empires. The Italian empire in Africa and Germany's short-lived eastern empire were lost in war. In the East, successive defeats, by Germany first, then more completely by the Soviet Union, have, for almost 50 years, stripped many European countries of any independent interest in the rest of the world.

The now universal image of a painfully beautiful blue and white planet, photographed against the deep black loneliness of space, has become the most potent symbol of our era. Yet whilst planetary consciousness has been expanding, European horizons have been shrinking. We have become parochial players of the great game. Only in the sparsely-populated Scandinavian countries has there been any real vigour of response to the fate of the earth. In this sense, at least, it was no coincidence that the World Commission on Environment and Development was chaired by Gro Harlem Brundtland, Prime Minister of Norway.

But the reflexes missing from official Europe have not been lost to the European people, especially among those born since 1945. This generation, now on the verge of power, and its successors form an emergent majority.

Three experiences, wholly new to humankind, have marked their lives: the threat of nuclear war, the magnitude of global poverty and the degradation of the environment. The vigour of the political impulse to which these experiences have given birth cannot be denied. The staggering response to the Band Aid concerts was the most spectacular event to give testimony to its force. Massive popular movements, intensely international both in spirit and practice, led for the most part by the emerging generation, have swept across Europe in the past three decades.

Their abrasive attempts to break the stifling grasp of the post-war orthodoxy on Europe's political agenda have been the only sure source of originality and vitality in European policy-making. It is as mistaken to think of these movements merely as spasms of reaction against the side-effects of progress as it is to think of them simply as movements of the left against the right. Rather, they represent deeper shifts in the emotional ground of European politics. A new generation is giving voice to new concerns pressed upon it by the new, and intolerable, conditions under which we all live.

The sheer scale of the problems posed by the existence of nuclear weapons or the ecologically destructive capability of human numbers armed with modern technology has created a new realm of politics, global in extent. Nothing in history has equipped us with the personal, institutional or political ability to cope with events of this magnitude.

The price of failure in this effort is no longer simply delay in the upward march of historical development. It may literally be annihilation and the end of history. Perceptions of such awesome consequences have a tendency to disable: they suppress rather than stimulate response. The overwhelming sense of urgency, often expressed as anger, that permeates the peace, environment and development movements is in large part an antidote to political disablement.

Of these three movements that most reflect the emerging voice of the post-war generation, the environment movement is pivotal. Intellectually, it integrates the other experiences. The nuclear winter which would follow, and be the most destructive effect of, a nuclear war is, in effect, the environmental aftershock. The grinding poverty of the landless poor is often a consequence, as well as a cause, of environmental degradation. Institutionally, too, the environment movement is older and stronger than the other movements, being built on foundations largely created in the first half of the century as the environmental consequences of industrialization became apparent.

Thus it is that 'green' has become the new colour in European politics. The environmentalism that is at the leading edge of the post-war generation's assault on the orthodox agenda spans the great European divides. It is as common in the communist East as it is in the capitalist West, albeit in different forms, and as deep in the Catholic South as in the Protestant North. It evokes responses equally on the authoritarian right or democratic left; among working class poor and middle class affluent. It contains within its compass the traditional European tensions between idealist and pragmatist (witness the power plays between the 'fundi' and 'realo' wings of the West German Greens), between romantic and rationalist, between revolutionary and reformer. It also reflects and transcends the newer tensions between parliamentary and extra-parliamentary politics.

The sharpest assaults on conventional European politics have taken place in Germany and Britain. Between them they cover the continuum between the parliamentary and extra-parliamentary approaches. In Germany, the parliamentary thrust is strong, the pressure groups relatively weak. In Britain, the position is reversed. In Holland, where there is a highly organized and influential non-governmental movement, there is also a long tradition of small party participation in Parliament. A formal Green Party was founded there in 1984 and has run as high as 12 per cent in the polls, well above the 4 per cent needed to enter Parliament. In Belgium, there were soon one Green Member of the European Parliament, five Senators and four MPs, in addition to more than 100 local councillors.

It was in France, though, that the environment first made a significant national electoral impact. When Brice Lalonde stood in the 1981 presidential elections, his million-plus votes represented 3.7 per cent of the vote. Internal divisions have prevented much further development of the Greens in France, despite occasionally impressive showings in the polls. Nonetheless, several hundred ecologists have been elected to French local councils. This reflects the political position of environmental organizations in France: they are nationally weak, but occasionally very powerful regionally. And so it goes through the rest of Europe. Ironically, only Norway among the 17 Western European countries did not have a Green Party by the time the World Commission on Environment and Development reported.

Much of what passes for radical politics, whether of left or right, occurs simply on the level of ideas. Too often it becomes a search for difference for difference's sake and, recognizing no limits to its imaginings, drifts remorsely into intolerance and extremism. The greening of European politics is radical in a more genuine, less self-conscious manner. It reflects the experience of many millions of Europeans. There is nothing ephemeral about what is occurring.

Although it may appear differently from country to country as circumstances, culture and political structures modulate its manifestations, the underlying experience, and the anxieties and aspirations it evokes, is common to Europeans of the post-war generations. The greening of politics is important not just for its impact on the immediate agenda, but because it represents the first attempts by these emerging generations to grapple with the politics of a wholly altered world. Doing business with these people, whether you are selling them a political party or a can of beans, is not going to be the same as doing business with their parents.

Chapter 3

BOTTOM LINES

> One of the key difficulties which industrialists face in
> talking to environmentalists is that they operate on
> very different time-scales. Most businesses consider a
> two-year time horizon a luxury, focusing instead on
> quarter-by-quarter results. Ironically, the failure of
> many major industries can be traced to this myopia and
> the environmental challenge can help by forcing
> industrialists to raise their sights.

'In one sense, our job is to make decision-makers' jobs more difficult,' admitted Jeremy Russell, describing the work of Shell UK's business environment group. 'We aim to provide them with information which increases the number and complexity of factors to be taken into consideration when deciding upon a strategy. In certain cases,' he noted, 'the information may encourage them to consider issues from an entirely new perspective.'

In a growing number of cases, too, this is turning out to be a 'greener' perspective than they would have adopted even a few years back. The boards of leading companies may not welcome the growing complexity of the decisions they have to take, but many of them recognize that a much closer eye needs to be kept on the ways in which their business environment is changing. Russell and his team of six assistants focused on energy, economic, societal, political and environmental issues. The environmental aspects of this type of work are becoming increasingly important. 'Ultimately,' as Russell put it, 'it is the survival of our external environment which will enable us all to survive, and Shell UK has always recognized this very clearly. Now, more than ever, environmental factors play a central role in our considerations.'

In fact, if one looks around for the major trends in business thinking, one of the most striking changes has been the growing interest of companies in capturing a major slice of global markets in the longer term, rather than simply in quarter-by-quarter financial results. One reason for this has been the fact that the quarter-by-quarter results in many companies have been so frighteningly bad.

Corporate myopia has been particularly marked in the United States. 'It is remarkable how willing American business people are to make the current quarter look better at the expense of the future, to sacrifice the future to make this year's bottom line a little more attractive or less embarrassing,' business consultant, John Naisbitt, noted in his best-selling book, *Megatrends*. Naisbitt is not the only critic of the blinkered focus of many leading industrialists. Listen to Lee Iacocca, the man who brought ailing Chrysler back from the brink of bankruptcy and co-author of a best-selling autobiography, *Iacocca*.

Downsizing Detroit

'As long as Detroit was making money,' Iacocca recalled in a damning indictment of the American automobile industry's myopia in the key labour relations field, 'it was always easy for us to accept union demands and recoup them later in the form of price increases. The alternative was to take a strike and risk ruining the company. The executives at General Motors (GM), Ford and Chrysler have never been overly interested in long-range planning. They've been too concerned about expediency, improving the profits for the next quarter—and earning a good bonus.'

Iacocca admitted that he had behaved in the same way. 'I sat there in the midst of it all,' as he put it, 'and I said: "Discretion is the better part of valor. Give them what they want. Because if they strike, we'll lose hundreds of millions of dollars, we'll lose our bonuses, and I'll personally lose half a million dollars in cash". Our motivation was greed. The instinct was to settle quickly, to go for the bottom line.'

In the end, the auto industry paid dearly, as Japanese imports swept many American models off the board. Indeed, Iacocca noted: 'Today we're all paying for our complacency.' As far as the environmental pressure was concerned, Iacocca had few kind words to say, recalling that the outpouring of emission control and other environmental regulations involved Chrysler and its competitors in seemingly endless paperwork required by the Environmental Protection Agency (EPA). Chrysler, he recalled, was overwhelmed by 'the sheer volume of staff time and paperwork necessary to report on our EPA regulatory confirmations. In 1978 alone, we had to file 228,000 pages to the EPA!'

Because bigger companies like GM and Ford could spread such costs over larger auto production runs, Iacocca concluded that the EPA and other regulators had played a key role in pushing his company to the brink of collapse. 'The government helped to get us into this mess,' he argued, when applying for a $1.5 billion federal loan, 'so the government should be willing to help get us out.'

Yet the sort of short-term thinking which originally involved the American auto industry in such problems was illustrated by the resistance to 'downsizing' new models after the 1973 OPEC oil embargo. Iacocca was then at Ford and keen to develop smaller cars. 'Small, fuel-efficient, front-wheel-drive cars were the wave of the future,' he had concluded. 'You didn't have to be genius to figure this out. All you had to do was read the sales figures for 1974, a terrible year for Detroit. Sales at GM dropped by a million and a half vehicles. Sales at Ford were off by half a million. The Japanese had most of the small cars, and they were selling like crazy.' But as far as Henry Ford was concerned, 'small cars were a dead end. His favorite expression was "minicars, miniprofits".'

In the end, Ford came up with smaller models like the Fiesta, but not before Japanese and European manufacturers had severely dented its market share. The large companies had spent too long making cars they wanted to make and were tooled up to make rather than focusing on what the market was likely to demand.

One of Iacocca's early mentors at Ford had said to him: 'Make money. Screw everything else. This is a profit-making system, boy. The rest is frills.' Unfortunately, as Iacocca and other leading industrialists now found, the rest was not frills. The rest, including energy efficiency and pollution control goals, was increasingly shaping the central goals of auto design.

As far as future levels of emission control were concerned, the big auto companies needed to look no further than California, where unusually restrictive emission standards were introduced in response to the photochemical smog problems that have plagued Los Angeles. 'California has contributed some things that we in Michigan aren't too happy about,' said Iacocca, with masterly understatement. 'One is the import boom. Californians buy more imported cars than the residents of other states. Second, they've given us some supercharged standards that have already transformed California itself into a foreign country. It's been said before, but it's worth saying again: California is really the mirror into the future. Sometimes we don't like everything we see when we gaze into that mirror,' he agreed, 'but we'd be crazy if we didn't take a good, hard look.'

Different Clocks

Whichever mirror they use, environmentalists are concerned about the future and about the world which future generations will inherit. Their central message: We do not inherit the planet from our parents and grandparents, we borrow it from our children and grandchildren. This perspective, however hard business environment specialists may try and get it across in the boardroom, does not integrate particularly well with most business thinking. This is not to say that there are no industrialists who think in these terms: there certainly are. Bruce Smart, who was chairman and chief executive officer of The Continental Group before joining the Reagan Administration, has been one such industrialist (see page 22).

The problem, however, is that industrialists and environmentalists are generally working to different clocks. This is more than a matter of simply operating in different time-zones. It is more like two cultures colliding, producing inevitable culture shock. The time-scales are completely different. How, for example, can someone who is thinking about the implications of the felling of today's rainforests for the global climate in the year 2050 even begin to converse with someone who thinks of the 'long term' as 18 months to two years at the outside?

This is not an invented problem. It is a real issue even in the best-run businesses and for perfectly understandable economic reasons. 'Too many managers feel under pressure to concentrate on the short term in order to satisfy the financial community and the owners of the enterprise, the stockholders,' warned the retiring chairman of General Electric. 'In the United States, if your firm has a bad quarter, it's headlines. Real trouble ensues. The stock price falls out of bed. That's far different from Japan and Germany.' Anyone trying to massage a company's results into a shape likely to keep Wall Street happy is unlikely to have much time for developing a business strategy capable of taking the company through the next couple of decades.

'People talk of sustainable development,' as ICI group environment adviser Mike Flux summarized the problem, 'but it's a difficult message to sell in industry. There's an inherent conflict in time-scales. The idea of sustainable development is something I can accept philosophically, but the time-scale can be measured in decades, even generations. Even oil, for all the scares, is a resource which will prove finite outside our lifetimes. The facts are that most people in industry operate on a two year time-span. Hopefully the board operates on a somewhat longer time-frame, but it will be hauled back every time the economy goes into a nose-dive.'

As environmentalists begin to address the practicalities of real-world problems and as industrialists adapt to the longer-term thinking forced on them by the competitive pressures in international markets, however, there are moments when the different clocks seem on the verge of synchronizing, or when that culture shock begins to look like an essential part of a global learning process.

In many companies, the time-frame for key decisions is stretching significantly. 'Although Japan's example inspired part of the shift to long-range thinking,' John Naisbitt concluded, 'there is another important factor behind the changes American business is beginning to make. During the past decade the debate over the environment and nonrenewable resources has raised our collective consciousness about the dangers of the short-term approach. As a general proposition, we have become much more sensitive to the longer-range implications of our short-term actions.'

However, it would be misleading to ignore the long-term planning that does go on in some parts of industry. Indeed, a growing number of companies operate on a longer time-scale than most democratic governments, with their 4 to 5 year cycle of re-election. Many of us, in fact, are unaware of the length of time that it takes to bring an industrial product to market.

'When we talk about the "near term" in some areas,' explained Ford vice president, Helen Petrauskas, 'we are talking about 25 years. For example, in the waste disposal field what's happening in the US is that disposal sites are being closed, sites are being abandoned, the capacity of the entire waste disposal industry is being cut. I need to be assured that we can find secure access to well-run disposal sites for at least 25 years. And even in our mainstream business areas, you are often talking of time-scales in excess of a decade. If you invest in a new engine, you are often talking of 10, 12 or 14 years; that's far from unusual.'

Maps of the future

So while environmentalists place a shift to longer-term thinking high on their wish-list, many industrialists now see they *need* to make such a shift. Environmentalists talk of the transition to a more sustainable society, a more sustainable economy, while a growing number of industrialists are wondering whether such a transition could, at worst, undermine their markets or, at best, open up totally new market opportunities.

Environmental professionals are increasingly thinking about ways of getting industry involved in the drive for sustainable development. William Ruckelshaus, during his second term as Administrator of the US Environmental Protection Agency, described the private sector as 'a vast reservoir of untapped creative talent'. Despite tight budgetary constraints, he argued 'this is where many solutions will be generated'.

The key to tapping industry's enthusiasm and ingenuity may be to get sympathetic companies involved from the very earliest possible moment. Baron Leon de Rosen, a former director of the United Nations Environment Programme's Industry and Environment Office, put it this way: 'Whether you talk of deforestation, or desertification, or soil erosion, or acid rain, there always comes a moment when industry is called upon to provide, say, environmental monitoring equipment, earthmoving machinery, fertilizers, and other products or services. Since they are going to be involved eventually anyway, it makes sense to get them in at the beginning.'

Baron de Rosen also stressed that many of the problems now causing such concern have been severe for many years, but appear more acute because public opinion is only now becoming aware of them. This is clearly a positive development, although there is always the danger that politicians will be stampeded into adopting the wrong solutions simply because they have been caught off-guard.

Anyone who has been carefully following the trends in environmental policy and legislation will recognize that we are entering a new stage in the environmental revolution. Jim MacNeill, when director for the environment at the Organization for Economic Co-operation and Development (OECD), warned that environmental issues were taking on a very different complexion.

'The first environmental debate,' he suggested, 'focused on environmental pollution. It took off very quickly on a global scale and led, in a remarkably short period of time, to a wide array of institutions, policies and instruments designed to correct past abuses, reduce pollution and preserve and enhance the environment. Its objectives and the means required to achieve them were both relatively straightforward. They retain their importance, and some evidence suggests that they may even become increasingly relevant in the mid-term future.

'The second debate,' he continued, 'which is now under way, asks how the environment can be integrated into our society. It is characterized by an increased emphasis on policies that are anticipatory and preventive, reinforcing those that are reactive and curative. It reflects a heightened awareness in many quarters of the interdependence among economic growth, energy and resource management, product control and environmental quality. It presupposes that policies in these areas can be mutually reinforcing rather than always in conflict.'

This second debate has not taken off as fast as the first, but already MacNeill saw signs of 'a third, even more profound debate to come. It is based on the view that even anticipatory environmental policies cannot attack the fundamental forces underlying the continuing degradation of the environment. It argues that these forces are set in the personal habits and cultural traditions of our society and in the institutional forms which serve it. It raises questions of alternative lifestyles and alternative growth patterns compatible with the maintenance of a healthy environment.'

So how does an industrialist sum up the need for sustainable development? 'For society to be sustainable,' as Bruce Smart put it, when he was chairman of the Continental Group, 'world population must come to equilibrium within the carrying capacity of man's habitat—the ability of the earth to feed, shelter, clothe, care for, educate, amuse, and dispose of the wastes of its inhabitants. And that population must be sufficiently content with its lot to avoid triggering the destructive behaviour typical of species living in excessively crowded conditions.'

We may not like to think of our future, of our children's future, in these terms, but unless we take thought for what the future holds we could find ourselves backed into a rather unpleasant corner. Private industry has a very considerable role to play in the transition to more sustainable forms of development, as Smart himself recognized. If industry fails to respond to the challenge, the transition to sustainable forms of development will probably be impossible to achieve. Its willing support must be recruited, even if it is often currently part of the problems for which solutions are now being sought.

Private industry, as Smart noted, is among the largest institutions in most countries, 'commands the most resources, moves the most quickly and flexibly, is the least bound by traditional structure or ideology. It is the engine of wealth creation. It has learned the rule of the marketplace—*change or die*. The times call for massive change, and business knows how to manage change.'

This obviously is not to imply that adapting to change, or helping to drive change forward, is an easy business. For most companies, the 1973 OPEC oil embargo and its aftermath represented an incredibly difficult period of transition. Sadly, but perhaps predictably, corporate planners were blamed for industry's failure to predict the successive oil crises. As chemical manufacturers found they had built too many petrochemical plants or tyre makers found their longer-lived tyres meant they sold fewer new tyres, many companies concluded that long-term planning was simply not worth the effort.

In an era of increasing uncertainty, however, a new form of

planning began to surface: scenario planning. Shell is the oldest practitioner of this particular art, which it started developing in 1970. In fact, early scenario exercises predicted many aspects of the oil crisis, but went largely unheeded by senior management.

'Scenarios,' explained Peter Schwartz, then head of Shell International's business environment group, 'can be summed up as stories about the future. They function as a sort of mental map. Every one of us has a mental map of the world and, if our map is a good one, we are more likely to make good decisions. If our map is poor, we will be operating in a world of illusions.'

Some businesses, for example, are built on sand. They undermine their own future by undermining their natural resource base, as the whaling industry did, or the health of their customers or employees. An example of the latter case is the asbestos industry. Asbestos has been widely used for many years in buildings, ships, clothing and a broad range of other products, although there has been growing evidence that exposure to particular types of asbestos can cause such diseases as asbestosis and cancers. The difficulty here is that some of these diseases may take up to 40 years to surface. In the case of the US company Manville Corporation, thousands of individual law suits filed by those affected called for billions of dollars in damages and forced Manville, keen to protect itself from its victims, into voluntary bankruptcy.

But the story did not end there. If the company had actually foundered, the claimants would have lost out. By filing for what is called Chapter XI protection, however, Manville was able to continue operating under court supervision. Here, the aim of the exercise was not only to keep the business running for its own sake, but to find ways of paying off its debts. The option preferred by Manville was to set up a trust fund for the victims and their families, with the initial money coming from Manville's insurers, after which the company would continue to pay perhaps 20 per cent of its profits into the trust fund.

Because Manville is not now dependent on asbestos for its profits, a solution has been devised where those who were damaged or suffered some loss now have a stake in the future of the business. However, Manville's plight illustrates how a problem can build up over decades and ultimately threaten the survival of a company or, in some cases, an entire industry.

Poisoning the future

'When you say Times Beach to people,' said the woman who was that blighted town's last mayor, 'I think they look you up and down to see if you're green or glow in the dark.' If any one town in the United States symbolizes what has been wrong with the way in which industry has chosen to draw its bottom lines, it surely is this Missouri ghost town. A waste contractor sprayed dioxin-contaminated waste on roads throughout the area, making Times Beach effectively uninhabitable. None of his corporate clients checked to see what he was up to.

When the toxic waste issue grabbed the US headlines in the early 1980s, Congress reacted by voting through an emergency five-year clean-up programme, backed by a $1.6 billion 'Superfund'. Many politicians hoped that that would be the end of the story, but when the five-year programme expired in 1985, the Environmental Protection Agency's third director, Lee Thomas, admitted that: 'We have a far bigger problem than we thought when Superfund was enacted. There are far more sites that are far more difficult to deal with than anybody ever anticipated.'

The American dream, it transpires, has been bought at the cost of turning many areas of the country into toxic nightmares. The Office of Technology Assessment estimated that there could be at least 10,000 major hazardous waste sites in the United States, with the costs of clean-up likely to be in the region of $100 billion, or over $1,000 for every US household. Worse, the General Accounting Office reckoned that there could be as many as 378,000 sites which would eventually need to be cleaned up to some degree. As veteran environmentalist, Barry Commoner, told *Time* magazine: 'We are poisoning ourselves and our posterity.'

Companies which devote considerable resources to environmental protection are keen to set the problem in perspective. 'We're doing a lot better than a few decades ago,' was the way Du Pont executive vice president, Robert Forney, put it. 'If we clean up our past mistakes and adhere rigorously to recent improvements in managing toxic wastes, we'll catch up in time.'

Perhaps so, but evidence continues to build up which suggests that even today's high technology companies are still causing pollution problems of their own. Fairchild Camera and Instrument, for example, one of the Silicon Valley pioneers, discovered that a storage tank under its plant had been leaking, contaminating a local well with 1,1,1-trichloroethane, a degreasing agent used in the microchip industry. This substance is known to damage the central nervous system, liver and heart. While there is still considerable uncertainty about the precise links between such groundwater pollution and human health problems, local residents began suing the company, alleging that the pollution of their drinking water had caused miscarriages and birth defects among their children. Fairchild immediately spent $14 million trying to clean up the mess, but test wells still showed contamination. A leak-proof tank and leak detection equipment would have cost $100,000.

In some cases, what the economist would call the environmental 'externalities' of industrial activity are felt within minutes. Nowhere is this clearer than in the Third World. 'A plant starts dumping something into the atmosphere and this place immediately fills up with people begging for oxygen,' said Claudimir Rodrigues, a doctor working in a clinic in Cubatão, possibly the most polluted town on earth.

The Brazilian government, prepared to modernize at almost any cost, selected the town as a centre for industrial growth and Petrobras was the first major company to set up a petrochemical plant there. Although multinational companies like Monsanto and Union Carbide also have operations in the area, it is generally agreed that the main problems are caused by Petrobras and other Brazilian companies, including the Sao Paolo Steel Company, known as Cosiba, and Fertilizantes IAP.

'We became aware of environmental problems only in the 1970s,' explained Cosiba's environmental manager. 'We will spend $90 million to update our pollution control equipment over the next few years. But these things take time to implement. They don't happen overnight.' In 1983, voters chose a new governor for the state of Sao Paolo, Andre Franco Montoto, who began to take a much tougher line with the industries clustering around Cubatão. 'He tripled the number of pollution control experts at the environmental protection agency,' the *Wall Street Journal* reported a couple of years later, 'and turned it loose against the biggest polluters. The agency now routinely closes down factories when emissions sky-rocket and is requiring companies to install full anti-pollution systems.'

However, once such an industrial ulcer forms in the environment, it can take a very long time to heal. Hazardous wastes have been dumped with very little control, an approach which will inevitably turn out to have been painfully short-sighted and many of the health effects of the extraordinary levels of pollution which have been typical both in workplaces and the open environment will not show up for many years.

Some substances, carcinogens, will eventually prove to have triggered cancers in those exposed to them, as they already have in the developed countries. Others may prove to have been mutagens, capable of causing mutations. Any attempt to assess the risks imposed by an increased mutation rate, however, tends to be quite different in kind from most other risk-benefit analyses carried out today.

When the US Committee on Chemical Environment Mutagens reported the findings of its study on the genetic impact of chemical mutagens, it pointed out that 'it is not unusual for the benefits and risks to go to different persons; ideally there is some form of compensation. However, it is unusual for the benefits and risks to be many generations apart. In the case of chemical mutagens,' it stressed, 'most of the beneficiaries are living now, whereas most of those at risk have not been born and perhaps will not be born for many centuries.'

Even such concerns as these pale beside those associated with the use of nuclear technology. Nuclear wastes contain some extraordinarily long-lived health hazards. For example, when Greenpeace launched its campaign against the French government's use of the Muroroa atoll for atomic bomb tests (see page 48), France replied that it was carrying out the tests within a mass of basalt, the remains of a volcano which has been extinct for seven million years. It claimed this rock was iron-hard and the wastes generated by the explosions were safely contained for all time. However, a team of scientists from New Zealand, Australia and Papua New Guinea concluded that the series of nuclear explosions has already caused fissures and subsidence in the rocky foundations of the atoll.

Even if the tests stopped immediately, they argued, these nuclear wastes would begin to escape within 1,000 years. Among the materials likely to escape is neptunium, the most stable isotope and also produced in commercial nuclear reactors. Neptunium has a 'half-life', the period which half an element's radioactivity takes to decay, of 2.2 million years.

The French government has tried to play down the risks. President Mitterrand himself, however, appointed France's first Secretary of State for the Prevention of Major Natural and Technological Disasters. Known familiarly as 'Monsieur Catastrophe', Haroun Tazieff warned that: 'The quantity of potential disasters is increasing. There are more and more factories dealing with dangerous chemicals, more and more dangerous materials being transported by road and rail, and ever larger and more concentrated population centres at risk.' The transport of nuclear fuels, he admitted, was 'one of my biggest concerns.'

Moreover, Tazieff put his finger on the key problem when dealing with governments. 'When it comes to the point,' he concluded, 'governments hate to be warned. They prefer not to see or hear anything about possible disasters, whether natural or technological.'

The shifting bottom line

Monsieur Catastrophe's reaction to his brief, which he nonetheless felt would become a much more common feature in the thinking of other governments, is worth noting. 'I feel I have been preaching in a desert,' he said. Too often, in an increasingly complex world, governments prefer to impose controls only in the wake of disasters. This is nothing new, of course, as the story of one of Britain's most publicized clean-up successes shows.

'Your Mississippi,' a Battersea-born Briton once chided an American champion of that river, 'is plain mud, but the Thames is *liquid 'istory*.' Indeed, and an ecological history of London's river provides an embarrassingly sensitive barometer of the environmental pressures generated by those who have lived and worked within the river's extensive watershed.

During the eighteenth century, for instance, it was recorded that salmon were so plentiful in the Thames that apprentices protested that they were eating nothing else. Yet a survey in 1957 was unable to produce any evidence at all of fish life from Richmond down to Gravesend. The only life-forms surviving were those which either literally kept their heads above the water, such as the gulls and a few adult eels breathing at the surface, or those, such as certain types of worm, which thrive only in highly polluted conditions.

The word 'Thames' derives from the Celtic *Taom-Uis* or pouring out of waters. There have been complaints about the quality of those waters for well over five centuries, but early attempts at pollution control simply pushed the environmental 'bottom line' from one place to the next, with the emphasis on the principle, 'out of sight, out of mind'. The problem was progressively shunted from doorstep to street, from street to river bank, and thence into the river itself.

Environmental legislation was enacted as early as 1388, prohibiting the 'corruption' of London's air and water, with little effect. The real problems, however, began with the widespread use of water as the medium for much waste disposal. With the invention and diffusion of the water closet, 'night soil' was no longer spread on the fields around the city. Instead, it was discharged into the town drains and channelled thence, untreated, direct into the Thames.

The problem was acute by the early nineteenth century, with many major outbreaks of cholera. Dr John Snow presented evidence to show that contaminated drinking water, drawn direct from the Thames, was the main culprit, but the government of the day was slow to react. In 1856, however, the 'Year of the Great Stink', the Thames gave off such mighty clouds of hydrogen sulphide that the nation's legislators were overcome at their work. Consequently, 1857 saw the foundation of the Thames Conservancy, charged with preventing the pollution of the river, and the 1860s saw intensive investment in Sir Joseph Bazalgette's magnificent new sewerage system.

The Bazalgette system was a radical improvement on its predecessors, which had been poorly co-ordinated, built to different standards and were often tide-locked and stagnant. However, even Bazalgette's design simply relocated the problem, this time a few miles downstream. The complaints of those living near the new outfalls at Beckton and Crossness, respectively 11 and 15 miles downstream from London Bridge, stirred few consciences, even when the Barking inquiry of 1869 confirmed that fish were unable to survive in the vicinity of the outfalls, owing to a miscalculation about the rate at which the crude sewage would be carried out of the estuary on the ebb tide.

It took the foundering of a pleasureship, the *Princess Alice*, near the Beckton outfall, to bring the subject back into the headlines of September 1878. The inquest on the 640 victims concluded that there was a high probability that some had been poisoned, not drowned. Experimental sewage treatment soon followed, with elementary treatment plants built at Beckton in 1889 and at Crossness in 1891. New intercepting sewers were built in the early 1900s, but the momentum was not maintained. During the Second World War, in particular, bomb damage to sewers, sewage works, and factories had an adverse impact on the quality of the Thames. The dispersal of industry, especially of munitions manufacturing, meant that there were many small sources of heavy metals and other pollutants which were almost impossible to control.

By the late 1940s, the Thames was again black, foul-smelling and anaerobic. New pollutants were also emerging, such as the synthetic detergents introduced during the 1950s. Sometimes called 'surface active agents', these detergents spread on the surface of water and slowed the natural processes whereby oxygen is absorbed from the air. The most damaging of early 'hard' detergents was alkyl benzyl sulphonate, which was not decomposed in the biological treatment of existing sewage works. Indeed, it reduced the efficiency of such plants by some 30 per cent and buried at least one works under 15 feet of foam. Biodegradable detergents were increasingly adopted, with most hard detergents phased out by the end of 1964.

Other industrial pressures on the river included the thermal pollution produced by the warm water discharges from the cooling systems of some 20 Thames-side power stations, causing oxygen depletion. Nonetheless, the improvements achieved in sewage treatment and effluent discharges meant that fish began to return to the river in 1963. By 1967, a regular survey of fish caught in the cooling water intakes of Thames-side power stations was instituted and over 90 species were soon identified. The real stamp of approval came with the discovery of the first salmon at West Thurrock power station, a fish which had been absent from the river for over 100 years.

Even today, however, the clean Thames is primarily achieved by the dumping of sewage sludges out at sea. Properly managed, this approach will probably be acceptable for some time, but it seems likely that future generations will not want to draw this particular bottom line on the floor of the North Sea. There are still many other rivers around Britain whose quality is unbelievably poor. Indeed, the Thames clean-up probably owed more to the fact that it flows past the Mother of Parliaments than to anything else.

Around the world, meanwhile, other rivers are still running several hundred years behind the Thames in terms of pollution control. For example, there is Mother Ganges, the 1,550-mile sacred river through which passes a quarter of India's surface water. 'The Ganges is not yet totally polluted,' Professor Verr Bhadra Mishra, president of the Clean Ganges Campaign, told *The Guardian*, 'but wrinkles have started appearing on the face of the mother.' Indeed, he warned: 'There is more and more pollution, less and less dilution. Nature can no longer take care of it. The river is very dear to all of us, but its powers are not infinite.'

It remains to be seen whether the sacred river can, like the Thames, be resurrected. The Indian government has set up a Ganges authority to start cleaning up the river, with £180 million promised for the five years to 1990. An indication of how seriously the problem was being taken was the fact that Prime Minister Rajiv Gandhi took the chair.

The size of the challenge is indicated by the fact that the city of Benares alone discharges some 20 million tonnes of sewage into the river every day, while a tremendous array of factories also dump their noxious wastes into the river. If you visit Ghazipur, you may well come across the ultimate symbol of Ganges pollution: a tribe of monkeys which have become addicted to the effluent pouring out of a government opium factory.

Something in the air
Question: What have the Taj Mahal, the Acropolis and the Statue of Liberty got in common? *Answer:* They have all taken the acid test and are crumbling as a result.

Acid rain has been one of the hottest environmental issues in recent years, or perhaps one should rather say 'acid deposition', as the scientists prefer to call it, because acid pollution can either come in wet forms (mist, rain or snow) or in dry forms (gases, particles or smog).

Most people tend to think of sulphur dioxide when acid rain problems are mentioned, but other gases and substances are also now thought to be implicated. These include nitrogen oxides, hydrocarbons and ozone, whether acting alone or in concert. As the municipal forestry director for the West German town of Regensburg put it: 'The mixing of sulphur dioxide and nitrogen oxides is not one plus one equals two. It is one plus one equals three.' Sometimes two compounds combine to produce a more damaging compound, but in this case it may be that one compound depresses a tree's ability to protect itself against the other. Whatever the truth of the matter, this issue, more than any other, has highlighted the way in which a world of nation states tends to draw its environmental bottom lines around national boundaries.

Countries which have been victims of environmental acidification, such as the Scandinavian nations, have campaigned long and hard for tighter controls on the gases which are causing the problem. Countries like Britain which produce more than their fair share of these gases have lobbied vigorously against tighter controls, largely because of the cost likely to be involved in solving problems from which local politicians will get no real electoral benefit.

However, that is not to say that the issue is not political: it is in fact extremely highly charged. Canada has had a long-standing quarrel with the United States, which is responsible for much of the acid deposition affecting Canadian lakes, while countries like Norway have at times hardly been on speaking terms with Britain. In Britain's House of Commons, the Opposition environment spokesman actually warned the Government that its rejection of a £1.5 billion plan to curb acid pollution was tantamount to waging chemical warfare on the country's neighbours.

This sort of concern is not confined to the Opposition benches. Several of the countries most affected by acid deposition invited members of the House of Commons Environment Committee to see the evidence for themselves. The Committee's chairman, the Conservative MP Sir Hugh Rossi, returned with no doubts that the problems were real ones.

The point to remember about the Select Committee, as Sir Hugh himself put it, was that: 'We are not Greens or militant environmentalists. We are a group of 11 MPs, with a sizeable Conservative majority.' Needless to say, however, their report was not popular in Government circles.

'I think the turning point for us was our visit to West Germany and Scandinavia,' Sir Hugh recalled. 'Whether flying in a helicopter over the Black Forest, its lush green complexion stained brown and blotchy; or climbing, somewhat shakily, up Cologne Cathedral to inspect the repairs to crumbling spires and grotesquely disfigured statues; or walking by the Tovdal River in Norway, once a major salmon river, where no fish have been caught for ten years,' he reported, 'in each case we were horrified at the visible and tragic effects of an unseen pollutant.'

The Germans, not surprisingly, have a word for it: *Waldsterben*. The word means the dying forest syndrome. 'The Germans have always had a great ambivalence towards industrial civilization,' explained the director of the Cologne-based Institute of Applied Social Research. 'The woods for them are an alternative world to industry.' Now the evidence suggests that industry is helping destroy that other, greener world. Air pollution is not the only factor involved in the death of Europe's forests, but as one forester put it: '*Waldsterben* is not possible without air pollution.'

As recently as 1982, around 7 per cent of West Germany's trees were visibly affected, but just a year later 34 per cent of the country's trees were thought to have suffered some needle and leaf loss, or discoloration. By 1984, one tree in every two was affected to some degree. In southwestern Germany, home of the Black Forest, as many as 75 per cent of the trees were damaged or killed in some areas. Public opinion polls have shown that the West German public ranks the problem right at the top of national priorities.

Countries as far apart as Czechoslovakia and China are now showing alarming forest damage, together with other symptoms of acid pollution. Statistics are generally harder to come by for the communist bloc countries, however. In East Germany, 86 per cent of the country's three million hectares of woodland are thought to have been affected, while in Czechoslovakia at least 20 per cent of the nation's trees are recorded as irreversibly damaged.

Even the Arctic environment is showing signs of acid pollution, with airborne scientists reporting a 'brownish haze' in the atmosphere, and air sampling filters turning 'flannel grey' or 'sooty black'. 'Acid pollution,' as John McCormick explained in his book *Acid Earth*, 'is a classic instance of economic and industrial development proceeding at the expense of the environment. It may well be the most universal and most pressing transfrontier environmental issue of the century, proving a test case for the lip service paid to environmental management by more and more governments over the past decade.'

Some governments are making a stand, however. Canada, for example, plans to force four of Ontario's largest polluters to cut their sulphur dioxide emissions by 64 per cent of their 1980 emission figures within nine years. The heaviest cut, of 77 per cent, is being imposed on Inco, whose Sudbury smelter is North America's biggest single pollution source.

Few environmental problems more graphically illustrate what Garrett Hardin, professor emeritus of human ecology at the University of California at Santa Barbara, dubbed 'the tragedy of the commons'. The tragedy of the commons is that if each person with a right to loose animals over a particular piece of common land pushes his or her right to the limit, then the commons will be overgrazed and everyone will suffer. Today, though, we are talking about global commons, such as the atmosphere, the world's rain-forests and oceans, not village greens.

Indeed, if there is one major environmental challenge which may yet outrank acid rain, it is the build-up of carbon dioxide in the atmosphere. Scientists are tracking down old air, trapped in bottles, compasses, telescopes or old brass buttons, which might tell us how much carbon dioxide there was in the atmosphere when these products were manufactured. Two Connecticut companies have offered to supply samples of their hollow military buttons spanning almost two centuries. This sort of research, however, will simply fill in the details: what is not in dispute is that carbon dioxide levels have risen consistently since 1860, presumably in large part because of the growing use of fossil fuels.

The earth's atmosphere as a whole operates very much like the glass in a greenhouse, trapping solar radiation, so scientists have been asking what would happen if this trend continued unabated? Given long enough, the oceans might well absorb much of this carbon dioxide and the world's forests also act as an important 'carbon sink', but the rapid rate of deforestation around the world is reducing the absorptive capacity of the forest sink. If carbon dioxide build-up does turn out to be a significant problem, altering weather patterns and even climate, it will prove an unparalleled bottleneck for future industrial development, although perhaps not an insuperable one in the very long term.

Meanwhile, however, many other forms of economic activity continue to erode the environmental diversity which we have borrowed from our children and grandchildren. Even the transition to a 'leisure society' is having a major impact on the environment, which remains tourism's basic resource. The turtles of Zante offer a ready example. The uncontrolled growth of tourism around Laganas Bay, on the Greek island of Zante, is threatening the Mediterranean's main nesting ground for the endangered sea turtle. These need darkness and an undisturbed sandy beach if they are to lay their eggs, conditions which tourism is banishing.

'Speed-boats plough the bay all day and frighten the sea turtles which gather in the shallow waters by the hundreds to prepare to come ashore,' said Lily Venizelos of the Sea Turtle Protection Society. When they finally emerge from the sea at night, they are faced with cars and motorcycles, beach parties and the blare of discos. If they succeed in running this gauntlet successfully and lay their eggs without incident, the resulting hatchlings, which find their way to the sea by the faint natural light at the horizon, can be misled by the dazzling hotel lights, falling easy prey to predators such as gulls and ravens.

The turtles are part of the global commons, so they have been seen as of little economic value by the people of Zante, particularly when compared with the value of tourism revenues. Interestingly, however, the Greek environment ministry and the European Commission have been looking at ways in which the turtles might be saved. The idea is to establish a marine park, so that scientists can study the turtles and the tourists can enjoy them too. 'The idea,' explained project co-ordinator, Dimitri Margaritoulis, 'is to get the local landowners and the villagers to become shareholders in this venture in order to give them a vested interest in the survival of the sea turtles. This is the only way to save them.'

When future generations look back at this period of economic history, they may well conclude that we, like those hatchling turtles, were seduced away from sustainable development by the bright lights of consumerism. They will certainly draw the environmental bottom line very differently. But the tale of the Zante turtles symbolizes a rather surprising fact about today's world: private ownership and private enterprise, far from being endangered forms of economic activity, are playing an increasingly important role in the transition to more sustainable forms of development. And as consumers begin to demand more in terms of quality, both in the products and services they buy, so the pressures on industry to move further down this road will inevitably intensify.

II
COMPROMISE
The Corporate Chameleons

Chapter 4

THE GLOBAL GUSHER

If any one industry has shaped the second half of the
twentieth century, it is the oil industry. We live in
the Oil Age. The onset of the era of tanker 'super-spills'
made the industry's problems headline news. But the oil
companies have also pioneered in such fields as
environmental management and environmental
impact assessment. In the long view, however, the
'global gusher' may well be seen as an aberration,
encouraging levels of energy use which are
unsustainable.

A sign on the desk of one Atlantic Richfield director read: 'All
business is making changes in anticipation of changes being shoved
down your throat.' Some of the changes that have been forced down
the oil industry's throat in recent years have turned oilmen a distinct
shade of green.

As recently as 1985, Atlantic Richfield, better known as Arco,
was the sixth largest US oil company. However, the merger
mania which swept the oil industry forced Arco to make itself less
attractive to 'corporate raiders' such as T. Boone Pickens, variously
described as a 'real-life J. R. Ewing' and the 'Dracula of the oil
patch'. The company wrote off $1.5 billion in assets, sold or
closed all its metal and mining operations east of the Mississippi
River and bought back some of its own stock, to the value of
$4 billion.

Few people had imagined in the midst of the worldwide energy
crisis triggered by OPEC's oil embargo in 1974 that just ten years
later the oil industry would be thrown into confusion by an oil glut
and falling prices. The pressure to increase the efficiency of oil
industry operations became intense. But one thing has not changed:

the world might be using oil more efficiently, but it still needs prodigious quantities of this commodity.

The exploration work pressed ahead even as oil prices fell. 'Our industry is one that has to look to the long term,' explained Amoco chairman, Richard Morrow. 'Many actions we are taking today will not have any impact on our financial performance in the next ten years. When prices start to move up, as they will in the late 1980s and getting on through the 1990s, the control of oil for a company like ours will be very important.'

For if there is one thing about which economists can be certain, it is that the law of diminishing returns applies to oil exploration. Nobody knows how quickly the oil industry's returns will diminish, but the trend is clear: oil is becoming harder and more costly to find.

Mobil, one of the 'Seven Sisters' of the oil world, poured $300 million into drilling a single borehole at Mukluk Island, in Alaska. This proved to be the world's most expensive dry hole to date. In fact, 48 of the first 49 wells drilled in Alaska's outer continental shelf proved to be dry. Shell, however, found a modest 300 million barrel field not far from Mukluk Island and various oil companies drilled as many as 40 wells before discovering the nine-billion barrel Prudhoe Bay field, which now accounts for over ten per cent of US production. Thus the oil companies often continue drilling even in areas where the initial signs are unpromising. However, to step back in time a little, the unhappy truth is that oil discoveries reached their peak before the first OPEC oil embargo, which was triggered by the October War of 1973.

'Even though surging oil prices spurred exploration and development in the following ten years,' as Herman Franssen, head of energy economics at the International Energy Agency, has put it, 'gross additions to the world's oil reserves were only 259 billion barrels (excluding the planned economies) between 1973 and 1984, compared with 328 billion barrels in the 1964 to 1973 period.'

Despite huge sums invested, and some experts say the oil industry's capital and exploration spending tripled over ten years to reach $60 billion in 1983, only western Europe and Mexico showed oil production gains that anywhere near reflected this effort. Production from the mature North American fields actually fell over the decade. Most of the giant and super-giant fields were discovered before 1970, Franssen noted in 1985, concluding that 'it is doubtful whether even the modest record of new discoveries of the Seventies can be matched in the next 15 years.'

In other words, oil market signals that the world has an abundance of oil are misleading and even dangerous. The geological facts of the matter are that the oil industry is exploiting a non-renewable resource at a rate which, on current levels of consumption, is projected to run through the world's remaining oil in little more than 30 years. Whatever else it may be, this cannot be described as sustainable development.

The human factor

When the oil companies do find oil, the chances are that they will encounter fierce opposition from environmentalists who fear that the search for 'black gold' will cause widespread ecological damage. And the oil industry can hardly plead total innocence in the matter.

The public is often accused of having a short memory, but companies like Amoco, Arco, Chevron, Exxon and Shell, all of which own rights to offshore oil off Santa Barbara County, California, have found that old memories live on. Their attempts to exploit that oil have been enormously hampered by the fact that one of the first major oil disasters happened in the area. On 28 January 1968, a line on an offshore rig in the Santa Barbara Channel ruptured. Before it could be closed off days later, millions of gallons of thick crude oil had spilled into the sea. Pictures of oil-coated sea birds, fish and sea lions made the front pages, triggering an outcry and doing a great deal to spur the growth of the embryonic environmental movement.

Amoco, too, has made headlines because of the 226,000 tonnes of oil which the *Amoco Cadiz*, while on charter to Shell International Oil, belched into the sea off Brittany in 1978. Amoco, the fourth largest US oil company soon faced a $2 billion lawsuit brought by the various interests affected by the resulting pollution.

Such accidents typically result in large-scale pollution, with damage to beaches, fisheries and coastal wildlife. Less obvious, but equally worrying threats include operational discharges by tankers while at sea. New approaches, such as the 'load-on-top' technique, have gone some way towards solving this problem, but there are still those who are only too happy to cut corners and to run any risks this may involve. 'Unfortunately, no matter how well founded and reasonable the regulations,' admitted Ian Blackwood, director of the Oil Companies International Marine Forum, 'it is inevitable that they will sometimes be circumvented through ignorance, laziness, or to gain commercial advantage.'

It is interesting to note, however, that economic pressures often work hand in hand with conservation pressures. The load-on-top and crude oil washing (COW) techniques were developed, in part at least, to keep as much precious oil as possible inside the tanker, rather than letting it out into the environment. Load-on-top, for example, reduced the amount of oil discharged to the marine environment during a tanker's ballast passage to just one fiftieth of its previous level.

In the meantime, oil has become one of the most widely dispersed pollutants of all time, finding its way into the environment from the Arctic to Antarctica. Given that most of the oil resulting from oil industry operations comes from routine tanker operations, the hunt is on for methods to pinpoint the culprits. Aircraft armed with side-looking airborne radar (SLAR) can already spot oil slicks from distances of up to 17 kilometres, in all weathers, day or night. Work with laser fluorosensors promises to provide methods of detecting the particular type of oil from the air, which can help both to identify culprits and to pick the most appropriate clean-up response.

However, even while the technology may evolve, a lot depends on how it is used. The *Amoco Cadiz*, for example, was considered to be one of the best equipped and operated very large crude carriers (VLCCs) of its kind. The ultimate challenge, as Blackwood argued, is to ensure that oil industry personnel identify with environmental protection objectives. 'Human conduct,' he noted, 'is the least amenable subject for legislation. The acquisition of skill requires a considerable commitment of time and resources, and even then its application is still dependent on proper motivation of ship's staff, management and government officials. Our eventual success will be measured in our progress from merely reducing pollution towards the goal of preventing pollution.'

The role played by chairmen, presidents, managing directors and other senior managers in ensuring that such objectives are taken seriously cannot be overvalued. For another example of the greening of capitalism, recall Arco chairman Robert O. Anderson, who finally stepped down from that role in 1986. He struck it rich shortly after merging his original company, Atlantic, with Richfield Oil in 1965. Richfield had extensive oil exploration leases in Alaska, which gave Arco a 22 per cent stake in Prudhoe Bay, discovered by BP and the largest US oil find to date. However, the environmental pressure on the industry was so intense that Anderson funded a Sierra Club study of the impact of the Alaska oil pipeline on caribou migrations.

Anderson also aggressively defended the environmental record of capitalism when he took the platform at the World Industry Conference on Environmental Management (see page 18). 'Out of enlightened self-interest,' he argued, 'business is likely to become involved in social problems concerned with the environment.'

It is one thing to say such things in the centrally-heated Palais des Congres at Versailles, however, quite another to ensure that oilmen on the ground in the frozen wastes of Greenland toe the green line. 'It's the harshest, most remote terrain we've ever had to work on,' as Arco's man on the spot put it. 'It could be described as an Arctic desert,' explained Dave Kofahl, head of the company's Greenland Mobilization Task Force. The problem with these Arctic deserts is that they are extremely sensitive both ecologically and politically.

Arco, like oil companies the world around, is on trial. 'But they know it,' noted Jonathan Motzfeld, the Greenland Prime Minister who helped negotiate the deal with the American company. 'They have been pinned down to a set of promises that will guarantee, we believe, that East Greenland is respected for what it is: the Inuit people, the polar bears, the seals; everything will still be there and just the same. That's what they promise, and that's what they hope.' But no-one suggests that it is going to be easy.

There are only six weeks in the year, for example, when the fjords leading to Arco's concession area are free of ice, and even when they are, ships still have to smash their way through a 100-mile wide permanent ice-field. This makes getting the oil out very difficult. A pipeline, along Alaskan lines, is out of the question, so industry thinking has been revolving around ice-breaking tankers. These, noted a Dane involved in the negotiations with Arco, are 'a totally new concept. They are very big and very expensive and potentially very dangerous. Can you imagine a million-ton tanker going down off East Greenland? It would ruin this place forever.

Oil in East Greenland could be a blessing. It could also be the most monstrous nightmare.'

The collision between industry's dreams and the surrounding community's nightmares is an age-old problem, and those nightmares are fuelled every time there is another *Amoco Cadiz*, Bhopal or Chernobyl. But each successive disaster also influences the way in which entrepreneurs and industrialists define and pursue their dreams. Those who carry on in the old ways risk going out of business. Some do, of course, but most adapt, to a greater or lesser extent. So how far has the oil industry allowed 'enlightened self-interest' to green its thinking and operations? One good place to start when looking for an answer to this question is Sullom Voe, in the Shetlands.

Oil's Stonehenge
There is something druidic about the brilliant flares that blaze in the sky over Sullom Voe. You first catch sight of them as your plane banks in towards Skatska airport, winging across a landscape of peat moors, exposed rock and small lakes, and they continue to hold your attention as you sink towards the runway.

As you step out of the aircraft, into a howling wind, you get a closer view of the orange sheets of flame which roar up from the flare stacks on the Hill of Garth, overlooking the oil terminal. A flame length of 20 metres has been recorded on the main flare, which means that you can see it over an enormous distance. Indeed, given the right night-time conditions, you can sometimes see the glow reflected from low cloud as far away as Sumburgh, some 80 kilometres away. The flare stacks may be a great deal thinner than the stone columns of Stonehenge and there are fewer of them, but you are left in no doubt that you are in the presence of an elemental force, the raw energy which powers today's industrial societies.

The architects of Stonehenge, however, did not have to file an environmental impact assessment before setting to work, and it is unlikely that anyone paid much attention to the temple's effects on its surrounding environment once it opened for business. Sullom Voe has been another matter entirely. Even the flares are closely monitored to ensure that they do not pollute the Shetland skies. A TV camera and video recorder have been installed in the process control room to keep a record of the amount of smoke produced by the main flare stack, following a number of complaints to the Shetland Islands Council (SIC) and to BP, the company which operates the terminal.

The Sullom Voe terminal sits at the end of two pipelines, the Brent and Ninian systems, which bring North Sea oil to land. As you walk and drive around the 1,000-acre terminal site, Europe's largest, it is difficult not to be impressed by the sheer scale of the enterprise. For example, over three million tonnes of peat and rock had to be stripped from the site to achieve the desired contours. Arrayed around the terminal are giant oil storage tanks and, alongside the jetties in Calback Ness, you see very large oil tankers and liquid petroleum gas carriers loading their tanks. In addition, in case there is a surge of pressure from the oilfields or a process breakdown at the terminal, both pipelines have their own massive surge tanks, each able to hold 220,000 barrels of oil, equivalent to four hours' maximum production.

Despite the number and scale of these facilities, however, careful landscaping and local geography combine to ensure that if you drive just a couple of miles from the terminal, it disappears from sight. The main concerns, therefore, have not been about the terminal's visual impact but about its effect on Shetland's economy and ecology.

In fact, the terminal's construction involved a unique process of co-operation between the SIC and nearly 30 companies involved in developing the offshore oilfields whose oil was destined to pass through Sullom Voe. Shetland has tried hard to ensure that its economy benefits from the oil boom. Indeed, the SIC actually filed a suit against BP and Shell, demanding an annual rent of £90 million for the terminal site. Shetland had had its booms before, with the herring fishery and the whaling industry, and it had also lived through the ensuing crashes. This time it wanted to make sure that it did not suffer when the oil ran out. 'It's absolutely vital that we sort this thing out with the oil companies as quickly and as fairly as possible,' said Michael Gerrard, chief executive of the SIC, 'so that we give the next generation of Shetlanders a chance to build a secure future for themselves.'

The natural environment was also a major consideration. BP, because of its experience in developing Alaska's oil resources, was one of the first major companies to recognize that ecology was becoming a fact of business life. It carried out a thorough environmental impact assessment for the proposed terminal and has since devoted considerable resources to environmental monitoring and auditing.

Ironically, the major pollution incident in the Voe happened because of a sequence of events which had not been foreseen in the impact assessment. The company had spent over £500,000 on oil clean-up equipment. When the *Esso Bernicia* was holed shortly after the terminal opened, the tanker spilled over 1,000 tonnes of heavy fuel oil into the Voe. The problem was that no-one had imagined that this sort of oil would ever get in the water: the terminal's equipment was designed for coping with light fuel oil, not the heavy fuel oil used in the *Esso Bernicia*'s engines.

The damage to local wildlife, including the otter population, was considerable, but most of the oil was eventually cleaned up and the Voe today is remarkably clean. Moreover, BP and the other companies involved have funded a considerable amount of ecological research, which has helped develop new environmental management techniques. But, even with the best will in the world, it is often impossible to please everyone. When the Brent and Ninian pipelines first came ashore, for example, the Nature Conservancy Council wanted the pipeline routes restored to moorland, whereas local crofters insisted that they should be fertilized and turned into grazing land. The result was compromise. In most places, the pipeline routes have been successfully restored to their original condition, except for a distinct green band running up to the radio mast on Firth Ness: the improved pasture the crofters had demanded.

Getting the green light

All over the world people, meanwhile, have been turning up in the most unlikely places in pursuit of oil. Despite the importance of oil to today's economies, however, they have often found it extremely hard to get the green light for their exploration and development plans. In Britain's beauty spots, for example, the arguments have centred around the question whether it makes sense to 'sacrifice' the Cotswolds, the Yorkshire Dales or the New Forest to onshore oil exploration and development. Shell Oil, which wanted to prospect in the New Forest, ran into problems when environmentalists learned that the oil the company expected to find might keep Britain in oil for less than a week, although a Shell spokesman stressed that the company might spend £1 million and find a 'big fat zero'.

What many people forget, however, is that countries like Britain often have a long history of oil exploitation. The Romans, for example, used oil from natural seepages to provide raw material for road surfacing and waterproofing, while some of Britain's seepages were set alight in the seventeenth century as tourist attractions. Oil encountered while digging mines and tunnels in the nineteenth century was processed to provide kerosene, wax and lubricants. Britain's first oil well was drilled in Derbyshire as long ago as 1918. Small fields have been producing since the 1930s, with Nottinghamshire's Eakring oilfield contributing 300,000 tonnes of oil to the country's war effort during the Second World War.

Between 1918 and 1973, over 300 exploration wells were drilled in Britain. 25 of these produced oil and perhaps a dozen of them are still in production. In most of the areas where the onshore oil industry operates, its operations are dwarfed by the operations of larger mineral extraction operations, including coal mining. Indeed, local people are often scarcely aware that the oil industry is there, but try to drill a borehole in an unexplored area of the country and the reaction can be very different. In this age of television, inevitably, many people's image of oilmen is taken direct from the soap opera worlds of *Dallas* or *Dynasty* and their image of the oil business is based on the Machiavellian dealings of J. R. Ewing of Ewing Oil.

Not surprisingly, the oil companies have tried hard to play down this image of rapacious capitalism. Several of them have prepared and published environmental impact assessments when applying for planning permission to develop onshore wells and they generally have tried hard to satisfy genuine objections. Carless, to take just one example, shifted the location of one of its drilling sites following complaints from the Nature Conservancy Council that the proposed exploration site would disturb the natural habitat of the Duke of Burgundy's Fritillary.

BP's own Wytch Farm oilfield, Britain's largest, was originally developed by British Gas. It is sited in one of the most sensitive and prized landscapes in the country and is very hard to spot even if you know it is there. However, further exploratory drilling discovered another, much larger oil reservoir lying beneath the original Bridport reservoir, which itself lies under Poole Harbour. Whereas the Bridport reservoir had been producing at the rate of 4,000 barrels a day, BP proposed to draw oil from the new Sherwood reservoir at the rate of at least 36,000 barrels a day. What troubled environmentalists was the fact that the industry was beginning to outgrow the limits at which they had been led to believe it would stop.

Now, instead of being able to locate their facilities in the midst of a forestry plantation, the Wytch Farm operators found they needed to venture out into some very much more sensitive locations, such as Furzey Island and the Studland Peninsula. It would be hard to think of areas which environmentalists would fight harder to protect.

Furzey Island, for example, is not only a Site of Special Scientific Interest in its own right, but sits in the midst of an Area of Outstanding Natural Beauty. It is also part of Dorset's Heritage Coast, which was awarded a Council of Europe Diploma in 1984. The Studland Peninsula itself is seen as a jewel in the crown of British nature conservation. It is also the only place in the British Isles where all six native British reptiles are found. If further expansion was planned, environmentalists asked, would Bournemouth and Poole be transformed into another Aberdeen?

In the event, BP got permission to drill exploratory boreholes on Furzey Island, despite the fact that Dorset County Council recognized that full-scale production from this small island at the mouth of Poole Harbour would be the logical next step. Two key considerations swayed Dorset and behind them the Government: the unparalleled richness of this new onshore field and BP's undisputed reputation for environmental excellence.

Wildcats and wildlife

Onshore technology is evolving rapidly, meanwhile. Even with today's technology, the onshore oil industry can generally reduce the environmental impact of its wildcat, or exploratory drilling, operations to acceptable levels. It has developed new, smaller rigs which are much quieter than earlier versions. It has worked out ways of concealing its rigs and other facilities from sight, although it must be admitted that in some areas, like Furzey Island, it simply is not possible to hide the entire rig. But once the oil production phase starts in such environmentally sensitive areas, as BP points out, the pumps and other equipment can be buried below ground level.

At the same time, operators such as Elf, the French oil company, are developing new drilling techniques which will enable the oil industry to drill at an angle, and in some cases horizontally, to tap into oil reservoirs from less sensitive sites some distance away. Elf began testing its horizontal testing technology in Italy, to tap the large offshore Rospo Mare field. The problem here is not environmental protection, but water-flooding. 'If we drilled the conventional vertical way,' explained Jacques Bosio, Elf's deputy research manager, 'the water under the oil deposit would rapidly flood the well. Using the horizontal system, we can keep the water at bay for longer and extract more oil.'

Horizontal drilling is still much more expensive than conventional drilling, but more oil can be recovered in such tricky situations. 'At first people thought it would cost ten times more to drill horizontally,' noted Bosio, 'but we have now been able to bring the costs down to about three times more than a vertical well.'

To return to Dorset, the Nature Conservancy Council and other conservation bodies will continue to keep the pressure up on BP and the other companies, because they know how damaging a single spill can be in the wrong place, and Poole Harbour, with its highly prized salt marshes and coastal habitats, would certainly be the wrong place. If conservationists push hard enough, the oil industry may well be prepared to pay the necessary additional premium and use horizontal drilling and other environmentally acceptable techniques, tapping the oil without having to drive a drill-string through the heart of a treasured habitat.

Cooling the permafrost
In some ways it could be argued that BP has had an easy task in Dorset and, with its North Sea experience behind it, the company would be the first to admit the fact. For perhaps the severest constraint that oilmen now face, as the industry drives ever further northwards into ever more hostile conditions, is not the hostility of environmentalists but the hostility of the environment itself. One does not have to go north to find such problems: they can, for instance, be found in Australia.

BP has been a partner in Broken Hill Proprietary Company (BHP)'s programme of exploration for oil and gas on Australia's North West Shelf. The tapping of a huge offshore gas reservoir there could help convert Australia into one of the world's most important energy exporters. But the familiar difficulties of working out in deep water are compounded on the North West Shelf by the threat of cyclones, which plague the area. One drilling platform, the North Rankin A, can produce 1.2 billion cubic feet (34 million cubic metres) of gas a day, but its location in 380 feet (114 metres) of water some 80 miles (128 kilometres) northwest of the town of Karantha has meant that it has had to withstand 70-foot (21-metre) waves and winds reaching 84 miles (135 kilometres) per hour.

Conditions can be even tougher on Alaska's North Slope, where the sun dips below the horizon in November and comes up two months later. Oilmen here only see the snowscape briefly during a twilight hour around midday. Yet even with snow blanketing the land and the wind chill factor plunging to minus 115 degrees Fahrenheit (46 degrees Centigrade), the oil industry still has to work hard to protect the North Slope ecology. It may not look like much, with no trees or large plants and very few year-round animal residents, but it is in fact home to many species, and the greening of the industry is evident even in these white wastes.

Those animals that do stay in the area through the long Arctic winter, such as the caribou, lemming, arctic fox, musk ox and polar bear, have evolved ways of surviving the harsh conditions. The oil companies, too, have had to evolve to cope with the Arctic.

Given the harsh characteristics of the North Slope environment, it is perhaps not surprising that the oil companies have found it a major challenge not only to get the oil out of the ground without damaging the environment, but to get it out at all. As much as three-quarters of the oil and gas in North America is thought to lie beyond the Arctic Circle, where the average yearly temperature is below the freezing point of water. As a result, the ground freezes into 'permafrost' and does so to a depth of up to 400 metres. This makes it nearly impossible to dispose of waste water or sewage and there are even more serious problems when you get to the stage of building a pipeline to transport your oil to market.

Anything built on the permafrost changes the thermal characteristics of the nearby soil, often causing it to thaw. Buildings or pipelines built directly on the permafrost can sink into the ground as it thaws. If this happened with a major oil pipeline, the consequences can only be imagined. Alyeska, the company which opened the Trans-Alaska pipeline in 1977, found ways of keeping the pipeline from slumping into the permafrost, but only at considerable cost. The total price-tag for the pipeline was $900 million.

Where it proved impossible to bury the pipeline on a stabilized bed within the permafrost, Alyeska erected it on stilts. Even so, the heat from the pipeline was such that in many places the company also had to install heat pumps. These are ammonia-filled devices which absorb heat underground and then carry it up into cooling fins above the ground.

Gravel ramps have had to be built over some sections of the pipeline, to enable migrating caribou to cross it. Furthermore, a minimum height was set for the elevated sections, so that animals could happily walk under the pipeline. Once the pipeline had been built, the area surrounding its route was carefully replanted, since Arctic plants do not recolonize barren land quickly enough.

In fact the oil companies have funded a considerable amount of work on Arctic ecology. Sohio spent $1.2 million studying wildlife in the area of its planned Endicott Field, near Prudhoe Bay, before beginning to develop the field. Overall, the company spent $150 million a year to protect the Alaskan environment while it was involved in the development of the North Slope and it continues to study local wildlife as part of its environmental monitoring and control programmes. It also publishes an orientation booklet to help new North Slope employees to understand how to limit their effect on the Arctic ecosystem. Hunting is strictly forbidden and the general advice is to avoid any direct contact with wildlife. Environmentalists, however, generally remain unconvinced, arguing that the problems could get much worse if the industry needs to scale up its operations in these fragile areas.

The challenge, meanwhile, is far from over. The oil and gas riches of the Arctic are thought to be immense and companies like Panarctic are now struggling again with the problem of getting their oil and gas out of the far north. Another pipeline has been proposed, but critics point out that icebergs can gouge gashes two metres deep in the ocean floor as they pass overhead, which suggests that pipelines could be ruptured.

An iceberg with an estimated weight of over eight million tonnes was sighted south of the oilfields in 1972 and in the late 1970s Dome Petroleum tracked an ice island that had probably been cruising the Arctic for some 70 years. It measured seven miles by three (11.2 kilometres by 4.8) and stretched 120 feet (37 metres) from its peak above the water to the tip of its keel beneath. 'I don't know what kind of platform could withstand an iceberg of eight to ten million tonnes,' observed one Mobil executive, 'but I wouldn't want to be on one until I knew!'

Ice-breaking tankers capable of battering their way through three metres of solid ice seem to be the only alternative. Indeed, Canada has announced that it plans to build one at a cost of $3 billion, a project expected to take six years. Inevitably, ecologists are worried. One immediate concern is that many animals tend to congregate in the Arctic at certain times of the year, making them much more vulnerable to oil spills. The low temperatures mean that microbes would take much longer to break down any oil spilled.

'The tankers must cross Lancaster Sound, the most productive marine area in the Arctic,' warned David van der Zwaag of Canada's Dalhousie University. Over eight million birds nest there, alongside eight or nine out of every ten North American narwhals and large numbers of seals. Clearly, all eyes are going to be on the oil industry and if things do go wrong, the political impact could be tremendous. In these circumstances, oilmen have little option but to try and think of every possible eventuality, in an attempt to ensure that disasters do not happen.

Clearly, the oil companies are not going to be doing this sort of work simply to protect the environment. Accidents also cost human lives, which means that safety considerations are often at least as important as ecological concerns. In companies around the world, small groups of specialists spend their time imagining the worst of all possible worlds. So, for example, when Shell Expro was developing its Mosmorran gas separation plant in Fife, Scotland, it not only considered whether a liquefied petroleum gas tanker might collide with a ship from the nearby Royal Navy base at Rosyth, but it also tried to imagine what would happen if the worst possible accident happened directly beneath the Forth railbridge. Would the bridge melt?

Overall, Shell concluded, the towns closest to the plant are unlikely to experience a fire or explosion resulting from a marine accident more than once in every one million years. That does not mean that accidents will never happen: BP's experience at Sullom Voe showed that accidents do happen and often in totally unexpected ways. But risk assessment exercises such as these help the industry to prevent accidents and to develop contingency plans just in case the worst does happen.

Prevention or cure?

No-one disputes that oil pollution can cause serious environmental damage. In *Oil in the Sea*, a report published by the US National Research Council, there is clear evidence showing that oil pollution can have 'a seriously adverse effect on local environments, in some cases persisting unaltered for decades.' However, the report also stresses that monitoring studies following major spills always showed biological recovery taking place. In Britain, the eighth report of the Royal Commission on Environmental Pollution came to similar conclusions.

'We have concluded that oil spills are unlikely to cause long-lasting damage,' the Royal Commission noted. 'The marine environment appears to have a remarkable capacity for recovering from the effects of even the largest oil spillages. We have found no clear evidence that oil spills have significantly affected populations of sea birds or other marine species. We have found no grounds for concern that oil may pose a chronic threat to the marine ecosystem or, indirectly, a threat to man. We conclude that the threat of long-term and perhaps irreversible damage to the marine environment is insubstantial—and possibly less serious than that posed by other potential sources of damage, such as pollution by heavy metals and radioactivity.'

But there is a general rule in the pollution field which applies to all ecosystems: prevention is better than cure. To get a better idea of how scientists have built up our current understanding of how the marine environment responds to oil spills, we can consider some of the projects undertaken by the Oil Pollution Research Unit (OPRU), based near Pembroke, in Wales.

Established in the late 1960s, OPRU dates from the period when oil super-spills first started to hit the headlines. 'We all made some fairly wild accusations against the oil industry in those early days,' admits Eric Cowell, OPRU's first director, 'but it was a symptom of the fact that there was often very little hard information to go on. That was the gap which OPRU was set up to fill.' The Unit owes its birth largely to a Greek tanker, the *Chryssi P. Goulandris*, which spilled 250 tonnes of light Arabian crude oil into Milford Haven early in 1967. Two months later a far more serious disaster happened, when the *Torrey Canyon* went aground on the Seven Stones reef, northwest of the Scilly Isles. Seizing the moment, Cowell stepped up his lobbying of the oil industry for funds to support research on the ecology of oil pollution. Eventually, he won the support of the Institute of Petroleum and WWF.

'OPRU could perhaps have managed without the Institute of Petroleum funds,' says Dr Jenny Baker, who served as the Unit's second director. 'But it has been the most reliable long-term source of money and the successful working relationship developed between the Institute and the Unit provides a useful model for other forms of co-operation between industry and environmental interests.'

Even ten years ago, however, successful co-operation between the oil industry and environmentalists seemed highly improbable. But as Dr Brian Dicks, OPRU's current director, commented, 'even though the climate say 15 years ago was much more adversarial, if you got the chance to talk to people in the oil industry you generally found that they were normal people, with the same environmental concerns. That broke down a lot of barriers. Indeed, they would often give us the go-ahead without knowing quite what to expect. I suspect they were doing it with their fingers crossed!'

Much of OPRU's early work focused on the ecological impact of the oil dispersants used to clean up spilled oil. Early dispersants often proved at least as damaging as the oil itself. The Unit's scientists studied the fate and ecological effects of successive generations of dispersants, and of chemically dispersed oil, in a variety of marine habitats. Sometimes this involved the unlikely spectacle of ecologists spraying oil on unpolluted saltmarsh or hand-painting shoreline rocks with various grades of oil, to see how fast they weathered.

An important early finding of these studies was that rocky shores, indeed most elements of the marine environment, undergo major *natural* shifts in the abundance and distribution of species. Similar findings have emerged from OPRU's long-running monitoring studies of the Sullom Voe area, where the majority of the changes observed seem to reflect natural fluctuations affecting much of the region.

'Clearly, if you want to assess the oil industry's impact,' says Dr Dicks, 'one of the first things you have to do is to find ways of teasing out from your monitoring data those changes which are natural and those which are caused by pollution. As an example of these natural changes, the very hot summer of 1976 produced dramatic changes in the upper shore biological communities, and some of these effects were still apparent in 1979.'

Meanwhile, OPRU's changing workload symptomizes the changing nature of the world oil industry. A growing number of its contracts, for example, have come from overseas. In one study Jenny Baker looked at the effects of oil pollution on mangrove swamps. These are tremendously important both ecologically and economically, supporting oysters, crabs, barnacles, fish and other creatures in their complex roots, which are often immersed in sea water, while simultaneously harbouring dry-land animals in their upper branches. They are now under enormous pressure, not only from oil pollution but also from waste dumping and land reclamation, the canalization of rivers, hot water pollution from nearby power stations, felling for timber and from the growing use of herbicides.

Part of Dr Baker's task was to consider how oiled mangroves should be cleaned up. She concluded that the labyrinthine environment created by these trees often makes such operations almost impossible. In short, the old adage that prevention is better than cure is particularly apposite in mangrove swamps. At the same time, however, present trading patterns make it clear that the Pacific region, where many of the world's mangrove swamps are found, is going to be increasingly exposed to oil pollution, particularly in the area of the Malacca Straits near Singapore, where the tanker traffic between the Gulf and Japan is particularly dense.

OPRU has also been asked to look at coral reefs. 'Coral reefs are very difficult to survey,' says Dr Keith Hiscock, who was until recently OPRU's deputy director and did a great deal of the diving work. 'You've got such a broken surface with knolls, crevices, overhangs and caves, as well as all those fish swimming back and forth. How on earth do you survey that quantitatively?'

In fact OPRU has worked out ways of telling the oil company and government scientists what they need to know in order to make a decision. 'In essence,' says Dr Dicks, 'the oil companies don't want to know whether there are 46 or 47 species there. They want to know what effects oil operations have upon the ecology, whether these effects are acceptable, and how to avoid or reduce them.'

A good example of what can be involved is the work that OPRU did for the Suez Oil Company on the east side of the Gulf of Suez, at Ras Budran, where an oil trans-shipment terminal was planned. 'We got involved at the stage of producing baseline data,' Dr Dicks explains. 'So we gave them the data and then asked what they wanted to build. They had done the exploratory drilling and now wanted to construct an offshore field with three platforms and pipelines coming ashore to a marine terminal. The oil will be sent out through another pipeline to a single point mooring system, for loading into the tankers. It's a clean area, a beautiful area. The next step was to ensure that it stayed that way.'

In fact the relationship between the engineers and biologists worked very well. A pipeline was diverted through a natural break in the coral reef, rather than crunching through the reef itself. A solid jetty was redesigned so that water could continue to circulate behind the reef, while the effluent outfalls were located in such a way that the discharges were swept away from the reef.

'In the end,' Dr Dicks notes, 'it comes down to compromises. Very often, though, things will fall naturally into place. Perhaps 70 per cent of the time you will end up with a pretty good solution, leaving the other 30 per cent to argue about.'

In the longer term, there will certainly continue to be plenty of issues which the oil industry can argue about with environmentalists. Bodies such as the International Petroleum Industry Environmental Conservation Association (IPIECA) have done a great deal to ensure that the world outside the oil industry knows what it is doing on the environmental front and the way its thinking is going. But IPIECA, too, recognizes that there is going to be no immediate reduction in the industry's environmental agenda.

Not only will there be the environmental problems associated with the growing use of low quality crudes, but as conventional oils run out the industry will be forced to exploit tar sands, oil shale and coal. These trends will aggravate such problems as acid rain and the build-up of atmospheric carbon dioxide, in addition to raising other issues, of which oil shale exploitation has been just one example. A plant producing about 100,000 barrels of shale oil a day (or about half of one per cent of America's daily consumption) would have to get rid of about 20 million tonnes of waste material each year. If all the shale in Colorado were to be exploited, it has been estimated that the resulting spoil would raise the height of that part of the Rockies range from 14,000 feet to 18,000 feet.

Whatever environmental problems it may face, however, the oil industry's future is assured. We may find that we can do more with less energy, but we cannot do without it. Meanwhile, IPIECA and industry spokesmen are beginning to broaden their focus from immediate pollution problems to consider how the oil industry can contribute to sustainable development. No-one now doubts that our current willingness to expend the energy capital built up over millenia in the space of a few centuries is dangerously short-sighted. The key question, which is touched on in Chapter 9, is whether industry in general, and the oil industry in particular, can help the world switch to more sustainable forms of development before the pumps begin to run dry.

Chapter 5

CHEMICAL REACTIONS

Because of the environmental pressures on hundreds
of its products, from pesticides to aerosol propellants,
the chemical industry has had to carry out leading
edge research in such abstruse fields as ecotoxicology
and stratospheric chemistry. Despite the contrary
evidence of the Seveso and Bhopal disasters, the
greening of the chemical industry has been proceeding
at a spectacular pace.

Many of the people living in and around Bhopal before the disaster
may have owed their lives to the food, drugs and other products
provided by the chemical industry. But the fatal gassing of more
than 1,700 people, and perhaps as many as 2,500, around Union
Carbide's pesticide factory was just one of a series of incidents which
have convinced many people that the world's synthetic chemists
have opened the twentieth-century equivalent of Pandora's Box.

Bhopal may have seen the highest death toll to date, with a
further 17,000 people thought to have been seriously injured out of
over 300,000 affected by the gas, but the petrochemical and chemical
industries are no strangers to major disasters. 1984, in fact, had
already seen two other major disasters in the Third World: in
November liquefied gas storage tanks had exploded at the San Juan
Ixhuatepec plant in Mexico City, killing well over 400 people, while
in February an estimated 500 people had died in Cubatão (see
page 75) when gasoline leaking from a pipeline exploded in a
colossal fireball.

Nor were the disasters confined to the Third World. In 1978, for
example, a road tanker carrying propylene gas was responsible for
killing 215 tourists in San Carlos de la Rapita, Spain. In 1976,
a runaway chemical reaction at a plant owned by Givaudan, a

Hoffmann-La Roche subsidiary, led to a major release of dioxin in Seveso, Italy. Two years earlier, in the biggest explosion ever to occur in Britain in peacetime, Nypro's Caprolactum plant at Flixborough blew up and 28 workers died.

These catastrophes, however, were simply the most dramatic examples of the environmental damage caused by the world's growing chemical industry. For example, there had also been tremendous concern about the chronic environmental effects of pesticides such as DDT, of industrial chemicals such as polychlorinated biphenyls (PCBs) and of a wide range of other substances, including chlorofluorocarbon aerosol propellants.

Even so, Bhopal was different. While the Cubatão and San Juan Ixhuatepec disasters produced surprisingly little media interest in the developed countries, India was determined that Bhopal should not be forgotten and the people of the city shared this resolve. While troops patrolled the streets of the city on the first anniversary of the disaster, demonstrators burned 2,500 effigies of Union Carbide's chairman, Warren Anderson.

The world's smokiest factory?

The interesting thing about Union Carbide, however, is that the company had previously had a fairly good environmental reputation. There were some major blemishes on its record, of course, as there are on the record of a number of major chemical companies. In the late 1960s, for example, the company's iron-alloy plant in the West Virginian town of Alloy was described by local environmentalists as 'the smokiest factory in the world'.

The company had, in fact, invested a considerable amount of money in cleaning up its many plants around the world. By the time of the disaster, indeed, Union Carbide's track record in safety and environmental matters was considered to be above average. 'I am not surprised that something like this happened,' commented a hazardous waste specialist at the US Environmental Protection Agency, following the Bhopal deaths, 'but I *am* surprised that it was Union Carbide.'

Best known as the manufacturer of such consumer products as Eveready batteries, Glad bags and Simoniz car wax which it was later forced to sell, Union Carbide nonetheless made the bulk of its money from the sale of commodity chemicals such as polyethylene, industrial gases such as acetylene and argon, and pesticides. Ironically, though, the Bhopal pesticide plant had been so unprofitable prior to the accident that Union Carbide had been thinking about dismantling it. When government investigators entered the plant to find out why the gas cloud had formed in the first place, they reported that safety conditions there had deteriorated sharply during the months leading up to the disaster.

A cooling unit which could possibly have slowed the runaway chemical reaction had been switched off. A flare tower normally used to burn escaping chemical vapours had been dismantled and was awaiting repair. A scrubber designed to neutralize chemicals escaping from the faulty tank was also out of action.

It is worth noting, however, that, while there had been longstanding complaints about the safety of the plant from some of the workers there, no-one had previously known that methyl isocyanate, the gas released, could be so deadly. It was known to affect the eyes and lungs, but because it was an intermediate chemical, to which it was assumed the public would never be exposed, the toxicity testing requirements had been minimal.

Not surprisingly, a barrage of criticism burst around the world chemical industry. Many critics claim that such disasters are inevitable if economic development is left in the hands of multinational companies, but this is a travesty of the facts. You could shut down all the world's multinationals today and still have a major industrial pollution incident tomorrow. Indeed, just one day after those Anderson effigies burned around Bhopal, a cloud of sulphur trioxide escaped from the Indian-owned Sri Ram Chemical Fertilizers plant in Delhi. Thousands fled from their homes and workplaces. More than 200 people needed hospital treatment, although most were released after receiving first aid.

As usual, the picture at Bhopal was not quite as simple as it looked. Throughout the Third World, national governments have been pressuring the multinationals since the decolonization period to give up majority control of their local operations. In the wake of the Bhopal disaster, Warren Anderson noted that Union Carbide India had effectively 'operated as a separate company'. Restrictive foreign investment regulations in many developing countries not only mean that ownership is diluted, as far as the parent company is concerned, but also that *control* is diluted. Following Bhopal, one immediate reaction in some multinational chemical companies was to say that in future they would press harder to retain control over the safety and environmental aspects of such Third World operations.

The view inside Union Carbide itself was increasingly expressed in stronger terms. 'We're bitter,' said one company employee in the build-up to the disaster's first anniversary. 'A few incompetent, casual Indians put a black mark on my name.' Even Warren Anderson, who had flown to India in the wake of the disaster and there found himself held under house arrest, had begun to take a tougher line. 'The early days were traumatic,' he told *Business Week*, 'but then you step back. It's gotten to be manageable and non-emotional. Life goes on. I've got a big company here.' More aggressively, he told the *Wall Street Journal* that the Indians were to blame: 'We put the plant outside the city,' he said. 'They allowed the people to settle around it. The Third World has a lot to learn.'

In fact, Anderson knew that his company could not shrug off responsibility quite so easily and it was also proving hard to shrug off the financial aftermath of the disaster. If Union Carbide's financial position had been difficult before Bhopal, it was made dramatically worse as investors sold the company's stock, which fell dramatically, making the company a possible takeover target. No-one resigned or was fired following the Bhopal disaster, but over 4,500 Union Carbide employees were cut as part of a restructuring programme designed to make the company less attractive to potential predators. However, as Anderson himself pointed out, the litigation building up in the wake of Bhopal would probably prove to be the 'ultimate poison pill', scaring away anyone considering a Union Carbide takeover.

Clearly, there were faults on all sides, although the question remains whether any company should allow its technology to be operated in an unsatisfactory way while it is still technically under its control. Union Carbide's credibility was, in any event, further dented by a succession of pollution incidents at its plants in the United States. Although Anderson had stressed to a US congressional committee that 'it could never happen here,' a chemical cloud almost immediately leaked from the company's plant in Institute, West Virginia, injuring 135 people. 'I was deeply shaken,' Anderson recalled later. So, it is fair to say, were those who had tried to help the company rebuild community confidence around the Institute plant.

A month later, Union Carbide appointed Cornelius C. Smith to the new post of vice president for community and employee health, safety and the environment. The plan was that he would report direct to Anderson, who noted that Union Carbide's goal was now 'to achieve and maintain a level of health, safety and environmental protection in all of our operations that is second to none.' In fact, as we shall see, standards in this field are now very high. Because of the tremendous pressure on the chemical industry's products and operations, the greening of this sector of industry has proceeded at a very considerable rate.

'The auditing treadmill'

If you talk to any director or senior manager in the petrochemical and chemical industries, the chances are that they will tell you that one of the first things they did in the wake of the Bhopal disaster was to initiate reviews of their own operations to see whether they could come up against similar problems. A week after Bhopal, for example, Monsanto chief executive Richard J. Mahoney pulled together a company task force to carry out an urgent, worldwide review of Monsanto's safety policies and procedures.

'Monsanto are not complete strangers to industrial disasters,' commented Marek Mayer, editor of the *ENDS Report*, a British publication which monitors the environmental performance of leading industrial companies. 'In 1947, a massive explosion in two ships carrying ammonium nitrate killed 550 people in Texas City, including workers at a nearby Monsanto plant which was demolished by the blast. Two decades later, 11 people died following an explosion at the company's polystyrene plant in Montreal.'

It is worth stressing, however, that almost every major company has had similar problems: the main difference is that some companies have used such tragedies as a stimulus for their efforts to ensure that they develop a 'culture of safety', while others have simply tried to brush the problem under the corporate carpet.

Monsanto was one of the more positive companies as far as the management of health, safety and environmental issues was concerned. In 1983, for example, Monsanto and its subsidiaries around the world, a total of 136 manufacturing units and 19 research establishments, reported 1.07 cases of injury or illness for each 100 employees. This compared with a figure of 5.5 per 100 employees for the chemical industry as a whole, and 7.6 cases per 100 employees in the manufacturing and service industries as a whole. In 1984, Monsanto dropped below the one case per 100 employees for the first time. As Mayer commented, that achievement was 'due in part to the company's policy of ranking safety performance as one of the key criteria determining managers' salaries and promotion prospects.'

Each new Monsanto project is subjected to safety reviews when an authorization is first submitted to the board, when approved projects reach the detailed design stage and again when the plant is about to start up. Once in operation, the plant is then the subject of annual safety surveys and periodic audits to assess safety procedures and the management of the overall safety effort. Some audits are carried out by plant management, but external audits are also a strong feature of the Monsanto approach.

'A corporate auditing group is essential,' as Monsanto safety consultant Dr Stan Skinner put it. 'While self-auditing by plant management is vital, the people involved may be too close to the operations to pick out potential flaws.' The level of auditing may sometimes seem unduly onerous, but Dr Skinner noted that 'the auditing treadmill is one you have to keep treading all the time to achieve our safety results.'

Ultimately, one of the most visible impacts of the Bhopal disaster on Monsanto's safety procedures could prove to be the wider disclosure of information on hazardous substances. Although Monsanto already shared such information with local emergency services, chief executive Mahoney commented that, 'in view of what happened in India, we feel an obligation to become more pro-active in sharing information both on the hazards associated with our operations and the extraordinary precautions we take to ensure against mishaps.'

The question is how far this process should be taken. 'Obviously,' said Mahoney, 'whatever information we release must be consistent with ensuring the security of our operations and, in rare cases, the protection of legitimate trade secrets. But the emphasis of our efforts should be upon promoting public disclosure, not on reasons for withholding information.'

Nor is it simply a matter of generating and releasing information on risk. Monsanto has also been looking at ways in which it might reduce the hazards associated with some of its operations still further. Safety reviews were carried out at 14 plants which handled such highly toxic materials as acetone cyanohydrin, ammonia, chlorine and hydrogen cyanide. One priority has been to look for ways of cutting the amounts of such materials which have to be stored at such plants.

In one such exercise, at Monsanto's Texas City plant, changes in processes involving acrylonitrile have resulted in a reduction in the number of tanks of the material needed, from five tanks to one. With further process changes, it should be possible to use hydrogen cyanide as it is manufactured, eliminating the need to store this dangerous substance.

The environmental pressure is forcing growing numbers of companies to look at ways in which they can design toxic waste problems out of their processes. Dow Chemical, for example, produced one pound of waste for every pound of product in 1960. By the early 1980s, however, it was producing one pound of waste for every 1,000 pounds of product.

'In the design of our new plants,' noted Ciba-Geigy vice president Joseph T. Sullivan, 'automation *and* reduction of effluent load are the two items at the top of our list.' But, despite the experience of 3M (see Chapter 9), designing cleaner technologies can often be an economically hazardous business, as Bayer's experience indicates.

A green giant?

Risks are an essential part of business, particularly so when companies are having to invest in new technologies. 'If you don't want risks or surprises,' as Bayer chief executive, Hermann-Josef Strenger put it, 'then you should put your money in the bank. If you are engaged in business activity, if you are permanently ready to take risks, then you find that risks might lead to setbacks.' One such setback came when Bayer and Ciba-Geigy were forced to shut down a new plant they had designed to produce anthraquinone, used in dyestuffs manufacture, in an environmentally acceptable way.

One of West Germany's big three chemical companies, along with BASF and Hoechst, Bayer has been busily internationalizing its businesses. It also restructured its corporate operations in 1984. The new structure, explained Dr Heinrich Vossberg, the company's head of strategic planning, 'reflects the changes in both internal and external influences on the company.' Intriguingly, one of the seven committees servicing the board covers ecology.

Despite the recession which started in the early 1980s, leading German industrialists were distressed to find that the environmental pressures on their companies showed little sign of abating. Indeed, the pressure has increased dramatically in many areas. At Hoechst's 1983 annual meeting of shareholders, for example, it emerged that several thousand shares had been bought by members of the Green movement. They took the podium as shareholders and demanded that Hoechst should spend its entire dividend of DM259 million on environmental protection. Other shareholders, perhaps not surprisingly, were less enthusiastic.

Hoechst, in fact, was one of the companies which had been branded as 'pollution criminals' by a Rhine Tribunal organized by environmentalists from Switzerland, France, West Germany, Luxembourg and the Netherlands, all of which lie along the river's course. Other companies attacked at the time included BASF, Bayer, Ciba-Geigy, Hoffmann-La Roche, Rhone Poulenc and Sandoz. Greenpeace, however, did not support the Tribunal, deciding instead to pick on just one company which it had reason to believe was dumping considerable quantities of acid wastes into the North Sea.

The company was Bayer and the wastes, Greenpeace discovered, contained materials known to cause cancer, in addition to such substances as chromium, lead, copper, zinc, cadmium and mercury. The Dutch Minister for transport and waterways had already instructed Bayer to carry out its dumping 30 kilometres further out to sea and to reduce the rate at which the wastes were discharged, to ensure better mixing. However, Greenpeace was convinced that the company was acting in breach of the London and Oslo Conventions, which forbid the marine dumping of certain hazardous substances.

Greenpeace therefore began a blockade of Bayer's waste shipments, using inflatable dinghies, trapping the two coasters used for the dumping in harbour. The group also called on the company to explain what it was doing and why, and on the Dutch government to issue any future dumping permits only after rigorous ecological and toxicity tests had been carried out with the fauna and flora actually found in the North and Wadden Seas, where the dumping was taking place.

Bayer's first reaction was to ask the authorities for permission instead to dump 250,000 tonnes of treated acid waste into the Rhine, a practice which it had been the first to stop in 1969. It told the press that there were 4,000 jobs at stake if the ban was allowed to go ahead. Later on, it managed to end the blockade by taking Greenpeace to court and threatening the group with punitive damages. It did not leave matters there, however. First, it invited members of Greenpeace to immediate discussions with top management, including the managing director of the company's massive Leverkusen site, Professor Eberhard Weise. Second, it invited Greenpeace to send a small group of observers to see what the company was doing to overcome the acid waste problem.

Paradoxically, it turned out that Bayer had been one of the most environmentally sensitive of West Germany's chemical companies, featuring environmental protection in its annual reports and, indeed, in its corporate logo: a green linden leaf emblazoned with the motto, *Bayer research for a clean environment*. Greenpeace had known nothing of all this when it decided to launch its campaign, believing that it was a straightforward case of David against Goliath, with little inkling that Bayer considered itself something of a Green Giant.

Bayer, too, was taken aback by the blockade, having genuinely believed that its North Sea acid dumping was preferable to dumping the same wastes in the Rhine. To be fair, when Bayer took that small group, including Dr Alan Pickaver of Greenpeace, Friends of the Earth pollution consultant, Dr Brian Price, and John Elkington (as an independent observer with some knowledge of what other chemical companies had been able to achieve), around its various production sites, they were all impressed by the progress the company had made in dealing with a highly complex problem.

By the time they arrived, Bayer was recycling the equivalent of 122,000 tonnes of 20 per cent sulphuric acid each year. Acid recycling, however, can be a difficult business because of the corrosiveness of the various process streams. The recycled acid can end up costing five or six times more than acid produced from scratch, which hardly makes the exercise a commercial proposition. A much happier approach, and one which they saw in action at Bayer's new production site at Brunsbuettel, in northern Germany, involves the development and deployment of cleaner, low-waste technologies, although pollution control facilities are still likely to be needed. Among the first plants to appear on the site were incineration and wet air oxidation facilities, designed to detoxify or destroy toxic wastes.

Sadly, though, Schelde Chemie, a joint venture between Bayer and Ciba-Geigy, later decided to shut down its newly built anthraquinone plant at Brunsbuettel. The company had to write off an investment of around DM350 million, worth about £100 million at the time. As chief executive Strenger told the *Financial Times*, Bayer researchers had 'tried to find a way to make anthraquinone in a more economical and environmentally favourable process. The second stage: we built a pilot plant. This started operating and made large quantities of anthraquinone without problems. Third stage: to make a transition from the pilot installation to a large-scale installation. And now comes the crazy phenomenon of chemistry. We have not succeeded in transferring the knowledge that we gained from the pilot plant to the large-scale mass production plant.'

A cleaner, friendlier Dow?

On the face of it, Bayer's experience was scarcely reassuring for companies wishing to present a greener image to the public: Greenpeace was attacking a company which had already devoted considerable resources to cleaning up its image. However, again, the picture was not quite as simple as it seemed. Bayer's response to the blockade did deflect Greenpeace onto other problems and other companies, and the fact that it had been able to show convincing evidence that it was working on new solutions to pressing pollution problems helped influence the attitude of its critics.

Indeed, even some of the really hard-nosed chemical companies are beginning to recognize that it can pay dividends to try and establish common ground with the environmental lobby. Dow Chemical, which ranks second only to Du Pont in the United States, and occupies sixth place in most listings of the world's largest chemical companies, is a prime example. Like many major chemical companies, Dow has been rethinking its business strategy and, as a direct consequence, it has been rethinking its environmental strategy too.

Dow, which had been under fire for many years on the dioxin issue, had always played 'hardball' in the environmental field. The company combined an emphasis on scientific excellence with an aggressive impatience with those it viewed as amateurs, including most environmentalists. 'We play our cards close,' was the way Dow chairman Robert W. Lundeen put it, 'maybe because we have a high regard for the value of technical information. We don't back down easily or compromise. We are perceived as prickly, difficult, and arrogant.'

But while Dow could afford to shrug off the environmental pressure when its income was rising steadily, its operating income slipped badly in the late 1970s and early 1980s. Worse, the company saw that the future lay in the speciality chemical market, rather than in bulk chemicals. The obvious strategy was to go after speciality targets, but this raised a difficult question.

Whereas bulk chemicals are bought by small numbers of high-volume consumers, with the main concern being the price, speciality chemicals are generally bought by large numbers of small-volume consumers. Sometimes, in the form of cleaners or other household products, they are bought by individual consumers, who may find unacceptable the idea of buying something with *Dow* on the label. 'Will the consumer buy a Dow kitchen cleaner,' a company executive asked, 'if he thinks that Dow pollutes the environment with chemicals that give people cancer? Would you?'

As part of an attempt to rebuild its public image, Dow redeployed five senior executives to form an environmental action team. The company also invested $3 million in a series of independent studies of the most serious allegations which had been made against it. 'I have to say I was against it,' said the company's president, Paul F. Oreffice. 'It smacks to me of trying to buy people off. But if we say we know the facts on something, we are accused of being arrogant. If we say we don't know the answers, people say: "You are killing people and you don't know the answers?" To be guilty until being proven innocent is ridiculous, but it is something we have to learn to live with.'

Even some of the company's critics admit that Dow's science is excellent and accept that its environmental performance is better than that of some of its competitors, but they fault it for playing down the potential risks associated with toxic chemicals, its unyielding opposition to new regulations and other controls and its unusual readiness to take its opponents to court.

In fact, many saw an incident which happened in Dow's home town of Midland, Michigan, as typical of the company's aggressive style. On the same day that the *Rainbow Warrior* went to the bottom of Auckland Harbour, a small team from Greenpeace managed to plug Dow's main effluent outfall which at that time discharged around 20,000 gallons of effluent into the Tittabawassee River every working day. When the Environmental Protection Agency had earlier found traces of forty toxic chemicals, including dioxin, in Dow's effluent, Paul Oreffice had told the company's shareholders that the level of dioxin found, 50 parts per *quadrillion*, was equal to less than twenty drops in the plant's total annual discharge of nine billion gallons into the river.

Unfortunately for Dow, such statistics failed to reassure many of the company's critics. They pointed out that fish caged at the mouth of the effluent outfall accumulated 100 parts per trillion of dioxin, twice the level which the Food and Drug Administration had declared as safe for consumption.

It took the company three days to work out how to remove Greenpeace's stopper from its outfall, following which the Greenpeace team returned for a repeat performance. They failed and were arrested. They were held in gaol for three days while Greenpeace struggled to raise the $30,000 needed to bail them out. In the meantime, all three had been given a blood test. Shortly thereafter, the public relations officer at the Midland plant called the local Greenpeace activist and said that one of the team appeared to have venereal disease. This piece of information proved false, but the significant thing as far as Dow's critics were concerned was the fact that the information reached Dow in the first place and that once it did the story was circulated so quickly.

There was a strong feeling that this had been an attempt to discredit Greenpeace. Later, following an investigation by *The Guardian*, Dow took advertizing space in the *Midland Daily News* to admit it had made a 'serious error of judgement'.

Clearly old habits die hard, but Dow officials have continued to insist that the company aims to approach environmental questions in a more sensitive manner in future. 'We insisted on the soundness of our science and thought that would prevail,' explained Robert Charlton, public affairs manager at Dow's Washington office. However, that approach had failed, hence the new one. 'We've grown weary of confrontation,' Charlton continued. 'We recognize that there's a more savvy response. We're going to be more sensitive and tolerant. We're going to address issues head on. We want the new way to become part of our culture, much as confrontation used to be.'

This is not to say that there are not still those who favour confrontation: there are. Even Dow may yet change its corporate mind. In Europe, for example, the Greens have stirred deep passions in many industrialists, with considerable differences of opinion on how the challenge should be countered.

Some are adopting the hard line approach. 'It is high time that the industry stopped their pompous pretensions,' was the way Dr Peter King, general secretary of Britain's Society of Chemical Industry, summed up his views on the Greens. 'Don't call them the "Greens",' he suggested. 'Call them "green pygmies" and "the flat earth society".' Typical environmental activists, he argued, are often female (one might of course say they are often male, too), have no knowledge of chemistry and are opposed to capitalism. 'Rational arguments and the use of good independent statistics,' he fumed, 'are like throwing blunt spears at tanks.'

A way with pests

No-one who has seen some of the Greens in action against West German industry would dismiss such views entirely, but Dr King was soon under attack for presenting a distorted portrait of the chemical industry's critics. At the same time, however, many of the industry's critics have a distorted idea of the way the chemical industry itself views the environment.

Given the way the media cover environmental stories, this is scarcely surprising and industry has often seemed to go out of its way to give the media issues to feed on, particularly in the United States. Consider the position in California, for example. If you believe the figures in a recent report published by the US Economic Development Commission, some 2,500 Californians will die from cancers each year over the next decade because of their exposure to toxic chemicals. If the pace of clean-up activities is not accelerated, the Commission concluded, the necessary remedial steps could well cost $4 billion a year. 'We are in danger of polluting our own prosperity,' was the way California Lieutenant Governor, Leo McCarthy, described the situation.

McCarthy, who also headed the Commission, noted that the equivalent of a lorry-load of toxic waste is produced each year for every Californian living in the state. The Commission also estimated that it was already costing $1.3 billion a year to treat cancers caused by toxic chemicals, while another $32 million is spent each year to replace contaminated underground water supplies. Californian companies face lawsuits demanding more than $2.7 billion in damages because of toxic waste problems, while the cost of enforcing and complying with the relevant regulations works out at around $1.7 billion a year for industry and taxpayers.

At the same time, it is difficult to pick up a paper or watch television without hearing of some problem associated with the mismanagement of chemicals. The year after Bhopal, for example, a Union Carbide pesticide, Aldicarb, was in the news because some ten million Californian watermelons, about a third of the whole US crop, were marked down as unsaleable following the discovery of Aldicarb residues in watermelons produced in the state's central valley. Union Carbide claimed the product should degrade within 100 days of application, but there was evidence to suggest that some of the residues might have been caused by applications of Aldicarb to cotton crops on the same land some years previously.

The use of chemicals to control pests is not unnatural, however. Indeed, even starlings are now known to use this strategy. Because they re-use the same nests year after year, pest infestations can build up. So starlings select plant materials for refurbishing their nests which contain natural pesticides. No-one yet knows how they pick the right plant species, but the statistical evidence shows that they do. The question is not whether we should use pesticides, but whether we should use pesticides which are known to damage the environment.

Companies like Ciba-Geigy, ICI, Monsanto and Shell managed, by careful backstage lobbying, to outflank a campaign by the Pesticide Action Network (PAN), co-ordinated by Oxfam, which was designed to place much tighter controls on Third World sales of particularly hazardous pesticides. At least 10,000 people are thought to die of pesticide poisoning every year in the developing countries, which is equivalent, as Oxfam's David Bull put it, to 'four Bhopals each and every year.'

Even so, all these companies have impressive programmes designed to produce ecologically-safe pesticides. Shell, for example, launched 'Fastac' in 1983. 'It has the two vital ingredients of a top insecticide,' said product co-ordinator Neville Craig, 'high activity and broad spectrum of control, balanced by minimal environmental effects.' The extraordinary aspect of Fastac was that it could be sprayed on flowering crops without affecting any foraging bees.

ICI has also found some 'dream' compounds. 'If you sat down and wrote out what you wanted from a compound, both commercially and environmentally,' said Dr John Leahey, a senior ICI scientist, 'you would find that you had come a long way towards describing "Fusilade". It was a dream compound, the first on which I have worked where everywhere you looked it was the way you wanted it.'

However, the herbicide Fusilade was simply an example of the luck of the draw at work: eventually something must fit the bill in every respect. Most compounds which prove to have some quality which could be of value in crop protection also prove to have at least some environmental side-effects which need to be carefully evaluated both in the laboratory and in field tests.

Even with a product like its pirimicarb aphicide, marketed as 'Aphox' and 'Rapid', ICI had a fairly difficult time persuading both regulators and potential customers of the product's extraordinary selectivity. 'It took a lot of testing to convince people that it is safe to spray an insecticide on a flowering crop where bees are present,' Dr Leahey recalled. 'But it is safe. In fact it is so safe that it is an excellent chemical for use in integrated pest control programmes.'

According to ICI, the average cost of taking a new pesticide from discovery to large-scale manufacture increased from about £1.5 million in 1965 to about £3 million by 1970. By 1979, that figure had reached £15 million, with toxicological, ecological and environmental testing taking up to seven years to complete for each new product. This element of product costs grew at a rate of around 30 per cent a year through the early 1980s.

The problem is that many of these new pesticides are more

expensive than Third World countries can afford. Indeed, many developing countries continue to use environmentally hazardous pesticides, including DDT, because they are effective and cheap. Faced with a market for such products, some chemical companies continue to supply DDT and other products which have been banned in the developed countries.

Green lights for ICI

Ask Sir John Harvey-Jones, who, as chairman of ICI until early 1987, whether he expected the environmental pressure on the chemical industry to slacken and he replies: 'I doubt it. I think it's a continuing situation. The rate of climb may vary, but I think it is an inevitable trend. First of all, our understanding of the environment, of the trigger effects in the environment, is growing the whole time. And as we find new cause and effect links, it is right and proper that we should deal with the resulting problems. Secondly, we are further and further into a situation where people have more and more leisure. People appreciate more and more the opportunity to enjoy the environment as part of their quality of life, so the pressures are not going to get any less.'

The world's fifth largest chemical company, ICI makes or sells products in almost every country. Its product range includes petrochemicals, plastics, fibres, dyes, explosives, paints, pharmaceuticals and agrochemicals, all of which have come under fire from environmentalists at some time. The company, however, has been in pursuit of environmental excellence for many years and its approach provides a useful model for other companies.

Dust, sulphur dioxide and ammonia were the main problems at ICI's Billingham site, until the company launched a £3 million clean-up campaign in the late 1960s. By the time the 'doomwatch' literature really began to take off in 1972, the company had already reduced Billingham's grit and dust emissions by a staggering 98 per cent. During the same period, too, the massive site's sulphur dioxide emissions had been cut by 97 per cent and ammonia emissions by 90 per cent.

In other words, technologies can evolve to meet changing environmental conditions, just as organisms do. Indeed, the economic pressures operating on the chemical industry at the moment are intense and environmental and energy efficiency considerations are often key factors influencing the direction and pace of technological evolution. A good example of this trend is the FM21 membrane cell, developed by ICI for chlor-alkali production. The FM21 is based on a simple, compact design and uses a third less energy than conventional processes. Additionally, it avoids the significant costs involved in making competing mercury cells or asbestos-based diaphragm cells environmentally acceptable.

Yet, however clever the engineering achieved with a particular plant or complex, industry is always going to be left with some form of waste requiring treatment and disposal. The example of ICI's new Wilhelmshaven complex shows what can be achieved.

This former shipbuilding town, on the shores of West Germany's Jade Bay, had been largely bypassed by the country's 'economic miracle'. Its main asset was its deep-water harbour, a feature which was the key to ICI's decision to build its £250 million production complex there. Other advantages included the fact that Wilhelmshaven had the longest jetty in Europe and, equally important, there is enough salt just a few miles down the road to supply the company with chlorine for 100 years.

However, Wilhelmshaven also had one major disadvantage: Jade Bay itself. 'The whole area is like an enormous nature reserve,' explained the effluent process design adviser for the project. A 'cradle-to-grave' system was designed to ensure that all chemicals used or manufactured on site were properly handled from production (or purchase) through to the final disposal of any waste products. The main problems in the effluents proved to be formates, glycol and salt. The salt can be discharged into the Bay, which is partly estuarine, but, while the glycol proved fairly easy to treat, the formates were a problem.

In designing the effluent treatment plant, ICI's Brixham Laboratory had to juggle with a number of conflicting requirements. If, for example, the treatment plant held on to the effluents long enough to break down the formates, there was a risk that filamentous fungi would grow in the sludges, introducing further complications. In the event, these problems were solved and, like Billingham before it, Wilhelmshaven demonstrates the way in which new investment can boost output while dramatically cutting any undesirable effects. The level of environmental quality achieved at Wilhelmshaven is indicated by the fact that copper is so effectively removed from the plant effluents that more goes into Jade Bay from copper-based anti-fouling paints on the hulls of passing ships than from the entire ICI complex.

A leaf from Nature's book

A whiff of almonds is often the last sensation reported by those lucky enough to survive poisoning by cyanide gas and they can count themselves lucky indeed to be alive. Cyanide is a peculiarly nasty chemical.

Swallow as little as 300 milligrams (just one hundredth of an ounce) of cyanide salts or inhale a mere 100 milligrams of hydrogen cyanide gas and this rapidly acting poison will disrupt the fine chemistry of your cells. Breathing air containing as little as 200 to 500 parts per million of hydrogen cyanide can prove fatal within half an hour. However, hydrogen cyanide is also an extremely useful industrial chemical, being used in the manufacture of acrylic fibres, synthetic rubber and plastics. The uses of cyanide have extended well beyond the manufacture of the synthetic fibres which are now such a feature of modern life. They include the manufacture of synthetic dyes and the hardening of iron and steel.

As a result, most developed countries are dotted with tanks and other containers filled with cyanide residues and sludges. Once these wastes would simply have been dumped in the nearest river or canal and no doubt some still are. But with today's stricter controls many businesses find themselves with quantities of waste cyanide, without the slightest idea of what they should do with them. ICI, however, has developed an economical and effective process for breaking down such cyanides into harmless substances, using an approach taken directly from nature.

'It's an elegant process and a simple one,' said Professor Christopher Knowles, head of microbial biochemistry at the University of Kent, the man whose original research had sparked ICI's interest in the new cyanide detoxification process. 'A range of natural organisms produce cyanide,' he noted, 'while others are able to degrade it. 20 per cent of all plants produce cyanide, for example, using it as a defensive mechanism to ward off micro-organisms which would otherwise invade damaged leaves. We knew some fungi and bacteria seemed to be able to get around this defence, by breaking down the cyanide. Once we had realized that, we began to wonder whether there might not be some commercial applications of this natural detoxification process.'

An ICI research team based at Billingham started work on the idea in 1982, screening nine different types of fungus for the sort of enzyme which was thought to be involved in breaking down the cyanide. An enzyme was found and a fermentation process was developed to produce it. ICI is convinced that the potential international market for its enzyme product, called 'Cyclear', will be very considerable indeed.

'We are probably talking about tens of millions of dollars in North America, Europe and Japan,' said Dr Peter Rodgers, head of the company's biochemical group, and the cyanide project 'is seen as a platform for ICI's aspirations to use a wider range of biotechnology processes in the management of effluents arising from oil, petrochemical and chemical industries.'

Ahead of the legislation

One of the chemical industry's fundamental problems is that environmental issues are getting more and more complicated. To start with, it was simply a matter of dust, grit, black smoke and dead fish in nearby rivers. Today, with issues such as 'acid rain' surfacing, the chemical industry is having to carry out fundamental research at the very frontiers of environmental science.

'Certainly our biggest problem is in establishing the links between cause and effect,' said Sir John Harvey-Jones. 'The outstanding example of this, of course, is acid rain. Although quite plainly some linkages have been established the process is still not fully understood. And, understandably, we are fairly windy of overreacting until we have reasonably clear evidence that what we are doing is causing problems—because nearly everything you do environmentally costs money. But even if the evidence is contradictory, if there are alternative technologies which are economically viable, they should be used.'

Aerosols, however, point up some of the constraints on this approach. 'The difficulty with aerosols,' as Sir John put it, 'is that when you mention the word most people think of air-fresheners or hair-sprays, yet there are a hell of a lot of applications where aerosols do things that you cannot get done in any other ways.' But who, even 15 years ago, would have imagined that companies like ICI would soon have to develop front-rank expertise in such an esoteric area as stratospheric chemistry in order to protect its aerosol propellant business? However, since two American scientists came up with the idea that certain aerosol propellants could be upsetting the chemistry of the upper atmosphere (see Chapter 6), ICI has had to spend millions of pounds on such research.

Another business which has encountered environmental resistance is the production of nitrogenous fertilizers—in which ICI is a market leader. The company has carried out many experiments over the years to produce an overall picture of where nitrogen in the soil was coming from and going to. The objective has been 'to account for every kilogram of nitrogen, if possible.' Given that the top layer of soil can contain about 10,000 kilograms of nitrogen per hectare, it was obviously vital that the fertilizer nitrogen should be clearly identifiable, so it was flagged with the heavy isotope nitrogen-15. This meant that the fertilizer nitrogen could be tracked through the soil system, whether it was taken up by the crop, temporarily stored in the roots, immobilized in the soil humus, or lost from the soil either as leachate and run-off, or as gases vented to the atmosphere after microbial denitrification.

The research showed that average applications of nitrogen to grassland were unlikely to cause significant pollution problems in nearby rivers, although local conditions could result in unexpected problems. Meanwhile, however, government scientists had pinpointed a much more important source of nitrate pollution: arable farming itself. If you plough a field which has been under grass for some years, or leave a field without a crop, you can trigger a burst of nitrate run-off from the natural nitrate reservoir in the soil. Chemicals, in short, were only part of the problem. Once you opt for intensive arable farming as it is currently practised, nitrate pollution seems to be inevitable.

Clearly, though, high nitrate levels in surface or underground water are undesirable, whatever their source, so ICI is providing advice to farmers on ways in which they can cut the nitrate loss from their fields: a loss which, from the farmer's point of view, is simply money down the drain.

ICI's policy, Sir John pointed out, 'has always been that we should be in advance of the legislation in the environmental field.' As the company decentralized during the major restructuring he initiated on taking over as chairman, he noted, 'it was important that we had a coherent statement of company values and that environmental responsibilities were given to those people best able to do something about them, the people on the ground.'

A company environment policy was adopted, highlighting ways in which new projects, processes and products could be made environmentally acceptable. The company aims to 'achieve environmental standards which are socially acceptable in the areas in which it operates.' Given the vital importance of the political factor in that acceptability equation, ICI has long recognized that a company which wants to thrive rather than simply survive must have finely attuned environmental antennae. Indeed, it employs several hundred technical staff to ensure that it keeps abreast of the relevant environmental trends and concerns.

A basic problem which the chemical industry still has to come to terms with, however, is the public's suspicion about what might emerge next from the Pandora's Box of industrial chemistry. This suspicion, Sir John Harvey-Jones suggested, 'has a great deal to do with the way we are taught chemistry at school. I remember that when I learned the very little chemistry that I was taught at school, the very first thing we did was to make a stink bomb, the second thing was to make something which went bang, and the third thing we did was to burn a hole in something with acid. So we start with the thought that chemicals are smelly, explosive and corrosive and it's almost impossible to persuade people that chemicals are friendly.'

This task obviously becomes effectively impossible for some considerable time in the wake of such disasters as Seveso or Bhopal. Indeed, very few industrialists now believe that they can avoid further environmental pressures, however hard they try to persuade the public that chemicals are essential. 'The chemical industry is going through a crisis of confidence,' admitted the chairman of Bayer's supervisory board. 'For many people, it arouses negative emotions, suspicion and even fear.'

In Hamburg, the Greens actually managed to have a plant operated by Boehringer Ingelheim shut down, because it had been contaminating the nearby environment with dioxin. 'We were very surprised to discover dioxin,' recalled the company's scientific adviser, Werner Deckers. 'We had never looked. We never imagined that this chemical reaction would take place.'

That approach is no longer adequate. Increasingly, the world's chemical companies are being forced to adopt different styles of thinking. As the new managing director of Union Carbide India put it a year after the Bhopal disaster: 'We are asking "What if . . . ?", which we didn't do before.'

Chapter 6

INTELLIGENT PRODUCTS

From lighter cans to jet engines which are cleaner,
quieter and more fuel-efficient, industry is coming
up with new generations of products which are
beginning to win significant shares of existing
markets and also look set to open up enormous new
markets. In the age of the microchip, too, a degree
of 'intelligence' can be built into many products,
cutting their energy consumption and pollution output.

Question: What have an aerosol, a tin can, a yacht, an outboard
engine, an automobile and a passenger aircraft got in common?
Answer: They, and a growing range of other industrial products,
have had to be completely redesigned to cut pollution or the
consumption of energy and other natural resources.

It has rarely been an easy task, although it is an increasingly vital one. Some products have proved almost impossible to
redesign and have had, or will need, to be banned outright. The
environmental problems they caused were an inevitable result of
the way they are built or formulated. However, remarkable
progress has been achieved in making many other industrial products more environmentally acceptable. This chapter outlines
some of these success stories and the work that underpinned
them.

In an industrial society, almost anything we do and almost any
product we use can affect some aspect of our broader natural
environment. Even when we try to get away from it all, jetting to
distant climes or casting off from the jetty for a day afloat, this
unwritten law of ecodynamics holds true. You can see this if you
put on a face mask for a moment and dive beneath the hull of your
yacht, skiff or dinghy.

Anyone who has kept a boat moored in the water for any length of time knows only too well that its hull will soon be coated with a thriving community of barnacles, limpets, seaweed and other unwelcome fellow travellers. This growth acts as a brake on the hull as it slips through the water, which means that the hull has to be scraped regularly. Eager to avoid this back-breaking and time-consuming work, boat-owners were delighted when the first anti-fouling paints appeared.

Initially, all sorts of strange compounds were used, with their inventors jealously guarding the formulations. Some worked, some did not. Gradually, however, the paint industry found mixtures that were more effective, often based on copper and sometimes ending up as a cocktail with such compounds as arsenic. These paints were certainly preferable to scraping, but they proved to have problems of their own. They could be dangerous and they were often difficult to apply. The active compounds rapidly leached out of the paint, which meant that the hull had to be painted regularly and, as a result, it still had to be scraped periodically, to strip back the accumulated layers of paint.

Consequently, when the paint industry came up with longer-lasting paints based on an organotin, tributyl tin (TBT), which could be formulated in a resin base to give a slow-release anti-fouling coat, boat-owners were delighted. However, evidence then began to emerge that the paints were damaging sensitive parts of the shallow coastal ecosystem. Copper, it transpired was soon rendered innocuous in the marine environment, whereas the newer TBT degrades very much more slowly and is much more toxic to marine life.

Initially, concern was voiced by oyster farmers, who claimed that TBT in seawater seemed to be stunting the growth of Pacific oysters. The yacht-owning community was unsympathetic. 'We are talking about a luxury delicacy against a type of paint developed to give us easier and safer sailing,' growled an editorial in *Yachts & Yachting*. Why should 90,000 yacht-owners be forced to give up TBT to keep oysters on the table?

This argument was unsuccessful: Britain's Department of the Environment retorted that the oyster problems were 'just the visible tip of a potentially massive environmental iceberg.' Oysters, it explained, are a particularly sensitive indicator of the damage TBT can cause. TBT had also been found to damage many other marine species, including algae, clams, crabs, Dover sole, plankton and shrimp. Infinitesimal amounts of TBT, between 0.2 and 0.5 parts per billion, proved harmful to marine micro-algae. Indeed, environment minister William Waldegrave, used the pages of *Yachting Monthly* to warn boat-owners that he had 'seldom been faced with clearer scientific evidence of the need for environmental action – and fast.' He stressed that TBT was too effective for the good of shallow coastal waters. 'Less than one teaspoon of TBT in 20 million gallons of water,' he noted, 'is sufficient to stop the growth of phytoplankton, the marine equivalent of grass.'

Following evidence that TBT was deforming oyster shells and cutting oyster reproduction rates, France banned the use of TBT-based paints on hulls under 25 metres in length. Britain, on the other hand, moved more slowly. Three years after the French ban, it also decided to ban TBT-based anti-fouling paints. As a result, the paint industry had to redouble its search for substitute products. Also, for the first time, anti-fouling paints became subject to formal toxicity testing requirements.

The one per cent solution
Castrol, a manufacturer operating in a very different line of business encountered the same problem: it, too, had to reformulate its product.

The Swiss have been increasingly concerned about the oil found in the sediments of the Bodensee, or Lake Constance as the English know it. The Lake forms part of the course of the Rhine and its waters afford both trout and salmon fishing. Its Alpine scenery, coupled with a mild climate, have long made it a popular resort area. But the Lake has been increasingly polluted since the 1950s, both by sewage effluents and by agricultural run-off.

When research showed a surprisingly high oil content in lake sediments, suspicion inevitably fell on the growing number of outboard engines being used in the area. As a result, in 1981 the authorities banned all outboard motors above 10 horsepower, and more recently they have been considering a total ban.

For companies supplying the oil used in the formulation of

two-stroke outboard engine fuels, this looked like the thin end of a rather unpleasant wedge. So they formed a joint research team to see whether their oils were, in fact, at the root of the problem. 'We began to suspect that something was awry,' said Castrol engineering manager, Mike Beggs, 'when monitoring studies showed more oil in the lake than had ever been sold for outboard motors. Under pressure from the Greens, the authorities had failed to ask themselves what *type* of oil they were dealing with.' Work by the independent Oil Pollution Research Unit (OPRU: see page 103) suggested that outboard engines were very unlikely to have been the main source of the sediment oils.

Outboard engines do cause oil pollution, however. It is generally accepted that between 15 and 40 per cent of the fuel used in even the most modern outboard finds its way into or onto the water. But, while these emissions can cause unsightly oil films on the water, OPRU found no evidence to suggest that they cause significant biological damage. It also indicated a number of other sources of oil pollution, including sewage and industrial discharges, stormwater run-off from roads and other built-up areas, outboard and inboard engines in shipping, as well as the natural erosion of sedimentary rocks and coal measures. To complicate matters still further, OPRU pointed out that oil can also be formed by the decomposition of vegetable or animal matter.

However, the outboard ban stayed in force and the implication was that a similar ban might be imposed in other areas. As a result, Castrol, an oil company which had won a major share of the Swiss market for outboard oils, began to look at ways in which its oils could be made to break down much more readily once out in the environment. Ordinary mineral oil is totally biodegradable, but in order to withstand the environment inside an outboard engine, two-stroke fuels need to be fortified with a number of chemical additives, which have the incidental effect of making them less biodegradable.

A Castrol Research Laboratories team began to screen different oils and different components of oil to check on their biodegradability, toxicity and likely pollution effect. Soon they had identified an oil formulation which appeared to have all the desirable technical features, such as stability, cleanliness and anti-corrosion properties, as well as greatly enhanced biodegradability.

The product successfully passed the rigorous tests to which it was subjected, but, Mike Beggs recalled, 'it was a rather pricey product. It worked out at around 150 per cent of the cost of a normal can of two-stroke oil. The Swiss were often willing – and able – to buy it. But the rest of the world asked why it should pay so much more. The fact is,' he noted, 'that this oil has a number of other extremely important benefits, with biodegradability very low down on the scale of attractions for the normal user. Indeed, a more immediate environmental benefit is that the oil is very heat-stable, so that it produces almost no smoke. But clearly we needed to put more work into the product to make it competitive.'

By careful reformulation, Castrol managed to produce an oil which had all these desirable properties, but could be used at the rate of just one part in a hundred of gasoline, rather than the more usual blends of one part in 50 or even one part in 25. This made the price much more acceptable.

'This isn't just a question of ecology, of a nice warm feeling in your breast,' Mike Beggs stressed. 'The Swiss police were soon requiring boat owners to have their outboards tested every year. If they produced smoke, they failed. In many cases, the police were telling people that if they used our product, Biolube 100, they would pass.'

However, as the first company into the field, Castrol had the task of convincing the outboard engine manufacturers that Biolube 100 would not harm the performance of their engines. 'Johnson accepted our evidence first,' Beggs said, 'and they were followed by Evinrude and mercury.' Today, for every can of ordinary outboard oil Castrol sells in Switzerland, it sells several of Biolube 100 and the company calculates that it has cut the oil emissions from outboards using its oil by 65 per cent. Indeed, the company stresses the environmental performance not only of its Biolube but also of oils like GTX3, which helps the catalytic converters installed in cars such as Mercedes, BMWs and Volkswagens to control air pollution more effectively.

A can of worms

Castrol, in short, managed to keep its product on the shelf. A very different type of can, meanwhile, had run into a different problem. Companies making aerosol cans and propellants suddenly found themselves accused of eroding the planet's protective ozone layer, letting through deadly ultraviolet radiation from the sun and boosting skin cancer rates around the world.

When the ozone layer first appeared in the world's headlines in the early 1970s, there were two main concerns: supersonic aircraft such as Concorde and aerosols. In the event, the proposed fleets of Concordes or Concordskis never really took to the air, but aerosol propellants did. Although the first aerosol was invented in 1926 by a Norwegian who wanted a better way of putting polish onto his skis, the idea was not taken up until the Second World War, when disease killed more Allied soldiers in the Far East campaigns than did enemy action. The US Government, looking for a better way of spraying insecticides, tried aerosol 'bug bombs' and the aerosols industry is the end result. Then, in the late 1960s, an independent scientist raised some important questions about some of the propellants used by the industry.

Scientist-inventor Jim Lovelock had shown in 1968 that chlorofluorocarbons (CFCs), widely used as aerosol propellants, were present in the smog-like haze which blew over his holiday cottage in the far west of Ireland. His measurements, using his own invention, an electron capture detector, showed that the concentration of these substances was three times higher in the airstream from Europe than it was in clean Atlantic air. Much more interesting, at least as far as Lovelock was concerned, was the fact that his detector was picking up CFCs in the air coming from the open sea too. 'Could it be that we're breathing polluted air blown right across the Atlantic from America?' he asked himself, 'Or are CFCs accumulating in the world at large because they are so stable?'

Since CFCs were known to be chemically inert, a major attraction as far as the aerosol manufacturer is concerned, the discovery that the atmosphere was permeated with them did not cause immediate alarm. At the time, the US aerosol industry was still in the final stages of fighting off an earlier challenge to the use of CFCs from parents whose children had taken to CFC sniffing, some of them dying as a result. However, in the interests of caution, the world's largest CFC manufacturer, E. I. du Pont de Nemours (better known as Du Pont), invited other manufacturers to a meeting on what it called the 'ecology of fluorocarbons' in 1972.

The company's invitation noted that 'fluorocarbons are intentionally or accidentally vented to the atmosphere worldwide at a rate approaching one billion pounds per year. These compounds may be either accumulating in the atmosphere or returning to the surface, land or sea, in the pure form or as decomposition products.' The important point, as Du Pont continued to say, was that 'under any of these alternatives, it is prudent that we investigate any effects which the compounds may produce on plants or animals, now or in the future.'

It would be inappropriate at this point to review the history of the debate about the chemistry of the ozone layer. Suffice it to say that the aerosol industry's deliberations were considerably accelerated by the publication in 1974 of a scientific paper by two American scientists, Rowland and Molina. There are a number of naturally occurring chemicals which destroy ozone, which is itself constantly being formed by the action of solar radiation on atmospheric oxygen. These natural ozone scavengers maintain a balance in the global ozone budget. The worrying thing about the Rowland-Molina hypothesis was that it introduced a new scavenger: chlorine. The break-up of a single CFC molecule, it appeared, could set off a chemical chain reaction which could destroy hundreds, and perhaps thousands, of ozone molecules. The results, Rowland and Molina predicted, could include higher skin cancer rates around the world, significant crop damage and disturbed weather patterns.

The science was continuously in dispute, but environmentalists argued that CFCs should be banned because two-thirds of their uses, in products such as hair sprays and anti-perspirants, could be considered frivolous in the light of the presumed risk to the atmosphere. In the event, and after a great deal of heated debate, countries like the United States, Canada and Sweden brought in legislation to control the use of CFC propellants in such non-essential uses. Then, in 1979, the EEC environment ministers agreed, as a precautionary step, to freeze CFC production in the European Community and, by 1981, to cut the use of CFCs in aerosols by 30 per cent of the 1976 production figure.

Meanwhile, the CFC research had opened up an atmospheric can of worms. The fate of the ozone layer, it is now recognized, is intimately bound up not only with the level of present and future

CFC emissions, but also with emissions of other gases, including carbon dioxide, methane, oxides of nitrogen and water vapour. These gases are now known to act and react in some unsuspected ways in the atmosphere.

Then, in 1985, British scientists discovered the 'ozone hole' opening up over the Antarctic. The evidence had been in American hands for ten years, in the form of data collected by orbiting space satellites, but the computers which processed the data ignored the ozone hole because they had been programmed to treat such things as impossible. The size of the hole, it turns out, varies throughout the year—but can cover an area as large as the United States. Soon other scientists were finding evidence of at least one more ozone hole, this time over the Arctic.

A mass of new research results and growing public concern led to the signing of the Montreal Protocol by the USA, the EEC and 23 other countries late in 1987. The aim was to cut world CFC consumption by 20 per cent by 1994 and by another 30 per cent by 1999. But, for the foreseeable future, this agreement will simply slow down the rate of ozone depletion because of the longevity of CFCs. Montreal II is now very much on the cards. Consequently, the destruction of the ozone layer is likely to be in the headlines for many years to come. The race to switch to CFCs which are less damaging to the ozone layer—and to other forms of propellant or dispenser—can only intensify.

One key factor which helped trigger the move out of CFCs in Britain was a campaign mounted by Friends of the Earth. Initially, FoE published *The Aerosol Connection*, a pamphlet spotlighting aerosol brands that were CFC-free. Then, just days before FoE followed up with a list of the brands that did contain CFCs, the eight largest aerosol manufacturers announced that they would phase out CFCs by the end of 1989. Those companies alone accounted for 65 per cent of the UK toiletries market and other companies—including some of the major supermarket groups—followed suit. The age of the Green Consumer had arrived.

Lighting and lightweighting
While CFC manufacturers have been gathering information on the impact of their products on the distant ozone layer, other manufacturers have been responding to another challenge thrown

up by the 'environmental revolution'. They have been trying to do more with less, to squeeze more product out of a given quantity of natural resources. For example, consider the progress already made with such everyday products as tin cans and light bulbs.

The conventional light bulbs that we switch on and off with hardly a thought are 'incandescent' bulbs, and have been around for over a hundred years. Incandescent lamps were in use in Britain's House of Commons by 1881, for example, and the country's first domestic installations were made in 1886. Today these bulbs are relatively cheap but, as a Philips scientist put it recently: 'If you buy an incandescent bulb, you are simply buying an electricity bill.'

Fluorescent, 'discharge' lighting came somewhat later. Although the first experiments with discharge tubes date from 1857, the first commercial use of fluorescent lamps was in 1938, with domestic use following in 1942. Whereas incandescent bulbs are cheap and simple, discharge tubes are expensive and more complicated to manufacture. For one thing, they need electronic circuitry to control the flow of current. So, at the time of writing, a discharge lamp such as the Thorn 2D tube costs around seventeen times as much as an incandescent bulb. However, the discharge approach offers a number of key advantages: the lamp lasts five times as long and uses a fraction of the energy used by an incandescent bulb.

Now new manufacturing technology is helping the industry shrink the size of discharge lamps, opening up new applications. By squeezing all the electronic circuitry needed onto a single silicon chip, Philips and its US semiconductor subsidiary, Signetics, have brought the technology to the stage where, as one Philips executive explained: 'It's the first time in history you can put a fluorescent tube in your pocket.'

Whichever type of bulb you buy, however, it is bound to come in some form of package. When environmentalists attacked the packaging industry in the 1960s and 1970s, they saw packaging as the ultimate symbol of the throwaway age. In their view, it squandered resources and, many felt, should be banned. But packaging often serves a very real purpose. It can prevent the spoilage of products, such as food and medicines, and the loss of the energy and raw materials which went into making them. Substantially more energy goes into such products than into the packaging used to protect them.

Packaging can also reduce the amount of energy needed to transport products to market (although, obviously, the converse can also be true). Packaging materials can be recycled, as are considerable volumes of glass, tin, plastic and paper. In addition, a trend which would have surprised many early environmentalists, packagers have found new ways of protecting products, which use less energy and less material.

In a process known as 'lightweighting', the packaging industry has progressively reduced the amount of tin-plate or glass needed to protect a particular product, whether it is mulligatawny soup, baked beans or milk. Since 1957, for example, there has been a 30 per cent reduction in the thickness of can walls and tin coatings are 50 per cent thinner. In 1970, an empty can and its two ends weighed 68.9 grams, whereas by 1980, the weight had been cut to 58.4 grams. By the time of writing, the weight was down to 56.5 grams.

Another example of lightweighting is the wrapping used on bars of chocolate. Chocolate is very sensitive to oxygen, light and tainting, so it needs to be well protected. It used to be wrapped in a waxed paper laminate weighing 56 grams per square metre, whereas it is now wrapped in a plastic film which gives better protection and weighs 45 per cent less. That may not make much difference in terms of the chocolate bar you hold in your hand, but when you are moving tonnes of the stuff around it can begin to save materials, energy and money.

A third example of this trend takes us above the clouds. The energy cost of a refillable glass bottle designed for twenty reuse trips is just a tenth of that of an equivalent-sized plastic bottle. But, although glass uses less energy in manufacture, it is heavier, which can mean that you use *more* energy in certain situations. If you are supplying the airlines with miniature bottles of spirits, for example, the fact that a glass bottle is five times heavier than a plastic bottle is an important consideration.

If an airline uses plastic bottles on a single intercontinental 747 Jumbo, it can currently save fuel worth £12,000 in a single year. This is a tiny amount if you are running an airline, but even such small savings can add up rapidly if you are running a large fleet of aircraft over many years. The savings can be very much more significant if you apply the lightweighting principle to rather heavier parts of the aircraft, such as the engines.

Flying into the 21st century

The roll-out of the first 757 aircraft at Boeing's Renton airfield, early in 1982, was an even tenser event than usual. For the first time in its history the company had picked a non-American engine as the recommended powerplant for a major new commercial airliner. If the gamble failed, company officials knew, the political backlash from US politicians who had supported US engine manufacturers would be intense.

As the months passed, however, and the 757 began to build up a track record, Boeing found that it had picked the most reliable engine ever to enter airline service, a key consideration in twin-engine aircraft like the 757. However, it also found that the performance of Rolls-Royce's RB211-535 engine was exceptional both in terms of fuel efficiency and environmental acceptability. These, indeed, had been key elements of the early Rolls-Royce design brief for the 535 project.

Even those who fly today's jet airlines recognize that they can cause environmental headaches. 'I was sitting on the deck of the QE2 once, sipping a gin and tonic,' recalled Concorde captain Brian Walpole, 'when Concorde went overhead. The noise was like a pistol shot – it was bloody unpleasant.' Environmental considerations, ranging from noise concerns to fears that aircraft emissions might, like CFCs, modify the weather, have become ever more important for jet engine designers.

'The annual growth in the number of jet airliners went as high as 50 per cent in the 1960s, and the public reaction became overwhelming,' explains Mike Smith, chief of noise technology at Rolls-Royce. 'In the early days of the Boeing 707, the noise problems were such that they had to take off for America with too little fuel for the whole trip, just to get out of the airport. Then they refuelled at Shannon.' The 707's engines, he notes, were 'ideal sirens. They moved a small amount of air very rapidly, whereas today we try to move a large amount of air more slowly. In early designs, the air was moving at supersonic speeds. Today we have virtually halved those speeds and have achieved enormous noise benefits as a result.'

The 535-E4 engine, the latest variant, is also a more powerful engine. Normally, this would have meant a greedier, noisier engine too, but the use of remodelled fans, an exhaust nozzle buried within the engine, improved noise control and combustion efficiency, together with weight-saving measures, brought a further ten per cent saving in fuel consumption. While the 535-E4 consumes slightly more fuel than its closest rival, it is an astonishing 40 per cent more fuel-efficient than the previous generation of Rolls-Royce engines. The company believes that it can knock a further three to five per cent off the engine's fuel consumption by 1990 and even today the 757 saves enough fuel in a year to fly 12 times around the world.

As far as exhaust emissions are concerned, Rolls-Royce was trying to improve the pollution performance of its engines ahead of legislation. Even a military jet which produces smoke is in trouble. 'An exhaust plume is a give away of the plane's position,' says Graham Pilkington, who was responsible for ensuring that the 535-E4 was a clean-burning engine. However, as he notes, engine design is a complicated juggling act.

'Whatever we do to control one set of pollutants produced by a new turbofan engine,' he explains, 'can affect the production of other pollutants.' As we have seen, the Rolls-Royce designers were not simply trading off one set of pollutants against another. They were also trying to design a quieter and more fuel-efficient engine. It is an uncomfortable fact that a quieter engine is often a heavier engine, while a cleaner engine is not necessarily more fuel-efficient.

To cope with the complexities of the internal physics and chemistry of such engines, Rolls-Royce spent between 30 and 50 man-*years* on developing sophisticated computer simulation programmes, to ensure that all the variables were monitored as one component after another was designed and redesigned. In the event, the 535 series of engines proved to be much cleaner. They emit between 10 and 20 per cent of the carbon monoxide, smoke and unburned hydrocarbons emitted by the jet engines of the 1960s, for example. The Rolls-Royce Spey engine produced some six gallons of unburned hydrocarbons while carrying 65 passengers, while the 535-E4, with 200 passengers aboard, produces less than three pints, a 50-fold improvement.

The 757 fitted with the 535-E4 is as quiet as, and in some cases quieter than, many existing aircraft of only a quarter of its weight and is well in advance of the legislation. Indeed, so quiet is the aircraft that the US Federal Aircraft Administration decided that the 757 with the E4 version of the engine should be the first large commercial aircraft to be permitted to operate at the extremely noise-sensitive Washington National Airport at night.

However, as the company's director of technology, Phil Ruffles, points out: 'You can't have a quieter engine without simultaneously making major strides in weight reduction. You could make a quieter engine, but commercially it would never take off.' Engine weight, notes John Sadler, who was responsible for this aspect of the 535-E4 project, 'has a very powerful effect on an aircraft's performance. If you are dealing with a twin-engine aircraft, one pound of engine needs another pound of aircraft to carry it. And that cuts the amount of fuel or passengers you can carry.' New high strength, low weight materials have been used extensively, while the fan-blades have hollow, honeycomb centres, again to cut weight. Compared with the jets of the 1960s, the weight saving embodied in the 535-E4 means that the equivalent of 22 extra passengers can be carried.

Not only is the 535-E4 engine an intelligently designed product, it is an increasingly *intelligent* product. Its electronic control system detects significant changes in engine conditions and responds, ensuring that it operates in the most fuel-efficient way, whether the aircraft is cruising, approaching the airport, or taxi-ing to the terminal. It is a measure of Rolls-Royce's achievement that it has simultaneously managed to produce an engine that is not only cleaner, quieter and more fuel-efficient, but also looks like capturing a major share of a market likely to be worth £15 billion over what remains of the twentieth century.

A computer on wheels

Pick up your bags from the baggage claim and make your way through customs. Once inside your car, a taxi or the airport limousine, relax: but do not imagine that your contribution to environmental pollution has stopped. The relative contribution which motor vehicles make to air pollution problems has soared as their numbers have grown and as static sources of air pollution have been more tightly controlled.

As far as the car industry in Europe and North America is concerned, the 1970s and 1980s have been a period of almost constant crisis. First there was the OPEC oil crisis of 1973 to 74, following which manufacturers struggled to improve the energy efficiency of their latest models. Then there was the invasion of the Japanese, with car buyers buying Datsuns, Hondas or Toyotas, in ever-increasing numbers. Meanwhile, the world's cities have become increasingly congested and polluted by vehicles, with photo-chemical smogs forcing some cities to forbid cars to move at all on critical days. An undercurrent to these crises was the continuing question of whether the private motor car actually had a future of any kind.

The car industry was reassured when the MIT International Automobile Program finally produced its report, *The Future of the Automobile*, ten years after the OPEC oil embargo forced people to ask whether there *was* a future for the auto industry. MIT concluded that the car will endure as the prime means of transport, partly because of its flexibility and partly because of the strengths of the technologies which underpin it. However, environmental pressures now mounting against the industry will ensure that those technologies will be pushed to, and beyond, their limits.

The drive to improve the energy efficiency of cars has now been overshadowed by another pressing need, to make cars run more cleanly. Mercedes Benz, for example, launched a new line of cars fitted with anti-pollution catalytic converters at least three years before they were required by European Community legislation. Shortly thereafter the sales director of Daimler-Benz launched a scathing attack on the European Community's compromise agreement on exhaust pollution. Stressing that his company supported the drive for tighter controls of auto emissions, Hans-Jurgen Hinrichs argued that the 'half-hearted compromise which the European Community has now reached is environmentally unsatisfactory. In our view, a great European chance has been missed to reach political agreement on such an important question as air pollution control.'

Daimler-Benz, spurred on by West Germany's Greens, who had been campaigning for controls to stop acid rain, was content to install catalytic converters in its cars, as long as everyone else did. The problem was that the European car industry was far from being in agreement on the matter. Some companies argued that cars were simply not responsible for the problems which were decimating the country's forests. Others argued that catalytic converters were an unduly expensive halfway house technology, a band-aid approach instead of the ideal solution of redesigning the car around the so-called 'lean-burn' engine.

Some manufacturers pointed out that catalytic converters could increase petrol consumption significantly. All the gains made in fuel economy during the previous five years could be wiped out, they argued, if catalytic converters had to be fitted to new cars. They also need to run on lead-free fuel, since lead 'poisons' the catalysts within a few hundred miles, although this should not be a problem since Europe should have lead-free petrol by 1989. The news that the levels of lead entering the US environment have dropped by 40 per cent since the country limited the use of lead additives in gasoline have encouraged European activists who want to eliminate lead from European petrol too.

Meanwhile, the companies involved in the manufacture of catalytic converters, which use catalysts like platinum in a 'three-way' format to remove more than 90 per cent of the nitrogen oxides, carbon monoxide and unburned hydrocarbons spewed into a car's exhaust, have also lobbied hard for regulations requiring that their products should be fitted. They were scathing about the auto industry's resistance to catalytic converters.

'Before the American Clean Air Act,' noted the head of Johnson Matthey Chemicals' catalysts division, 'the US motor industry spent a lot of money vilifying catalysts, but it failed to get the law changed. Then General Motors (GM) broke ranks and announced that it would fit all its models with converters. It was not long before the motor industry was promoting the catalyst as the answer to a maiden's prayer.' Along with other manufacturers, such as West Germany's Degussa, which held 40 per cent of the European catalytic converter market to Johnson Matthey's 30 per cent, Johnson Matthey knew that a European decision to force car manufacturers to install their equipment would add at least 10 million units, worth around £500 million, to the world market of 22 million converters a year.

Once again, GM looked like the company which would break ranks. By 1985, GM catalytic converters were installed in over 60 million cars in the United States and the company was well set up to exploit similar technology in Europe. Even if Europe decides not to follow the United States along the catalytic converter route, however, GM is working on cars which should be markedly cleaner than those in use today. It has opened a $12.5 million European Technical Centre in Luxembourg to develop computer systems which would be used to build the next generation of 'intelligent' car.

The energy crisis and tough anti-pollution regulations brought in by the Environmental Protection Agency spurred the use of microcomputers in US cars. Now, just as the Rolls-Royce jet engine is constantly monitored by a microcomputer, so many car engines are monitored and tuned by computer.

The combination of computers, new materials which allow engines to burn hotter (and cleaner), and the emergence of lean-burn technology should help cut auto emissions considerably in the long term. The lean-burn engine, as its name suggests, will burn a fuel mixture containing a much higher proportion of air than that used in conventional engines. However, this is a complex area of science and technology, requiring that the industry find out what happens inside an internal combustion engine as it works. Using lasers, car industry scientists can now see what happens in the millisecond that it takes a cylinder of fuel and air to explode. 'We always thought unburned hydrocarbons in the exhaust were caused by rapid cooling as hot gases contacted cooler cylinder walls,' explained one scientist. 'They really come from gases trapped in crevices around the head gasket and pistons. Now that we know reducing the interior surface area of the cylinder is the wrong solution, auto companies can work on the right ones.'

The key question is whether the need to invest in catalytic converter technology will divert the car manufacturers from these other areas. One hopeful signal that it was not an insurmountable problem came with the news that Austin Rover, a subsidiary of British Leyland, had developed a new range of cars with low exhaust emissions to meet West German requirements and had done so without using catalytic converters.

One fact, though, seems inescapable. The car of the future will be very different from today's models. For one thing, it will be much lighter. At the time of the OPEC oil embargo, the typical American auto weighed around 4,000 pounds, or about 50 per cent more than Japanese and European models. Great strides have already been made to produce lightweight cars, but new materials such as engineering ceramics and plastics could speed the process. Even the disc brakes of tomorrow's cars will be made from plastic. Such cars should last longer, cost less to make and to run and should also produce less pollution.

To illustrate how environmental considerations are pushing almost every aspect of car technology, we can conclude this chapter by looking at recent progress cutting pollution from part of the car-making process which never reaches the headlines. In fact, a key element in this success story is that the car buyer will *not* spot the difference between the car he bought last time and the one he has just climbed into.

Coats of many colours

'The key point to remember,' says Dr Brian Letchford, director of ICI's Paints Division, 'is that we are selling products in the *world* market. The motor industry is now a world industry, with world standards. We must come up with world products. Around the world, pollution issues are increasingly important for the paints industry, so we have to achieve improved product quality and higher environmental standards simultaneously. And that's precisely what we have done with Aquabase and Tempro.'

During the last decade, the quality of a car's exterior finish has become a major selling feature. In Western Europe, approximately 50 per cent of all passenger vehicles produced are now painted with metallic coats. A low solids polyester 'basecoat' gives the metallic look and colour, while an acrylic 'clearcoat' provides the 'wet look' effect which so many of today's customers demand.

A major difficulty has emerged with this approach, however. Countries such as Sweden, West Germany and the United States are increasingly concerned about the growing levels of solvent emissions to the atmosphere. 'In West Germany, where the Greens are a major political force,' Dr Letchford explains, 'the emission of solvents from the paint industry is seen as a major problem. Paint manufacturers are not generating most of these emissions, paint users are. As paint manufacturers, though, we see it as our task to reduce solvent emissions from our paints, wherever they may arise.'

In Europe and the United States, it is estimated that industrial solvent emissions account for about one third of all the volatile organic compounds now discharged into the atmosphere. The automobile industry is increasingly seen as a major contributor to this form of pollution. In the process of painting a single car, some 12 to 15 litres of solvent are released. Consequently, one might expect that a medium-sized car factory would emit 2,000 to 3,000 tonnes of solvent each year. 'If you multiply this by the world's total car production figure,' says Dr Letchford, 'you can assume that something like 360,000 tonnes of solvent are emitted each year.'

When ICI looked at where most of these emissions were coming from, it discovered that 'up to 50 per cent of solvent emissions come from the use of metallic coats. These are typically sprayed at around 16 per cent solids, which means that 84 per cent of what you are spraying is solvent.' Other significant culprits are the surfacer (16 per cent), the clearcoat (13 per cent) and the wax protective coat applied to the car at the end of the production line.

Various methods have been tried to cut down on solvent emissions. These have included the use of after-burners to destroy solvents escaping from the ovens in which the sprayed cars are dried. This approach involves high capital and energy costs, however. As far as the spray booths themselves are concerned, about 90 per cent of the basecoat solvent and the majority of the clearcoat solvent are lost. After-burners cannot be used here, so expensive solvent abatement systems have to be installed. The cost of all this add-on technology is likely to grow rapidly as impending legislation comes into force.

The obvious, though not easy, answer is to do away with the solvents. Waterborne paints had been tried in the United States, largely in response to the air pollution concerns which had been expressed in California. But, says Dr Alan Backhouse, the scientist who was responsible for ICI's breakthrough in this field, 'those early waterborne paints produced results as variable as the humidity, which means as variable as the weather. Because of the environmental pressures in California, they were used for some time, but they proved extremely expensive. Drying and baking had to be carried out between each coat and the spray booths had to be dehumidified. The end result was that when the depression hit, the plants that had adopted this technology were more vulnerable and were closed down.'

The key to ICI's success in developing cheaper, more effective waterborne paints was the use of what are known in the trade as aqueous microgels. The unique paint structure resulting from ICI's patented microgel technology means that it will not run or sag as the humidity changes in the factory.

ICI had to overcome a considerable number of technical problems in developing its new basecoat, Aquabase. For example, under normal circumstances the aluminium particles in metallic basecoats would react with water, so they had to be formulated in special ways to ensure that they were stable. In addition, as Dr Mary Swords of the company's Autocolor marketing department puts it, 'there was also a certain amount of prejudice to overcome, because of the earlier failures of waterborne products.'

Perhaps the most impressive single fact about Aquabase is that it cuts basecoat solvent emissions by over 85 per cent. Taking the painting cycle as a whole, Aquabase cuts solvent emissions by 60 per cent when the car is finished off with a solvent-borne clearcoat. The only modification needed to existing car production lines is the installation of a drying tunnel between the basecoat and clearcoat stages.

Aquabase was given preliminary approval by General Motors in 1981 and numerous field trials followed in Canada and the United States, with the result that Aquabase won full technical approval from GM, the world's largest vehicle manufacturer. Trials have also been carried out by such European manufacturers as BMW, Daimler-Benz, Ford, Opel, Volkswagen, Renault and Volvo. Several of these companies are now going ahead with production lines using Aquabase. ICI's waterborne protective coating, Tempro, replaces wax-based coatings which need solvents to remove. Tempro not only does a better and quicker job of protecting paintwork, but it also cuts solvent emissions by between 80 and 94 per cent. It has now been adopted by Aston Martin Lagonda, Ford and Jaguar, with trials under way at Renault and Volvo.

Altogether, ICI spent £2 million on these two new products between 1980 and 1985 but stresses that they are only the beginning in waterborne technology. 'We can envisage a scenario, in say 10 years,' concludes Dr Letchford, 'when the whole car-painting system will be water-based.'

Chapter 7

BUILDING BRIDGES

If sustainable development is to be something more than a pious hope, business, government and conservation interests must work together on new solutions to priority problems. New types of 'bridging institutions' are emerging to promote greater dialogue and co-operation between these various sectors. The signs are that the pace of events is quickening.

'The only way to beat them is to join them,' suggested Dr David Bellamy, the British naturalist and conservationist. 'We have got to become the developers.' The extraordinary thing was that he was not recommending that conservationists and environmentalists should take up organic farming or the production of appropriate technology. He wanted them to work closely with Nirex, the Nuclear Industry Radioactive Waste Executive, to pinpoint an environmentally acceptable site for dumping nuclear waste.

Not surprisingly, and this was well before the Chernobyl disaster hit the headlines, the proposal provoked a storm of protest from other environmentalists. Some, indeed, saw it as a call to arms for green quislings. As usual in such matters, it all depended on your attitude towards the industry under discussion. Nirex, in fact, had been looking for disposal sites for low – and intermediate – level radioactive wastes, which have always occupied pride of place in environmental demonology. Dr Bellamy had chaired a successful protest meeting against a proposal to store the wastes in old salt caverns deep beneath ICI's massive Billingham production site on Teesside. Nirex thereupon switched its search to Upper Teesdale and Weardale, Bellamy's home turf. Once again, the environmental lobby was incensed. That was when Bellamy made his offer.

It is worth recalling that conservationists had previously worked with the nuclear industry to resolve specific problems. At around the same time, for example, British Nuclear Fuels had announced that it would spend £1 million to create a new breeding ground for some 500 rare natterjack toads, whose existing habitat was threatened by a new railway the company planned to bring into its Sellafield complex in Cumbria. However, helping the nuclear industry spend £2,000 a toad to create a replacement habitat was seen by some as rather different from helping the industry resolve one of its core problems.

Bellamy's offer nonetheless symbolized an emerging trend. There is a growing willingness on the part of many people in the environmental lobby to work with industry to resolve pressing issues in such a way that development can proceed, while the environment can be protected or even enhanced.

A key problem has been that many decision-making structures have been inadequate to cope with the additional strain of the environmental agenda. The costs have often been extraordinary. For example, the inquiry which looked into the question of whether Britain's first pressurized water reactor should be built at Sizewell, on the Suffolk coast, lasted 340 working days, spanning two years. It generated 16 million transcribed words, producing enough paper to stretch from London to Cairo, and it cost the Central Electricity Generating Board at least £15 million, while the Board's opponents spent an estimated £750,000.

Industry, not surprisingly, is now looking around for ways of achieving acceptable decisions without having to spend such enormous sums of money. Given the controversy surrounding the nuclear power industry, it is difficult to imagine that the industry will achieve any major breakthrough in safe waste disposal in the foreseeable future, but the prospects may prove to be considerably better for a number of other industries.

In short, there has been something of a sea-change in environmental thinking. 'The old hostilities are breaking down,' noted William Ruckelshaus, during his second term as Administrator of the US Environmental Protection Agency (EPA), 'and old grievances are giving way to a spirit of co-operation, a new willingness to listen.' He was addressing the World Industry Conference on Environmental Management (WICEM) and was focusing on a new breed of organization: the bridging institution.

Even with the best will in the world, he argued, the politicization of so many of the fora in which the environmental debate takes place often prevents reasonable discussion of the key issues. The answer to this difficulty, he suggested, could be to meet on neutral ground with those who are likely to influence policies or decisions.

This is a need that the new bridging institutions are being set up to meet. They aim to bring industry, government agencies and public interest groups together in a constructive atmosphere, in an attempt to break through environmental bottlenecks. Two examples mentioned by Ruckelshaus were Clean Sites, Inc. and the Health Effects Institute, which he put forward as 'possible models for public and private collaboration elsewhere.'

Clean Sites was set up by the chemical industry and environmental interests, most notably the Conservation Foundation, to accelerate the clean-up of hazardous wastes sites. Ruckelshaus, however, warned that the Clean Sites venture was 'not a substitute for the central government effort to clean up hazardous wastes, but a useful adjunct that may come up with new answers.' By the time WICEM opened its doors, the US chemical industry had already offered a total of $22 million as seed money for what could ultimately turn into a billion dollar programme.

Will it kill?

What is the industry view of such bridging institutions? In the case of the Health Effects Institute: 'I think the reaction of our senior management was positive, but it was a reaction born out of a great deal of frustration,' explained Helen Petrauskas, vice president for environmental and safety engineering at Ford. 'They were frustrated by the inability of our scientists, government scientists and environmental scientists to agree on many central issues. After the Health Effects Institute was set up, we expected agencies like the EPA to retain their freedom to make decisions, as we hoped to retain ours, but at least we would all agree on a scientific base for our decisions.'

Industry was worried initially about whether the EPA 'would accept HEI's conclusions when it suited – and ignore them when it didn't,' she commented and presumably the EPA reacted in the same way. 'But,' she reported, 'our experience to date has been very good. The disagreements tend to be on policies. They're not violent disagreements over basic facts. In the long run, for once, I think there is a hope that we can present to the public something other than one group of scientists saying "It's going to kill you", while another says "Don't worry about it".' Even if the consensus is that 'one needs to know more, that the studies that have been done are woefully inadequate, at least we have an agreement – and can proceed to the next stage.'

The interesting thing about WICEM, which was organized by the United Nations Environment Programme (UNEP) and the International Chamber of Commerce (ICC), was that it gave leading industrialists a platform for putting across some of the more positive facets of their environmental thinking. 'We face a modern challenge,' said David Roderick, chairman of United States Steel, 'to develop a co-operative effort for protecting the world's environment while achieving economic growth. We reject outright the false notion that environmental improvement and industrial development are mutually exclusive.'

However, while they may not be mutually exclusive, they can be mutually destructive if either is badly mismanaged. During the early days of the environmental revolution, for example, industry was forced to 'retrofit' its existing plants with expensive pollution control equipment. This expenditure was certainly necessary, but far from cost-effective. But the heat of the public debate on environmental issues meant that it was nearly impossible for industry to make a constructive contribution, even in those cases where it was actually inclined to do so. As time went on, however, industrialists began to realize that the environmental challenge to their businesses was not going to evaporate, while environmentalists began to realize that they needed working partnerships with industry. So they started looking for ways in which they could move from reactive to 'proactive' strategies, contributing the skills and other resources of their companies to the drive for environmental quality. It is, of course, vital that they continue to do so, because the old style of environmental regulation can sometimes act as an unnecessary brake on innovation and development.

They have been encouraged in this direction by the success of a number of the early bridge-building exercises. 'The maturing of the environmental movement has seen a diminution of rhetoric and an increase in problem-solving research and technology,' was the way Roderick summed up the change. 'The early problems included a proliferation of hasty legislation, myriad competing groups, overlapping bureaucracies and an unrealistic timetable for achieving the desired goals. These have given way to a more considered approach that has emphasized an intelligent, well-defined course of improvement in place of a highly charged emotional crusade.'

United States Steel, in fact, has been a striking example of the profound changes now taking place in the economies of many of the industrialized nations and of the new emphasis on the entrepreneurial approach to business. Once a pillar of the US industrial establishment, the company has shrunk to a shadow of its former self. At its peak, which in employment terms was 1979, US Steel employed 172,000 workers, whereas by 1985 the company employed only 88,000, including 20,000 workers at Marathon Oil. US Steel pensioners outnumbered active employees by around two to one.

But instead of going out of business, the company had in fact dramatically improved its efficiency. Since Roderick took over in 1979, many obsolete plants had been closed, aggravating the 'rust bowl' phenomenon in the United States. Simultaneously, however, new investment has gone into leading edge production technologies, so that by 1985 the company could produce a ton of steel with around five hours of labour, compared to the 11 hours needed in 1982. While it builds the foundations for what it hopes will be its businesses of the future, US Steel has continued to press forward with improvements in its environmental performance.

Many of its older, more polluting plants have been closed, of course, but equally important has been the selection of raw materials, the design and redesign of processes and equipment and the recycling of some process materials. As a result of all these activities, the company estimated that it had cut the amount of hazardous waste it produced by nearly 50 per cent in just five years, slashing its need for landfill disposal by 80 per cent over the same period. It substituted non-leaded for leaded greases and oils when lubricating its rolling mills and its coke plants now mix heavy sludges, which were once discarded, with tars for use as an industrial fuel.

Initially, many of the companies that got involved in the

early bridging institutions or exercises did so largely to publicize the fact that they are making real environmental progress. However, they have gradually tended to get sucked into a wider debate. Some, too, take it to the next stage, investing resources and staff time in pioneering projects designed to achieve sustainable development.

'There is no choice of either/or,' said Gro Harlem Brundtland, a former (and subsequently re-elected) Prime Minister of Norway and chairman of the World Commission on Environment and Development. 'We can only achieve sustainable growth provided we manage to protect the environment and we shall only succeed in protecting the environment if we can accomplish sustainable growth.' In the meantime, she warned, 'many of today's approaches to economic development simply are not working.' They are 'based on a squandering of our biological capital: our soils, forests, animal and plant species, even our water and air.' All too often, current forms of development 'consume their own ecological foundations,' she argued. 'They are clearly not sustainable as we move into the next century, building another world on top of the one we have, and doubling, at least, our demands on the planet's ecosystems.' The key question that emerges is: how to get industry involved in sustainable development.

A small number of bridging institutions are now working on the answers to this question. Among those represented at WICEM was the World Environment Center, founded in 1974 with backing from the United Nations Environment Programme. Through the Center, over 20 American companies had agreed to provide free technical advice to help Third World countries solve their industrial environment problems. 'One of the key elements of the WEC programme,' explained Dr Casey E. Westell Jr., industrial ecology director at Tenneco, 'permits technology transfer directly between our engineers and scientists and the requesting country. This direct contact provides better understanding, we believe, and a much better chance of success in the resolution of environmental problems.'

WEC president Dr Whitman Bassow agreed. 'The expert's role is similar to that of a physician,' he said. 'He or she examines the "patient", makes a diagnosis and prescribes the cure. Then it's up to the "patient" to do the rest.' The first country to request assistance was Tunisia. Seven projects had already been completed by engineers from Tenneco, Pennzoil, Calgon, AMAX and Koppers. In Jordan, too, a team of engineers from Dundee Cement and Kaiser Cement had completed an environmental evaluation of a cement plant.

The eyes have it

In the meantime, how have other countries, and other companies, been progressing? Some concern was expressed at WICEM that companies in Europe and Japan, for example, had so far been slower in taking action. Perhaps, though, they have been working in different regions, or have simply been less effective in publicizing the work they are doing?

Bridging institutions, in fact, are beginning to emerge in Europe. In Britain, for example, the Centre for Economic and Environmental Development (CEED) was established in 1983 'to take the lead in creating a partnership between conservation and development.' It was not an immediate success, but at the time of writing is showing signs of finding its stride.

One of the key factors influencing leading industrialists to support the drive for sustainable development, however, is not easily reproduceable. Often such people get involved because they have seen the damage caused by present development approaches with their own eyes.

'Despite the fact that I have spent most of my life in competitive, profit-oriented industry,' noted Sir Arthur Norman, at the time chairman both of De La Rue and of CEED, 'you may not be surprised to know that some of my friends and acquaintances classify me as an "eco-nut" and have fears for my sanity. My riposte is to say that over 50 years of manufacturing and trading, which has taken me all over the world, many times over, has taught me that the careful use and management of vital assets, physical, human and financial, is a prime requirement of successful activity and I have found that this concept seems to be all too rarely applied to the priceless riches of the natural world. I have also found in my life a curious dichotomy,' he noted, 'in that the less future I have personally, the more I become interested in what can happen in two, three or more generations' time.'

Just three days previously, he explained, he had been 'in a country which has taken only five years to lose 15 per cent of its forest cover and this fact, combined with the cultivation of steep slopes and land with shallow soil, has meant that heavy monsoon rains have triggered massive and frightening soil erosion. Soil loss each year is approximately 20 to 50 tons per hectare, 20 times more than the weight of grain produced from the same amount of land. Relatively peaceful rivers have become raging muddy torrents, giving rise to devastating floods many hundreds of miles downstream in neighbouring countries. Overgrazed pastures and cropland soil losses compound the problem and the human population, which took 70 years to double by 1970, will double again in 25 years or so.'

The overall picture was grim in the extreme. 'It was certainly difficult to claim that a process of careful management of vital assets existed,' Sir Arthur continued, 'despite the valiant efforts—local and foreign—to find remedies and to embrace, even at the eleventh hour, the concept of sustainable development now being advanced to people whose ancestors had practised it instinctively. Sustainable development,' he explained, 'means living off the income, not off the capital, which the natural world supplies.'

However, despite the evidence of his own eyes, Sir Arthur was not totally despondent. 'Public opinion has been marshalled effectively by environmental interest groups,' he noted. 'There *are* votes to be won and lost on environmental grounds. The scene *is* changing, and wise leadership *is* meeting changing requirements as early—rather than as late—as possible. The negative, reactive stance is just as damaging to companies as is, to the environmental cause, the unwillingness of some to accept the need for reasonable compromise at any time.'

Candid friends

As the world's environmental lobby has become more sophisticated, so it has often elected to fight its battles not over the ground it seeks to protect but in the courts, in the legislature and in public inquiries. It has also sought to cut the number and scale of the battles it has to fight by working assiduously to create a context of legislation, official thinking and public opinion favourable to its own point of view.

Thus, while the newer groups may attract the headlines with their campaigns and protests, the older, more established organizations often have an equally important role to play, working behind the scenes through established channels.

Max Nicholson, one of the founders of the World Wildlife Fund (now World Wide Fund for Nature) and the first director-general of Britain's original Nature Conservancy, distinguished between environmentalists who are *polarizers* and those whom he called *integrators*. He explained the difference between the two, a difference which he recognized was oversimplified, as follows: 'The polarizers,' he suggested, 'are the heirs of the pioneering, missionary and campaigning stage. Partly from temperament and partly through their reading of events, they cling tenaciously to the belief that modern culture, and above all modern industry, is incurably exploitative and destructive towards its natural environment and can only be curbed from ruining it by incessant warfare through the media, the law courts and by pressure groups operating with no holds barred.'

By contrast, he argued, the integrators, 'while sharing much of the same historical analysis, attribute environmental damage not to unalterable selfish attitudes and interests, but to defects in scientific analysis, in appraisal of costs and benefits, and above all in education and training which can be and should be remedied, especially in the ranks of many large economic agencies, both public and private.'

Nicholson, needless to say, had always counted himself as an integrator, as a 'candid friend of industry'. He was a driving force behind the production of Britain's response to the *World Conservation Strategy*, for example. The *Conservation and Development Programme for the UK* which resulted was produced by working groups composed of representatives from all sectors of society, industry included. Nicholson had always recognized the vital importance of the polarizers in keeping the media pot boiling, however. Friendly and constructive co-operation, he noted, is not news, but strife and heated words are. 'The polarizers,' he argued, 'are like predators in their role of keeping members of the industrial ecosystem alert.'

Related messages have been emerging from industry, particularly in the United States. 'Environmental policymaking during the past 15 years has been too confrontational,' was the way Louis

Fernandez, then chairman of Monsanto, summed up the problem, 'leaving as its legacy a cumbersome, inflexible regulatory process shaped almost entirely by adversarial proceedings. Litigation,' he noted, 'has become an almost automatic part of the process. Delays, inefficiencies and poor environmental regulations have been the result.'

In 1983, he recalled, Jay Hair, president of the National Wildlife Federation, had concluded that 'as more environmental rights are recognized, the potential for conflict increases.' But, Hair had continued, 'the courts simply do not have the time to be the exclusive arbiter of these rights.' So he predicted that in ten years more disputes would be sent for mediation rather than for litigation. The question is: what does environmental mediation actually involve?

Laying aside the baseball bat
Faced with a growing number of increasingly protracted environmental conflicts, hardline American industrialists have often called for the removal of environmental safeguards altogether, arguing that, in the final analysis, it is a question of America's economy or America's environment. But many more thoughtful industrialists have begun to think of ways in which apparently intractable environmental disputes might be resolved to the satisfaction of most of those involved. This goal, as one of the pioneers of environmental mediation put it, is certainly 'an appealing one,' but is it realistic?

On the evidence available, the answer has to be that it is. A basic piece of advice for anyone taking part in such exercises, however, is that they should try and see the problem from their opponents' point of view. Clearly, this is not an entirely novel concept. Indeed, one US company which tried this approach, in 1976, was the mining company, Amax.

Companies attain environmental enlightenment by a variety of routes, if, indeed, they achieve it at all. Some are born with it, as Shakespeare might have put it, some achieve it and some have it thrust upon them. The environmental history of Amax involved a combination of the latter two routes. At a time of growing environmental opposition to industry, the company was planning a new molybdenum mine in Colorado's Rocky Mountains, near Denver. If you drive up into the area today, the Henderson mine is hard to find, but such developments can cause considerable damage if they are not carefully designed and operated.

This mine was clearly a prime target for local environmentalists. However, a series of coincidences led to an impromptu discussion between an Amax lawyer and a leading environmentalist. In brief, the lawyer asked the environmentalist whether he thought 'a team of company people and environmentalists could possibly work together to develop a major mine on the soundest possible basis.' The answer was: It's worth a try.

One of the more intractable problems facing Amax was that only six pounds of molybdenum is extracted from each ton of ore. If you hold a section of drilling core in the palm of your hand, the molybdenum shows up as very thin streaks in the pale rock. Amax was talking about a mine able to produce and process 300 million tons of rock during its entire life, which meant that something like 299 million tons of tailings would need to be put somewhere, threatening water pollution and visual impact on a grand scale in an area of very considerable scenic value.

Eventually, the company people and environmentalists did indeed sit down together, even swapping roles, with environmentalists arguing for the mine while Amax executives argued *against* the mine. This so-called 'experiment in ecology' at the Henderson mine eventually cost Amax an estimated $50 million out of a total cost for the mine of around $200 million. A major proportion of these costs was accounted for by the construction of a rail tunnel stretching nearly ten miles under the Rockies, to transport mine spoil to an environmentally acceptable disposal site on the other side of the Continental Divide.

Asked why the company had been prepared to spend $50 million, Ian McGregor, at that time chairman of the Amax board, replied that 'carrying out a project in an environmentally correct way is a cost of doing business today. A lot of people will take the view that the way to solve the problem of opposition from environmentalists is to do it your own way and take a baseball bat in the other hand, beating away the people who want to stop you.' McGregor had built up a tough reputation for handling labour disputes, a reputation he later extended while chairman of Britain's ailing British Steel Corporation, but the baseball bat approach, he warned, 'belongs to another age.'

Different countries and different industries have obviously

evolved different approaches to environmental mediation. But for those who subscribe to the consensus model of society, and most mediators do, conflict is generally seen as a temporary aberration, within a system whose natural condition is some sort of equilibrium. The role of the outside mediator, in this view, is to remind those involved in a particular dispute that, while there are differences in their short-term objectives, they share long-term goals. 'The established judicial and administrative mechanisms have all too often polarized disputants and promoted a win-or-lose approach in deciding environmental issues,' noted John Busterud, a past chairman of the US Council on Environmental Quality and at the time president of Resolve, a centre for conflict resolution which later merged with the Conservation Foundation.

'Mediation,' as the Institute for Environmental Mediation put it, 'is a *voluntary* process in which those involved in a dispute jointly explore and reconcile their differences. The mediator has no authority to impose a settlement. His or her strength lies in the ability to assist the parties in resolving their own differences. The mediated dispute is settled when the parties themselves reach what they consider to be a workable solution.'

A growing amount of research is being done on the mediation process, partly to see whether it really is more effective than litigation. 'Few factors are absolute preconditions for success,' concluded Gail Bingham of the Conservation Foundation, although the key to success in implementing any agreements 'appears to be whether those with the authority to implement the decision participated directly in the process.'

Someone else who studied many mediation (or so-called mediation) projects was Kai Lee, of Washington University's Institute for Environmental Studies. 'It is far from clear,' he concluded, 'how (environmental mediators) can improve their arts and crafts. Like medicine before the germ theory of disease became dominant, conflict intervention is a collection of competing, somewhat incompatible techniques. It is still too early to tell which will turn out to be mere quackery.'

Codes of conduct

This sort of bridge building is obviously valuable, but its ultimate success depends on the answer to a rather bigger question, a question which surfaced time and again at WICEM. Can industry be expected to regulate itself, many wondered, or does it always need to be forced to behave sensibly by means of regulations? Voluntary codes of conduct, with industry left to work out how to meet mutually agreed objectives, whilst apparently an attractive idea, attracted both support and scepticism.

A strong supporter was Charles de Haes, director general of WWF International. 'In 1982,' he explained, 'representatives of the Greek shipping industry who wished to do something concrete about their reputation for being the worst polluters of the oceans, requested our assistance through the late Aurelio Peccei, founder of the Club of Rome and a member of the WWF International board. They wanted to adopt a voluntary code of behaviour to combat vessel borne pollution and to establish an association to educate members of their industry and members of the public on the value of their marine resources.'

The Greek shipowners had a problem, however. They knew that if they produced their own code, almost no-one outside the industry would take it seriously. If it was to work, they needed to get internationally known conservation organizations involved in preparing the code and in monitoring its operation. WWF was instrumental in bringing together a consortium of five leading organizations – the Club of Rome, the International Institute for Environment and Development (IIED), the International Union for the Conservation of Nature and Natural Resources (IUCN), the International Oceans Institute, and WWF itself, to sponsor and publicize the Greek initiative launched by the Hellenic Marine Environmental Protection Association (HELMEPA).

'However,' de Haes recalled, 'we also made it quite clear that we were laying our own credibility and reputations on the line in supporting them – and we warned them that we would not hesitate publicly to withdraw support and express criticism if there were insufficient progress.'

Just a few weeks before WICEM and two years after the launch of HELMEPA, a progress meeting was held. 'We were quite frankly amazed at the progress made by HELMEPA,' de Haes reported. The Association includes members from both the shipowners' and the seamen's unions, and also involves 'all ranks, from seamen to ships' masters.'

Environmentalists query whether such codes of conduct can be anything more than public relations exercises outside very special circumstances, while some industrialists are concerned that such voluntary guidelines are likely to be the first step on the road to more restrictive legislation and standards. In Britain, for example, the long-running Pesticides Safety Precautions Scheme (PSPS) was converted from a voluntary agreement between the chemical industry and government authorities into a set of formal regulations, although it is worth noting that in this case the pesticide manufacturers were in the forefront of the lobby for change. The reason was that so-called 'parallel imports' had been coming into the country which did not have to meet the standards set in the PSPS guidelines. The British manufacturers, in short, wanted regulatory protection against unfair competition.

A similar case happened in Belgium. According to Marc Renson, chef de cabinet at the Ministry of Public Health and Environment, the Belgian detergents industry had agreed in the early 1970s to move voluntarily towards biodegradable detergents. Unfortunately, imports of environmentally much less satisfactory products continued from France and, to a lesser extent, from the Netherlands. Ultimately, that voluntary code was also converted into statutory controls.

In some cases, however, codes of conduct and guidelines may well suffice. At the international level, too, they can help sensitize industrialists, developers and investors to the environmental dimensions of their activities. The International Chamber of Commerce, for example, published its *Environmental Guidelines for World Industry* in 1974, updating them in 1981. While these are fairly general, they have been supplemented by a number of guideline exercises targeted on specific industrial sectors, such as the oil pollution response guidelines developed for the oil industry by the International Petroleum Industry Environmental Conservation Association (IP-IECA). In Britain, too, the Nature Conservancy Council has worked closely with BP and other oil companies to develop conservation guidelines for the onshore oil and gas industries. In the United States, the Conservation Foundation has played a leading role in this area, developing a voluntary code covering advertising standards for use in the agrochemicals industry, for example, to reduce the misuse of agricultural chemicals in the Third World.

Where legislation turns out to be unavoidable, as OECD environment director, Erik Lykke, has argued, 'industry must be given maximum freedom concerning the choice of means of complying with regulations that are most efficient and best suited to its particular situation. Governments should avoid imposing "ready-made" solutions.'

A creative task

But if solutions are not going to be available off the shelf, industry needs to be involved in the process of tailoring solutions to the needs of the local environment and the resources of the local businesses. Increasingly, too, industrialists are playing an important role not only in the drafting and redrafting of new legislation, but also in defining the problems which such controls are meant to address. They recognize that they are no longer playing a 'no win' game. Instead, they are told, they are contributing to a vitally important area of human activity where their 'can do' approach can be enormously helpful. Environmental protection, as Bayer director, Dr Otto Koch, put it, 'must be seen as a creative task.' Its aim, he stressed, 'consists neither in restoring the past nor in maintaining the *status quo*, but in creating a contribution to the future.'

The trouble that many of them have, however, is a basic one: they are not sure that they know exactly what they are being asked to do. 'It's hard to get your arms around some of these problems as long as we continue to talk of them only in very, very general terms,' commented Phillip X. Masciantonio, vice president of environmental affairs at US Steel.

At ICI, group environment adviser Mike Flux, sounded a similar note of caution. 'I recognize that many thinking environmentalists do see a need to change our economic systems,' he explained, 'perhaps on a world scale. I understand and respect these views. But the point I wish to make is that to confront industry with these views is to present industry with an unmanageable problem which is unlikely to form the basis for a constructive dialogue. If such changes are to come about, then they will have to take root much more widely, not only in our own society, but within a majority of the major societies of the world. That would be a much wider process in which a whole variety of people, including industrialists, would wish to contribute views and discuss consequences.'

This type of advice is not offered in a negative way: indeed, there are many people in industry who are concerned to see their organization or company improve its environmental performance. The point, however, is that industry has to be approached in the right way. This does not mean that the future lies only with environmental 'integrators', nor that it can lie exclusively with the 'polarizers'. At different times, most people in the environmental movement have worn both hats. Instead, it means that the arguments for environmental protection and for sustainable development have to be presented to industry in such a way that it is seen to be a real, commercially viable option for business.

Many people in business, meanwhile, are concerned that their past and potential future contributions are consistently undervalued. For example, when the Brandt Commission's first report, *North-South: A Programme for Survival*, came out in 1980, the reaction of many industrialists was summed up by Britain's Trade Policy Research Centre (TPRC). It expressed concern that the Brandt Commission had shown a 'persistent, if implicit, belief in the efficiency and benevolence of governmental central planning and direction as the engine for economic progress and development.' It also, the TPRC suggested, displayed a 'pervasive mistrust about the working of the market and an assumption that it will, almost automatically, produce "wrong" results.' This suspicion had begun to dissipate, however, by the time the World Commission on Environment and Development published *Our Common Future*. Even the most straight-laced socialist states, like Bulgaria, have been advertising for western equity partners, in the hope of becoming industrially competitive.

'There is a great stirring out there,' commented Richard Richardson, director of development for the International Finance Corporation, the private investment affiliate of the World Bank. 'As the memory of colonialism recedes, countries are increasingly confident that they are able to deal on terms of parity with the multinationals that were once so feared.' Some of the new bridging institutions began to home in on the potential unlocked by this new realism. Foremost among them has been the World Resources Institute, which has produced a series of reports focusing on the ways in which multinational corporations can collaborate with developing countries to produce sustainable development.

There is every reason to hope, indeed to believe, that industry, and private enterprise in particular, will increasingly help drive forward the transition to sustainable forms of economic development. But there are a number of fundamental problems with the unregulated market system. For one thing, the market can act as a smokescreen, obscuring the environmental effects of industrial activities, particularly in relation to such transboundary problems as acid rain, or truly global problems such as the build-up of chlorofluorocarbons and carbon dioxide in the atmosphere. As long as the broader costs of particular industrial decisions or projects are not borne by the developer, there will always be those who are prepared to gamble with other people's lives and livelihoods.

Similar problems are found in respect of international development. During the 1970s and early 1980s, around 60 per cent of the industrial development in Third World countries originated outside those countries and much of this investment was made by multinational enterprises. A large proportion of this investment, as the Organization for Economic Co-operation and Development (OECD) noted, 'went into the exploitation of natural resources, such as minerals, fuels, timber and fish, for use largely by the various OECD economies.' The multinationals are also responsible for a growing proportion of the trade in minerals, manufactures and technology between the OECD countries and the Third World. But, as the OECD itself stressed, 'while this investment and trade plays an essential and beneficial role in development, there is no doubt that much of it has been associated with heavy inroads on exhaustible resources and avoidable damage to the environment and to the essential ecological basis for sustainable economic growth.'

Looking for green investors

Overseas investment is often a highly sensitive business, but in an increasingly interdependent world it must be of increasing importance. Multinational corporations have a major and growing stake (estimated to be at least $160 billion by the mid-1980s) in the developing countries, and they require a stable, predictable investment climate, free of environmental and resource disputes, if that stake is to prove profitable.

'Foreign direct investment is a *positive sum* activity that can benefit investor and host country alike,' concluded the World Resources Institute (WRI) in its report *Improving Environmental Co-operation: The Roles of Multinational Corporations and Developing Countries*. But such investment will only be of real long-term benefit if it is environmentally sustainable.

The world's multinational corporations, as WRI pointed out, represent a 'principal repository of data, technology, technical expertise and management capabilities with respect to the environmental consequences of their operations. Such information, technology and expertise is scarce and expensive in many developing countries.' So a key challenge is to find ways of harnessing these resources and skills to the sustainable development effort in the Third World.

Many of the newly industrializing countries are determined to try and avoid some of the environmental pitfalls which they know lie along the industrialization path. Turkey is an interesting example. With a population of 45 million, Turkey desperately needs to attract new investment. Historically, however, the country has not encouraged such investment, particularly between 1923 and 1950. However, its policies were liberalized in 1950 and a good deal of effort has since been devoted to ensuring that its investment climate is attractive to foreign capital.

There are now over 160 corporations active in Turkey which have some degree of foreign ownership, a dozen of them being totally foreign-owned. But this investment is coming into a country which is increasingly concerned about the environmental damage caused by previous industrial development. Turkey introduced its Environmental Law in 1983 and, said Engin Ural of the Environmental Problems Foundation, while 'nobody blames private investors *per se* for environmental pollution,' the Turkish public and press 'do hold industry accountable for pollution, especially in such areas as Izmit, Izmir and the Golden Horn.'

Just 20 years ago, Izmit had a population of 20,000, a few factories and a clean bay. Today there are 250,000 people, 200 factories and one of the most polluted bays in the Mediterranean. 'We were celebrating when these factories were established,' recalled Izmit's mayor, while a local shopkeeper mourned: 'The factories destroyed the bay. You see that park over there? I used to fish there as a boy. The last time I fished was in 1967.'

The country's emission standards are still amazingly permissive and its embryonic environmental agencies are typically poorly resourced and staffed. One government minister explained that environmentalism is a luxury which Turkey simply cannot afford, 'like putting a necktie on a *hamal*.' He was referring to the labourers who spend their lives carrying heavy loads. But even the *hamal* and his family may find their deteriorating environment unacceptable. Around the southern edge of Istanbul, for example, several hundred tanneries dump their noxious sludges into the Sea of Marmara. The stench is appalling by any standards.

With the ever-present danger that environmental concerns may be used to front an attack on the private sector, it is clearly vital that new investment projects should be subjected to a thorough environmental impact assessment study and their environmental performance should be carefully monitored once they are in operation. Increasingly too, as Ural warned, Turkish firms have been moving into the pollution control field and some of them are lobbying for tighter standards. Those Istanbul tanneries, for example, are being moved to a new site, which will have a waste treatment facility. Investors who ignore the growing interest in environmental quality, Ural suggested, will find that 'they will be bucking public opinion'. They may also find themselves out of business.

The emerging agenda

Turkey may have been a late starter in the environmental protection field, but it is still ahead of many Third World countries. Many of these countries are still well down the learning curve, although some are beginning to make real progress. In Africa, for example, countries like Botswana and Zambia have produced national conservation strategies, as recommended in the *World Conservation Strategy* of 1980. 'We hope to come up with something more comprehensive,' reported Seeiso Liphuko of Botswana's Ministry of Local Government and Lands, 'and once we have done that, we hope to home in on those areas of need which are most urgent.'

Inevitably, however, these countries are coming up against manpower and resource bottlenecks. A key bottleneck in Botswana has been the lack of technical expertise to screen major development proposals for possible environmental effects. 'We either have to bring in large numbers of expatriates, which has its political problems,' Liphuko noted, 'or we have to build up a bureaucracy which is out of scale with our current level of development.' Such difficulties make the bridging exercises carried out by the World Environment Center and other organizations all the more important.

Increasingly, the focus of mediation exercises is broadening to take in policy-related issues, rather than simply concentrating on site-related questions. This new approach is very much in the long term interest of the business sector, although many companies fail to recognize the fact. As a result, the World Resources Institute (WRI) has devoted a considerable amount of effort, for instance, to identifying and analysing the 'stake' which US industry currently has in the Third World and, in the longer term, in the sustainable development of Third World resources.

'Beyond a general interest in the global sustainability of natural resources and development,' explained WRI president Gus Speth, 'business has both direct and indirect reasons to care about environmental and resource-management issues. There are, of course, direct economic consequences for certain sectors of domestic and international commerce: the price and availability of oil, for example, or the marketability of food sprayed by certain pesticides. But indirect consequences are also important: the geopolitical effects of irrigation and fishing practices, for example, or the effects on agriculture of climate change caused by the build-up of carbon dioxide (CO_2) in the atmosphere.'

As a result, WRI is convinced that 'today a new environmental agenda is emerging.' Among the concerns it highlights are the health of the atmosphere, oceans, climate, soil and forests. 'Today's issues,' Speth noted, 'are arising from the spread of deserts, the loss of forests, the erosion of soils, the growth of human populations, the exhaustion of ecological communities, the accumulation of wastes and the alteration of the biogeochemical cycles of the planet. Today's environmental concerns transcend borders, national laws and local customs. As a result, the politics needed to meet present and future challenges require a new vision and a new diplomacy, new leaders and new policies.'

Speth and his colleagues point to three profound shifts in environmental thinking: a shift from traditional pollution control concerns to a broader interest in sustainable resource management; a shift from a nearly exclusive focus on local problems to a growing concern with long-distance, transnational and increasingly global concerns; and a shift, in the developing countries, from viewing the environment as a rich man's issue to a growing recognition that environmental conservation and economic development are inseparably linked and can be pursued simultaneously.

'The politics of the new agenda,' said Speth, 'must be a search for common ground. Popular support for the new agenda is now weaker than for the old: the issues are more remote, more distant in space and time. Although there are conspicuous exceptions (like acid rain), the new agenda addresses the relationship of environment and development in the Third World, the health of the global commons, and a series of resource and environmental threats that, while serious, are less visible, often slow to develop, or affect the US only indirectly. But, as if to compensate, the new agenda invites strangers and even old antagonists to work together. Economic growth is needed to attack poverty, the worst destroyer of the environment worldwide, so business and labour leaders and environmentalists must make common cause in promoting sustainable growth.'

Yet even if growing numbers of industrialists believe that the capitalist system has got to be overhauled to ensure it achieves sustainable development, many business leaders have yet to be convinced of the value of existing definitions of the basic concept. 'There is an evident lack of clarity,' as Sir Peter Parker told a conference in Cambridge, England, organized by CEED. Speaking as chairman both of the Rockware Group and the British Institute of Management, he commented that: 'The debate is blurred. The definition of sustainable economic development is still likely to prove elusive for a harassed management dealing with problems of profit, jobs and shareholders. Frankly, management is learning by doing.'

The concept, however, has an impressive pedigree. It featured prominently in the *World Conservation Strategy*, it occupied pride of place at WICEM and was central to the brief of the World Commission on Environment and Development. However, environmentalists aware of the difficulty industry faces in coming to terms with the concept. Sustainable development, is a compass point rather than a route map, offering a rallying point around which new alliances can form.

III

ENTERPRISE

The Environmental Entrepreneur

Chapter 8

THE GREEN SUNRISE

The emergence of a cluster of new technologies, from
the microchip through high performance ceramics to
genetic engineering, provides the building blocks from
which a sustainable future can be assembled—if that is
what we decide we want. But these technologies will
need to be carefully screened for potential
environmental side-effects.

The nuns of Sterkrade were understandably horrified when they
heard that a new iron foundry was to be built at nearby Oberhausen,
on the banks of the river Elpenbach. They feared that the foundry
effluents would kill the river's fish and make it impossible for them
to do their laundry. Subsequent events have shown that their fears
were well-founded. The St Anthony-Hutte foundry which started
production in 1758 merged with two other local foundries in 1873
to form Gutehoffnungshutte (GHH). These three foundries, in fact,
were the seeds from which the massive industrial concentration of
West Germany's Ruhr would eventually grow.

Now, in a move which is being repeated throughout the industrial
world, GHH is moving south, in this case to Munich. Following
the Second World War, GHH was compelled by the Allied forces
to shed the iron and coal businesses which had been its roots and
the company has since developed into Europe's largest mechanical
engineering firm. Unwittingly, the Allies had done GHH a kindness,
by forcing it out of the 'sunset' areas of its business.

The subsequent collapse of the so-called 'sunset' or 'smokestack'
industries has left many traditional heavy manufacturing areas with
the environmental scars of the past, but without the resources
needed to institute any form of clean-up. The problem, as those
charged with the task of trying to rebuild such areas know only too

well, is that most of the 'sunrise' industries want to locate where the markets are and where the environment is of a much higher quality.

'This system was a living thing which gave us our industrial capacity,' commented John Tavare, chairman of a major programme launched to clean up Britain's highly polluted Mersey. 'Unless we raise the quality of this part of the region, do not expect people to invest a lot of money around here. They don't like coming here because it stinks.'

The north west region's industrial belt, which includes Greater Manchester, St Helens and Merseyside, now contains some of the worst examples of pollution and environmental decay to be found anywhere in Europe. The Mersey Basin, with over five million inhabitants, reports 500 miles of rivers and other water-courses which are so polluted that little or no life can survive in them. Much of the region's sewer system was built over a hundred years ago, so that sewer collapses are now a regular occurrence. Some 500 million gallons of sewage are treated daily, but 60 million gallons of untreated sewage still go into the Mersey every day.

Change is coming, however. The European Commission, for example, has given £67 million to help fund the early years of an ambitious clean-up campaign in Merseyside which could ultimately cost £3.5 billion (at current prices) over the next 25 years. A key component of the campaign is designed to persuade private companies to clean up their premises, especially on riverside sites, to help in the drive to make the whole area more salubrious and to promote much-needed economic regeneration. As Tavare told the *Financial Times*: 'It's absolutely essential to come to grips with this environmental problem.'

The emerging industries are not without their own environmental problems, but the overall picture is one of very much cleaner industrial technologies, with new investment subjected to today's much more rigorous environmental standards. Indeed, there are many documented cases where major companies refused to locate new complexes in areas which desperately wanted to have them because the local environment was not clean enough. When Kodak were looking for a new site for the manufacture of film, for example, it turned down a site near Milton Keynes because of possible air pollution from nearby brickworks.

The contrast between the sunset and sunrise industries is dramatically clear to anyone who has had to close down a sunset production site. In the United States, it can now take longer to close down a factory than to open a new one, as increasingly tough clean-up conditions are imposed to prevent companies from simply abandoning polluted manufacturing sites. Ford, for example, agreed to pay $4.3 million to sort out groundwater pollution at its old auto production site at Mahwah, New Jersey. The new controls, said one Ford environmental specialist, 'brought everything to a head because of the problem of selling the property until the (clean-up) plan was approved.'

New Jersey's new environmental controls were prompted by the discovery of alarmingly high levels of dioxin at a former Diamond Shamrock herbicide plant in Newark. Diamond Shamrock said it knew nothing about the problem until the authorities told it about the dioxin. The bill for the clean-up of the site and a nearby residential area will be considerable and Diamond Shamrock has already agreed to contribute $22 million.

As usual, there have been striking differences in the way in which different companies have reacted to these controls. Some say they will simply steer clear of New Jersey in future, while others have looked around and seen that other States are preparing to enact similar laws. As a result, the more conscientious companies have begun to look much more carefully at the plants they may want to close in the coming years. Monsanto, for example, found contamination at three plants it planned to close and instituted a plan to deal with the problems. 'The earlier we identify these problems, the cheaper it will be to clean them up,' noted the company's hazardous wastes director. Increasingly, too, such companies are trying to ensure that similar problems do not surface next time around.

Doing more with less

'Coal, rail, textile, steel, auto, rubber, machine tool manufacture—these were the classical industries of the Second Wave,' noted Alvin Toffler in *The Third Wave*, 'based on essentially simple electromechanical principles, they used high energy inputs, spat out enormous waste and pollution, and were characterized by long production runs, low skill requirements, repetitive work, standardized goods and highly centralized controls.'

In one of the clearest explanations of the changes which are now going on around us, Toffler suggested that the 'First Wave' of the Agricultural Revolution and the 'Second Wave' of the Industrial Revolution were now giving way to the Third Wave. This, he predicted, will create a civilization as different from those of the First and Second Waves as the civilizations they created were different from what went before.

A cluster of new technologies seems likely to form the industrial base of this emerging world. The new industries, Toffler noted, are 'no longer primarily electromechanical and no longer based on the classic science of the Second Wave era. Instead, they rose from accelerating breakthroughs in a mix of scientific disciplines that were rudimentary or even nonexistent as recently as 25 years ago – quantum electronics, information theory, molecular biology, oceanics, nucleonics, ecology, and the space sciences.'

In this view, areas like the Ruhr and Merseyside were the birthplaces of the Second Wave, while the new sunrise regions, particularly those along the Pacific Rim from Silicon Valley around to Singapore, are among the birthplaces of the Third Wave.

Indeed, the very fact that a country like Japan went through the Second Wave of industrialization so late and so precipitately has meant that it has been almost literally bounced into Third Wave technologies. If you talk to Japanese industrialists today, for example, many will comment on the way that those industries which were forced by rapidly tightening environmental controls to invest in new, cleaner technologies are now much more profitable than those which stuck with the older, more polluting technologies.

Indeed, there has been growing interest in such technologies, variously described as non-waste, low waste, clean or cleaner technologies. Numerous examples of such technologies have been given in previous chapters, the key problem being not so much one of developing cleaner, quieter and more resource-efficient technologies, but of ensuring that they are adopted by the relevant industries.

French research has shown that about 50 per cent of such technologies have brought real energy and raw material savings, while Danish work has indicated that companies which invested in cleaner technologies experienced direct financial benefits in 44 per cent of the examples studied, with those benefits averaging 13 per cent of the investment cost. 'Nevertheless,' noted OECD environment director, Erik Lykke, 'clean technologies still remain little used in industry. They are used in about one third of polluting plants in Denmark and they represent about 20 per cent of pollution control investment in the United States, and probably much less in most other countries.'

Often such technologies spring out of work designed to increase production efficiencies, rather than directly from environmental protection work. A prime example is ICI's FM21 membrane cell for chlor-alkali production, which was developed to cut ICI's energy costs, but also brought the almost incidental, although highly welcome, benefit of cutting out mercury emissions.

This trend towards greater energy and resource efficiency is particularly evident in the most successful companies. 'The argument that where there is one ethylene plant today there will be 20 tomorrow is simply wrong,' as ICI chairman Sir John Harvey-Jones put it. 'The evidence of one's own eyes shows that whereas we originally had five ethylene plants at Wilton, we now only need one. Or, to take another example, we now make much better plastics, so you need less of them.

'The exponential growth argument, in my view, has gone out of the window. All the trends point towards smaller, more efficient plants. Our most important task is to get more and more out of less and less. That is the industrialist's mission. And actually we are getting pretty good at it. Incidentally, too, that's not because we are boy scouts. It's for bloody good business reasons.'

This argument holds not only for industrial manufacturing processes, but also for industrial products. Pesticides, for instance, have been under continual attack by environmentalists for decades. 'We are using tremendous amounts of pesticides,' admitted Brazilian environment minister Dr Paulo Nogueira-Neto, 'and thousands and thousands and thousands of people go to hospital, or become diseased, every year because of the improper use of pesticides.' However, he stressed that: 'We are not against the use of pesticides, but against the overuse or misuse of pesticides.'

We have seen that chemical companies are coming up with ecologically tested pesticides, which clearly represent a considerable advance. However, another objective must be to reduce the total amount of such biocidal chemicals entering the environment. An excellent example of the pressure to do more with less is ICI's Electrodyn pesticide application system. One of the key attractions of the Electrodyn sprayer is that it can achieve thoroughly effective crop protection with relatively small quantities of pesticide. The electrodynamic atomization technique, which involves giving each droplet of pesticide an electric charge, means that the droplets 'wrap around' the target crop plants, ensuring all-round, relatively rainfast coverage of leaves and stems.

The heart of the Electrodyn sprayer is the 'Bozzle', an amalgam of the words nozzle and bottle. The system produces small, evenly sized droplets. Normally, small droplets would magnify the environmental problem by increasing the amount of spray drift, but virtually all the spray homes in on the plants, rather than falling on the soil. In addition, the fact that the droplets are mutually repellent means that a uniform coating of each plant is achieved. The system is so efficient, in fact, that as little as a half litre of pesticide can protect a hectare of crops, compared with the 200 to 400 litres of water-based pesticide needed with conventional spray systems.

As far as the Third World is concerned, the Electrodyn sprayer has a number of powerful attractions. Unlike conventional sprayers, for example, it has no moving parts to wear out or break down. The entire system is also astonishingly light, at around 2.5 kilograms. Because a single Bozzle will typically treat up to 1.5 hectares, which can take about four hours to cover, the operator can readily carry enough spray for an entire working day. The sealed Bozzles mean that he or she does not have to work with large containers of toxic chemicals, with all the hazards of spillage.

While the system offers significant ergonomic and environmental advantages, however, its major contribution will stem from the increased crop yields it can bring. Following the adoption of the Electrodyn, there have been enormous improvements in crop yields: in Paraguay, for example, a 33 per cent increase in cotton yields has been reported, compared with conventionally sprayed crops, while Zambian trials on cotton showed an increase of nearly 60 per cent in yields.

Turning a glass eye on asbestos

The Electrodyn sprayer is a clear example, in short, of economic priorities coinciding with environmental requirements. In this case, the product was a direct development from the company's existing businesses. In Vitrifix's case, however, it was a question of working out ways to use an existing technology for a totally new environmental application.

Someone else's wastes can represent a fairly tricky raw material to work with, but a growing number of companies are making a living by developing new methods for the safe disposal of hazardous wastes. Asbestos is an interesting case in point. At times it is almost impossible to open a newspaper without being confronted by the latest asbestos scare. *Item*: 120 asbestos removal specialists had to be contracted to vacuum schools, nurseries and play areas in north and west London following widespread asbestos fall-out caused by a massive warehouse fire. *Item*: Work on new port facilities for Britain's Trident submarines was held up when 100,000 cubic metres of blue, white and brown asbestos were discovered at the former ship-breaking site.

In the United States, the *Financial Times* reported, 'asbestosis and asbestos-related injuries in the US have turned out to be the largest natural disaster to hit world insurance and re-insurance markets.' Insurers talk in terms of 'long tail' businesses, where there is a very long lag between an insurance policy being written and the claims coming in, with the asbestos industry being perhaps the most obvious example to date. The ultimate asbestos-related insurance liability could be anywhere between £10 billion and £50 billion. Many insurers now feel that this sort of business is no longer economic and Lloyd's syndicates which have written many policies in this field are now highly exposed, given that the claims could still be coming in well into the twenty-first century.

'The problem with asbestos is that we have no idea just how harmful it can be,' stressed Brent Council's health and safety adviser, responsible for co-ordinating the north London clean-up, 'but if disturbed the material produces asbestos dust fibres which have been known to cause cancer.' Britain's employment minister put it more strongly: 'We must assume that a single fibre could do real damage which may not be seen for 20 years or more,' he warned, noting that there is no known safe exposure limit.

Too often, asbestos has found its way into landfill sites, where it will remain as a permanent environmental hazard. Now, however, a British company has developed a process which converts all forms of asbestos into a totally safe glass material. Founded in 1918, King, Taudevin & Gregson (KTG) has supplied furnaces for glass melting since 1922 and has invested well over £150,000 in its new 'Vitrifix' asbestos vitrification technology. 'As far as R & D expenditure is concerned,' the company noted, 'this project stands head and shoulders over anything else we have done.'

It originally emerged from a certain amount of lateral thinking. 'The original idea was sparked by a television programme on asbestos hazards,' recalled KTG managing director Stuart Johnson. 'We asked ourselves: why can't we stick the asbestos in one of our glass-making furnaces and melt it?' When KTG first approached the asbestos industry, however, the reaction was far from enthusiastic. 'They were apparently not keen to do anything which would further publicize any dangers associated with asbestos,' said Dr David Roberts, KTG technical director. 'We therefore had to look for an opportunity to develop the process independently.'

All forms of asbestos are crystalline silicates. They are remarkable materials, with water so tightly bound into their crystal structure that it is not released until they are heated to more than 900°C, which is why asbestos has been so widely used as a high temperature insulating material. If you heat asbestos to the point where this 'water of crystallization' is driven off, however, it loses its fibrous structure and ceases to be a health hazard.

The problem, as Dr Roberts points out, is that any asbestos destruction process 'must be very, very safe. You can't hang up a litmus paper and check whether you have cured the problem. We tried simple heating, but you can't guarantee complete destruction; you could still be left with unconverted pockets. Since there was no way of detecting such problems, we abandoned simple heating processes and turned to glass melting technology proper.'

When asbestos is put into a glass-making furnace, operating at over 1,400°C, it is transformed both physically and chemically: once vitrified, the melted asbestos can never be re-formed. The system has also been designed in such a way that it is, in Dr Roberts' words, 'idiot-proof'. The glass leaves the furnace through a sub-merged 'throat', in the shape of a U-tube. As glass cools, it becomes more viscous and will eventually stop flowing altogether. If the furnace were to cool, for any reason, the glass would 'freeze' in the throat when the temperature fell below 1,100°C.

A pilot plant was tested at London's Fulham power station, where asbestos was being stripped. The system came through the tests with flying colours, demonstrating that up to 80 per cent of the final glass could be made from asbestos and asbestos-contaminated materials. The vitrification process worked out some 30 to 50 per cent cheaper than the more hazardous method of bagging the asbestos and trucking it to landfill sites. The resulting glass is either sent for disposal in landfill sites, or it may be used in low-grade commercial applications, as an aggregate in road surfacing, for example. The question is: will the pressures on the asbestos industry be sufficiently intense to force it to adopt this sort of technology?

Slick solutions

Even with over a hundred power stations in line for decommissioning in the United Kingdom alone, however, the ultimate market for this process is limited by the amount of asbestos currently in use, given that the future use of asbestos will be very much more restricted. Other companies have been looking at ways of dealing with substances which are likely to be in common use for consider-ably longer, like oil.

Although mammoth spills such as those caused by the *Torrey Canyon* or the *Amoco Cadiz* capture the headlines, even quite small slicks can cause considerable damage in areas where dispersants cannot be used. Many of the most serious problems stem from the fact that oil can spread over a wide area, wetting surfaces and clinging to them. During the early 1970s, oil industry scientists recognized that if the sticky black oil floating on the water could be converted into a compact, non-sticky solid, it could be removed by nets or some other simple physical means. Unfortunately, the first attempts to achieve this goal, using gelling agents, left scientists struggling with grease-like products, rather than the robust solids they had hoped for.

Ultimately, however, British Petroleum (BP) discovered that if slicks were sprayed with an oil-soluble polymer and a suitable cross-linking agent, the oil would gradually become trapped in the developing three-dimensional web of polymer. That, at least, was the theory. Later work showed it to have been essentially correct, although not before the BP scientists had run the gauntlet of mishaps and failures, interspersed with a number of tantalizing successes. On one occasion, the team lost a one-tonne oil slick they had just laid at sea. In another, a seepage of polymer into the pump reserved for the cross-linking agent froze the whole system solid. But eventually the approach was shown to work. Great lumps of oil slick could be lifted from the sea, like so many rubber mats, with nothing more complicated than boathooks.

BP initially developed its process for internal use, but the company has been putting considerable effort into marketing its oil solidification technology to other companies and countries. Indeed, one of the strongest messages which came across on the occasion when BP was presented with a Pollution Abatement Technology Award was that those with environmental technology should do a better job of marketing it. 'The ingenuity and enterprise shown here should not simply be applauded now and forgotten later,' said environment minister, William Waldegrave. 'They must be exploited to the full by vigorous and effective marketing.'

Sir Terence Beckett, as director-general of the Confederation of British Industry, agreed. 'We cannot afford to be coy about selling our ideas on the world market,' he stressed. 'The developed world is environmentally highly-charged at the moment and if we don't take the opportunities which present themselves, our rivals most surely will.' At the time, he noted, the water and effluent treatment sector alone employed 20,000 people, while British companies in this area had about £250 million of orders in 1984, some 60 per cent for export.

By 1987 Mr Waldegrave was reporting that the UK pollution control industry had a turnover of more than £2.2 billion, twice that of the UK pharmaceutical industry. The OECD market for pollution control equipment, he suggested, could be as much as £50 billion a year—with the world market obviously larger. But, he warned, the slow rate at which environmental regulations have been implemented in Britain in recent years has slowed the growth of the UK industry. Britain's exports of water effluent treatment plant had fallen from a peak value of £140 million in 1983 to £50 million by 1986, while its share of EEC exports of air pollution control equipment fell from 63 per cent in 1975 to 40 per cent by 1985. To help push UK markets for such technologies, he announced the Environment Protection Technology Scheme to provide £1–£2 million a year in pump-priming finance for research and development projects.

In the United States, according to Management Information Services, expenditures on pollution abatement and control totalled $70 billion in 1985, representing an enormous market. That same year, $8.5 billion in private business capital was invested in environmental protection, resulting in sales of $19 billion, business profits of $2.6 billion and 167,000 jobs.

However, the pollution control industry needs a healthy home market if it is to sell overseas, a fact often ignored by politicians concerned to ensure that the impact of environmental controls on industry is minimized. Acid rain is an example. While most European countries committed themselves to cutting sulphur dioxide emissions from their power stations by 30 per cent by 1993, Britain's government and the Central Electricity Generating Board held back, arguing that further research was needed. This caution owed a great deal to the fact that the necessary work could cost around £250 million for a single power station.

No-one would argue that money should be thrown away by being invested in technology to control problems which are not amenable to that form of control. However, on the other hand, Britain's reputation as the 'dirty man of Europe' is no help to its environmental companies when they come to sell their services and technologies in other countries.

'The environmental element of big contracts is more important than ever. Previously it was just the process that counted,' explained Neil Cherrett, managing director of Davy McKee Environment, part of the Davy Corporation, Britain's largest engineering and construction group. At the time, Davy McKee had just been approached by East Germany, one of the latest members of the '30 Per Cent Club', which wanted to cut the sulphur emissions from up to forty of its power stations. Davy, which has a proprietary desulphurization process, had already won four large contracts in

West Germany and another in Austria. But the British government's attitude, Cherrett observed, made his company's environmental export business considerably more difficult. 'It's like trying to sell Jaguars abroad,' he said, 'when you've got no roads of your own.'

A ceramic key to the future

Pollution control technologies are only one component of what one might call the 'green sunrise', however. Many new technologies are also now emerging which were not designed with environmental protection in mind, but which nonetheless look set to make massive contributions to the worldwide drive to build a sustainable future. Consider just two examples: high performance ceramics and fibre optics.

Gone are the days when young people, like Dustin Hoffman in the film *The Graduate*, were advised to 'get into plastics' for an assured, meteoric career. Today, the ceramics industry might be a better bet. Talk to the Japanese and they will tell you that the high technology industries of the 1990s will be based on non-oil energy sources; on micro-electronics and information technology; on biotechnology, health care and food production; and on the exploration and industrialization of the oceans and of space. However, an increasing number of Japanese will also stress, like Kunio Nakajima, head of the MITI Fine Ceramics Office, that research and development work on new materials 'holds the key to the future of high technology.'

In Japan, Nakajima explained, the term 'fine ceramics' is used to refer to 'ceramics made of extremely pure ultra-minute particles, formed, sintered and treated under highly controlled conditions and possessing outstanding performance characteristics. Depending on the raw materials used and the forming and sintering methods employed, fine ceramics can possess special properties which cannot be duplicated by metals or plastics. Great expectations,' he noted, 'are thus held for this fledgling industry.'

Indeed MITI, or the Ministry of International Trade and Industry to give it its full title, is increasingly convinced that fine ceramics could be the 'star industry of the 1990s'. If MITI is right, and it is investing growing sums of money in the underlying technology, then we are going to find an astonishing range of industrial products fashioned from ceramics, including car and jet engines, cutting tools able to outperform their tungsten carbide competitors and even artificial teeth or bones.

Anyone who has watched the Japanese adapting to the successive oil crises, will need no convincing that the 'land of the rising sun' thinks about the energy prospect very differently from some of the other industrialized countries which have been benefitting from lower oil prices due to the surpluses of the mid-1980s. While others have scaled down their investment in renewable energy technologies and energy conservation measures, Japan has continued to press ahead with its 'Sunshine' (renewable energy) and 'Moonlight' (energy conservation) projects.

Japan's achievements in applying mass production techniques to such renewable energy technologies as photovoltaic cells have been more than matched in its efforts to achieve greater energy efficiency. During the decade following the first oil shock in 1973, Japan's steel industry cut the energy needed to produce a tonne of steel by over 85 per cent, for example.

This staggering achievement resulted from the widespread introduction of continuous casting. This, in turn, depended on the use of refractory bricks which derived their resistance to heat and friction from a new ceramic ingredient, a synthetic compound of silicon nitride and alumina-carbon.

Whereas conventional ceramics, such as pottery and glass, are made from natural raw materials like clay and quartzite, using fairly simple refining and melting techniques, the advanced ceramic materials now emerging, including those used to make the insulation tiles which shield the Space Shuttle from the fierce heat of re-entry, are based on synthetic materials whose composition, particle size and degree of refining are rigidly controlled. By adding small quantities of certain speciality chemicals, or by tinkering with their crystalline structure, it is possible to give such materials special properties, such as electrical conductivity, semi-conductivity, translucence, novel magnetic properties or resistance to corrosion, heat, expansion or radioactivity. The phenomenon of superconductivity, where exotic materials can carry an electrical current with very little loss, holds great promise and is very much worth keeping an eye on.

A key target for the Japanese auto industry, meanwhile, is the 'ceramic engine'. Isuzu Motors has announced that it has developed an all-ceramic diesel engine with Kyocera, the ceramics manufacturer. The all-ceramic components used in the combustion chamber enable the engine to reach higher temperatures and eliminate the need for radiators and other cooling devices which normally cut engine efficiency. Some of the components can cope with temperatures as high as 1,200°C, while conventional cast iron and aluminium parts have to be cooled below 900°C if they are to survive.

Similar success stories are beginning to emerge in other countries. In Britain, for example, the efficiency of steel and glass furnaces has been improved three-fold by a new regenerative ceramic burner developed by British Gas and Hotwork International. Whereas conventional furnaces discharge hot flue gases into the atmosphere, the new design recirculates the gases through a bed of ceramic material, which is then used to preheat the next wave of air which is fed to two alternating burners, with the opening and shutting of valves controlled by a microprocessor. A well-managed conventional furnace can achieve perhaps 20 per cent process efficiency, but the regenerative burner can push efficiencies to 60 per cent. Fuel savings of 45 per cent can be achieved even where processes operate at temperatures as low as 1,000°C.

Aero engine designers, like Rolls-Royce, are also waking up to the potential of ceramics. If you take an engine which runs at 1,050°C and boost that temperature to 1,350°C by using ceramic components, you can use a cheaper fuel, use less of it and generate less pollution in the process.

Research by a team at Newcastle University came up with the Syalon family of ceramics, which have been described as 'almost as hard as diamond, as strong as steel and as light as aluminium.' Lucas Cookson Syalon, the joint venture company which is manufacturing Syalon components, can point to some extraordinary research results when marketing its products. To take just a single example, conventional metal weld locator pins typically wear out after about 5,000 welding operations, whereas locator pins made from Syalon have performed more than 7 million welding operations without any significant deterioration.

Many obstacles still have to be surmounted before ceramics break into all their potential markets, however. New techniques have to be developed to ensure the necessary purity and fineness of ceramic ingredients, for example. New mass production, machining and quality control methods are needed for these complex materials. Designers still have to work out ways of using them such that their strong points are exploited while their weak points are protected.

The new ceramics, in short, would have seemed near-miraculous to the authors of the 1972 *Limits to Growth* study, which warned that we were running out of energy, resources and environment. Apart from their structural and mechanical properties, ceramics can help industry switch from raw materials which are in increasingly short supply to others which are among the most abundant on earth. Also, since a hotter engine burns cleaner, they can help cut air pollution and they can clearly help save energy.

In case this seems like an isolated case of technological serendipity, consider fibre optics. The past ten years have seen extraordinary changes in the amount of information that optical fibres can carry. The transparency of silica glass fibre has been pushed to around the theoretical maximum, with light-pulses still visible after travelling 100 kilometres down such fibres. Research has shown that four billion 'bits', or about the same amount of information stored in 30 volumes of the *Encyclopaedia Britannica*, can be transmitted each second over a distance of more than 100 kilometres and the signs are that even greater capacities and speeds will soon be achieved.

Fibre optics, in fact, summed up the Third Wave as far as Alvin Toffler was concerned. 'Second Wave telephone systems,' he noted, 'required virtual copper mines beneath the city streets—endless miles of snaking cable, conduit, relays and switches. We are now about to convert to fiber optic systems that use hair-thin light-carrying fibers to carry messages. The energy implications of this switchover,' he concluded, 'are staggering: it takes about one thousandth of the energy to manufacture optical fiber that it took to dig, smelt and process an equivalent length of copper wire. The same ton of coal required to produce 90 miles of copper wire can now turn out 80,000 miles of fiber!'

Nailing the opposition

On the face of it, it looks as though industry could become environmentally acceptable almost overnight. However, this will not necessarily be the case. The mistake that many utopian thinkers have made is to imagine that because something is possible it will automatically happen. We may develop the tools needed to live in greater harmony with our environment, but will we actually use them?

Ceramics, for example, hold enormous promise, but even they can be used in unexpected ways. Already they have been used in acts of 'ecotage', or environmental sabotage. The radical environmental group, Earth First!, has been instructing people in Oregon on ways in which they can booby-trap the enormous, ancient Douglas firs which the US Forest Service and a number of logging companies want to fell. The best idea, the group advises, is to use ceramic nails when 'spiking' tree trunks. These do not show up, even if the lumber crews are using metal detectors. 'If enough people do it in enough wild places,' said Earth First! co-founder David Foreman, 'it will just become too expensive to exploit some of the last remnants of nature's diversity.'

Logging companies like Louisiana-Pacific have described this type of activity as 'environmental terrorism'. The ceramic nails can cause chainsaws to buck back at the lumberjacks, they point out, and bandsaws can explode if a spiked trunk gets into the sawmill, sending shrapnel everywhere. From the point of view of Earth First!, it might be said that ceramic nails are already working, however, for now they may be invited to participate in planning the future. 'It would be nice if these people would sit down with us and join in the forest-planning process and there would be no more spiking,' one forest supervisor observed to the *Wall Street Journal*. 'But,' he predicted, 'that's as likely to happen as being able to buy a good nickel cigar again.' He may yet prove to have been unduly pessimistic.

Many people also hoped that another form of high technology would help slow the rate at which our industrial societies consume forests. They saw in the computer and office automation a possible answer to the ever-increasing use of paper in offices. However, if the experience of Reliance Insurance is anything to go by, these hopes are at best premature.

In 1979, the company produced some worrying statistics: its employees were using 27 million sheets of inter-office paper a year, representing a paper-trail some 3,900 miles long. As a result, it launched a campaign designed to make it 'paper-free by 1983'. Former chairman, John Folk, told insurance executives: 'Eventually I believe the insurance industry will eliminate at least 75 per cent of its paper records.' 1983 came around, however, and there was more paper than ever. The campaign was dropped. 'Instead of having a room filled with memo forms,' as one Reliance employee put it, 'we now have a room filled with computer paper.'

The paper industry decided that it has no reason to start worrying about its longer term prospects. 'The paperless office is a myth,' concluded Don Korell, research director for Steelcase, an office furniture manufacturer. 'Corporate America generates enough paper each day to circle the world 40 times, and over half that comes off computer printers.'

So the basic message must be that, while we are beginning to develop the tools needed to build a more sustainable society, their longer term impact will depend on the ways in which we decide to use them. A microprocessor can be used to control a regenerative burner or an auto engine, for example, but it can just as easily be used in a timing device by a terrorist who wants to blow a jumbo jet out of the sky.

At the very same time that we are building solar power plants and developing cleaner production technologies, we also continue to build nuclear weapons which could take an estimated 2.5 billion lives in an all-out nuclear exchange. When the Scientific Committee on Problems of the Environment (SCOPE) reported the conclusions of its two-year study recently, it confirmed earlier predictions that a nuclear war between the superpowers could throw 100 million tonnes of soot and dust into the atmosphere, triggering a 'nuclear winter'. The result, SCOPE warned, would be devastating crop failures as incoming sunlight was interrupted for months on end. The seasonal monsoons could well be halted in India. Indeed, as Mark Harwell, one of the study's co-authors, pointed out: 'More people could die in India from a nuclear war involving only the US and the Soviet Union than in those two countries combined.'

Consequently, the idea that technology alone is going to solve our problems looks like something of a non-starter. If the new tools that are now being developed are to be used in the right way, the climate of opinion must be such that it is no longer acceptable to use them in the wrong way. Regulations and other forms of administrative control clearly have an important role to play here. At the same time, however, such tools must be used imaginatively if they are to have a positive impact on our environmental problems. We cannot simply trust that the sunrise technologies will bail us out. Instead, we must focus in on each emerging technology, vetting it for potential environmental defects and, simultaneously, considering how it might help in achieving sustainable development. Consider what is happening in biotechnology.

The living economy

Of all the emerging technologies, biotechnology is perhaps the most promising as far as sustainable development is concerned. The Japanese, in particular, increasingly believe that biotechnology will help us develop environmentally acceptable forms of economic development. If, for example, you went into the Midori-kan Pavilion at Expo 85, which was held in Tsukuba Science City, you were taken on a 15-minute journey to 'Bio-star', a planet where various biotechnologies helped conserve and recycle resources, supply food and energy and prevent disease, as well as solving pollution problems. The word *midori* translates as 'verdure', and the recurring message was that biotechnology can help green the world's industrial economies.

Everyone has a slightly different definition of what *biotechnology* actually means, however, perhaps because the word actually embraces a whole cluster of new techniques and the processes and products which spin off from them. However, the basic idea, as Dr Ralph Hardy (then life sciences director at Du Pont) put it, is that biological systems, including living organisms such as bacteria, fungi, yeasts or plants, are being used 'as a product, as a process to make a product, or as a service.'

Genetic engineering is what has made biotechnology such an important area of science and technology. Much of the early recombinant DNA work has been carried out in bacteria, such as *Escherichia coli* (better known as *E. coli*) and in yeast, although there is a growing interest in animal and plant cells. 'DNA can be thought of as a language,' explained Genex, one of the early biotechnology start-up companies, 'the language in which all of nature's genetic information is written. As with any language, it is desirable to be able to read, write and edit the language of DNA. Rapid methods for determining the substructure of DNA (DNA sequencing), developed half a dozen years ago, correspond to *reading* DNA. These methods now make it possible to determine the complete structure of a gene in a few weeks. New and still rapidly evolving methodologies for chemical synthesis of DNA molecules make it possible to *write* in the language of DNA much more rapidly than was possible only a couple of years ago. Finally, and most important, genetic engineering techniques themselves (recombinant DNA methodology) make it possible to *edit* the language of DNA. It is by this editing process that the naturally occurring text can be rearranged for the benefit of the experimenter.'

Genex also stressed that 'new words (genes) can be introduced into the text, and new and more suitable texts (organisms) can be chosen. In addition, the editing process allows more subtle changes to be made in the DNA molecule, changes that can result in focusing much of the cell's metabolic energy on producing a single, specific protein from a single gene of choice.'

Thus, whereas in the last phase of biotechnology micro-organisms were persuaded to over-produce products which they already produced in the wild, particularly antibiotics, the new genetic engineering companies like Genentech, Cetus or Celltech, have been coaxing various different micro-organisms to produce substances which they would never produce under normal circumstances, including human growth hormone and interferon.

Early environmental concerns about genetic engineering tended to focus on the accidental release of genetically engineered microbes. The sort of scenario which opponents put forward in the 1970s ran along the following lines: the bacterium *E. coli*, normally found in the human intestine, and now the work-horse of genetic engineering research, might be tailored to produce industrial alcohol. If it escaped into the open environment, perhaps by being flushed down a drain, it might recolonize the human intestine and create a world of unwitting drunks.

Most biotechnologists and many environmental regulators now believe that such fears are exaggerated. But, as several hundred biotechnology companies begin to bring products to market and the commercial pressures intensify, there is a growing feeling among environmentalists, and among some regulators, that tougher regulations *are* needed. 'Industry didn't police itself during the petrochemical age,' warned Jeremy Rifkin, one of the biotechnology industry's most persistent critics, 'and it didn't police itself during the nuclear age. It's unrealistic to ask them to do it with biotechnology.' Once described as the 'Paul Revere of biotechnology,' Rifkin had been a thorn in the flesh of America's bio-industry for some time, but never more so than when the industry began to apply for permission to deliberately release genetically engineered micro-organisms into the environment, whether to control pests or to prevent frost damage to crops.

Unfortunately, there is always the danger that companies will get fed up with waiting for their applications to field-test new products to work their way through the official channels and will try to cut corners. There was uproar, for example, when it emerged that one US biotechnology company, Advanced Genetic Sciences (AGS), had secretly carried out an illegal test of its (perfectly safe) genetically engineered micro-organisms on the roof of its research facility. The bacteria are intended to protect strawberries and other crops from frost damage, by displacing wild strains of bacteria that promote ice crystal formation on plants at low temperatures. Californians living in Monterey, where the eventual field tests were to be carried out, expressed alarm and welcomed the tough stand taken by the Environmental Protection Agency. 'The EPA has sent a clear signal to the biotechnology industry that it must behave in a safe and ethical manner,' said July Pennycock, vice president of a group called Action League for Ecologically Responsible Technology (ALERT). AGS finally field-tested its 'Frostban' bacteria early in 1987, despite continuing protests and vandalism of the strawberry plots on which it was testing the product.

In Europe, too, there has been concern about the likely impact of biotechnology. When Gallup carried out a poll in Britain for the magazine *New Scientist*, for example, it asked people which areas of science might have 'very dangerous effects.' Nuclear energy, predictably, came top. More surprisingly, perhaps, biotechnology and genetic engineering came second, above the world armaments industry! American (scientific) ecologists have warned the biotechnology industry that its growing obsession with commercial secrecy is making it increasingly difficult for environmental scientists to assess the risk involved in the industry's various activities. 'The most effective new approach,' advised one ecologist, 'would be for the biotechnology community to cease regarding ecologists as "fanatics" or as merely the equivalent of philosophical or political activists, and recognize that their discipline has much to offer in making biotechnology the success that it ought to be.'

Ought to be? Yes, indeed: a growing number of environmentalists believe that, in the long term, biotechnology has the potential to solve many of our most pressing environmental problems. In retrospect, the fact that the first patented genetically engineered microbe was tailor-made to relish and neutralize an important pollutant, oil, can perhaps be seen as something of a portent. Indeed, a number of recent market surveys have suggested that the environmental applications of biotechnology will represent one of the fastest growing bio-sectors.

One of the areas in which biotechnology could be most helpful in the short term is in the clean-up of hazardous waste sites. Although that first patented microbe was never used to clean up a real-world oil spill, Dr Ananda Chakrabarty, the scientist who developed it, went on to develop new microbial strains able to degrade a growing range of pollutants. Combining old-style breeding methods with new genetic engineering techniques, Dr Chakrabarty and his colleagues at the University of Illinois announced in 1981 that they had created a bacterium which could live on a diet of toxic chemicals, including the herbicide 2,4,5-T. The organism was an improved version of one they had originally found flourishing in a heavily polluted site.

Companies like Occidental Chemical are already using such microbes to clean up toxic waste dumps. One of Occidental's subsidiaries is Hooker Chemical, which was at the epicentre of the Love Canal toxic waste scandal. By isolating microbes from such dumps and genetically manipulating them, Occidental produced over 100 recombinant strains which it has since been using to break down chemical pollutants in specially designed reactors.

Meanwhile, another US biotechnology company, Repligen, has been working on enzymes designed to break down wood pulp to ensure that paper mills can extract more useful raw material from a tonne of pulp. These enzymes should help cut the amount of energy used in pulp mills, extending the life of plant (because they are less corrosive than the chemicals currently used) and eliminating the hazards associated with bleaching operations. Like ICI, with its cyanide detoxification enzymes (see page 125), Repligen is also thinking of using this lignin-degradation work as a platform for tackling much more intractable pollutants, such as polychlorinated biphenyls (PCBs) and dioxin. Another biotechnology company based in Cambridge, Massachusetts, BioTechnica International, is active in this field too. Its original British affiliate, Biotal, is working on the microbial decontamination of a derelict gasworks site in Blackburn, for example, where the pollutants to be biodegraded include phenols, coal tars and cyanide. In the United States, Biotal has been working with the Methane Development Corporation, a subsidiary of Brooklyn Gas, at MDC's Fresh Kills landfill site on Staten Island, New York. The company is looking at ways of producing more commercially valuable gas from the domestic refuse which is dumped in such sites.

Bugging the future

'The political pressures are building up in Silicon Valley and elsewhere, following the leak of solvents into aquifers,' noted Dr John Rees, who runs Biotal's waste management group BioTreatment. 'Recently, too, we were approached by a company which has a difficult waste which it has to dilute to treat, a process which needs a big reactor. We are looking at ways in which the use of a number of different microbes simultaneously might enable the company to shrink the size of the reactor. Overall, however we are moving away from simple problems involving adding microbes to liquids coming down pipes. We are now looking at waste disposal sites as bioreactors in their own right. Today we are more concerned with the microbial management of the environment.'

Biotechnology is also beginning to throw up products which, while they may not be directly designed to control pollution, have desirable environmental features. Companies like Ecogen, Monsanto and Mycogen, for example, are working on pest control microbes which could cut the damage caused by chemical pesticides. Microbial pesticides, Ecogen predicted, will be 'cost-competitive with conventional pesticides, non-toxic to humans, animals and non-target insect species, non-polluting and less likely to elicit the development of insect resistance after prolonged usage.' Mycogen president Dr Gerald Caulder agreed, predicting that 'over the next nine to 15 years, the whole concept of how we control pests will shift from synthetic organic chemical pesticides to new pesticides which are environmentally much more acceptable.'

As Ecogen vice president, Dr Bruce Carlton, noted, 'perhaps the ultimate accomplishment in developing new biological pesticides would involve incorporating their genes directly into a susceptible organism, thereby conferring the ability to synthesize its own pesticide and totally eliminating the usual delivery system. For example, it may be possible to transfer genes for bacterial insecticide toxins directly into the genetic backgrounds of various plants, enabling them to synthesize their own insecticidal material and bypassing the costly need for repeated sprayings.' Monsanto is one of the companies which has already made a good deal of progress in this direction.

More speculatively, biotechnology may help in species conservation. The plight of the California condor underlined one of the most difficult questions facing conservationists: do you leave the few remaining individuals of a threatened species in the wild, or do you go in for captive breeding? The latter option entails some difficult problems of its own, but with plant tissue culture methods it is now possible to increase the numbers of threatened varieties, an approach pioneered by Native Plants Inc (NPI) vice president Hugh Bollinger. He used such techniques to produce hundreds of plants from several remaining individuals of a threatened Sonora Desert cactus, for example.

Animals are more of a problem, but there is no reason why techniques such as artificial insemination (normally used to exploit high quality sperm) and embryo transfer (used to exploit high quality ova) should not be used in threatened animal species. Indeed, they already are being used in this way: scientists at the University of Florida have been looking at ways in which artificial insemination can help in the captive breeding of alligators, a normally very expensive process, which typically achieves poor results.

In general, species become threatened when their habitat is

eroded, so can biotechnology do anything to ensure that the loss of habitat is reduced? Consider the tropical rainforests, which house much of the planet's genetic diversity and yet which are fast disappearing in many parts of the world as they are logged or cleared for agriculture. There is now increasing interest in uncovering the genetic resources of such ecosystems before they are destroyed, not simply for academic reasons, but also to help prepare a commercial case for their conservation.

'Our goal is to bring high tech, in the form of extremely user-friendly microcomputers, to what in most respects is a bone age culture,' said Bioresources director, Dr Conrad Gorinsky. This British company, which was working in the rainforests of Cameroun and Peru, had been exploring ways in which biotechnology can contribute directly to the conservation and sustainable development of the world's remaining rainforests.

As the rainforests are destroyed, Dr Gorinsky points out, the indigenous people who lived in them are killed or dispossessed. With them goes the information they had built up over generations of the medicinal and other benefits to be had from the genetic diversity found in such areas. 'The Indians or Pygmies can be regarded as the "librarians" of these forests,' Gorinsky explained. 'We hope that the sort of data we are now recording on computers will provide the basis for securing the future of such forests. What we are trying to do is to persuade people, and particularly those who are now moving into Amazonia, that these forests are like libraries. The value of a library is not in the use of the books as fuel, but in the use of the information stored in those books.'

The idea of integrating environmental and development activities had not been an immediately obvious one as far as Bioresources chief executive, Dr John Meadley, was concerned. 'To be honest,' he recalled, 'I'd always seen the conservation movement as a negative force, a brake on development. Yet no-one who has travelled as extensively as I have would dispute that a growing number of countries, particularly in the Third World, are in danger of destroying important elements of their natural resource base in pursuit of much-needed development. But I don't think you are going to get very far by telling people they have to stop, you can't take away their livelihood. What we are trying to do is to find ways to generate new economic activity from existing natural resources without destroying them in the process.'

Handling the future

One of the most striking examples of the ways in which the commercial potential of such genetic diversity can be harnessed can be seen in Wales. If Biopharm managing director Dr Roy Sawyer will let you trail your hand through the water in any of his company's large plastic tanks, it will come out dripping and festooned with leeches.

Most people, perhaps remembering Humphrey Bogart dragging the *African Queen* through steaming, leech-infested swamps, would react in the same way, trying frantically to brush the clinging parasites from their skin. But Dr Sawyer, who first came across leeches during childhood visits to the local swimming hole in his native state of South Carolina, was more fascinated than horrified when they fastened onto his body. Blood suckers, he soon realized, have had to evolve in such a way that they are now exquisitely adapted to the physiology of those they prey on, including humans. 'The fact that we are working with blood-sucking species means that we have a built-in publicity factor,' he admitted, 'but we have to be careful: the last thing we want is to be seen as sensational and weird. We don't want headlines like "The Voodoo Farm!"'

Biopharm, which is rising out of the ashes of an old British Steel plant in Swansea, is convinced that 'secretions from blood-sucking animals will be to heart-related diseases what penicillin has been to infective diseases.' Leeches have been used medicinally for many centuries, but modern research is uncovering some remarkable facts which suggest that their use may often have had a real medicinal basis. 'We now know at least nine different biologically active substances found in the salivary glands of leeches,' Dr Sawyer reported, 'and we have only just started looking in this area.' Three of these substances are known to anaesthetize the wound, to dilate the victim's veins and to prevent the blood clotting. Taking just this last example, an anti-coagulant could be used to treat various heart conditions and stroke victims. Proof, if proof were needed, that the living world contains riches beyond the dreams of avarice, provided that we know where to look.

Meanwhile, an equally unusual environmental biotechnology company is British Earthworm Technology, which recruits its workforce in the dung-heaps of the world and is planning to build a profitable business out of some highly unpromising (and potentially highly polluting) raw materials. It aims to commercialize worm-farming, or 'vermiculture'. But is the use of worms to turn wastes into saleable compost really biotechnology? BET research director Dr Clive Edwards thought so. 'Earthworms feed mainly on micro-organisms growing on such organic wastes,' he pointed out, 'and in the process of feeding, they fragment the waste, thereby increasing its surface area and encouraging further microbial activity.'

But forget definitions for a moment and plunge your hand deep into one of BET's seething worm-beds. You will be handling the future, getting a truly intimate feel of the shape of things to come. The worms convert some highly intractable industrial wastes and animal manures into compost. Apart from trials on a wide range of manures, BET's worms have been tested with considerable success on brewery waste, paper pulp waste, potato waste and spent mushroom compost. Once the worms have worked their magic, they are promptly and unceremoniously converted into high-protein animal feed.

BET has estimated that the market value of the worms is £350 to £400 a tonne, although in certain circumstances, as in the feeding of young eels, their value may be £2,000 to £4,000 a tonne. If ten per cent of the available waste were to be treated in the United Kingdom, assuming a figure of £400 per tonne of worms, the market could be worth £160 million a year. If the *compost* were to be priced at £80 a tonne, a figure which BET has suggested may be conservative, then this market could be worth £1.8 billion a year.

Like any tool, biotechnology can be misused or abused. In the worst scenario, new germ warfare weapons might be developed and deployed. Less dramatically, biotechnologists working in support of environmentally unsound systems may help keep them going. Environmentalists, like Jack Doyle of the US Environmental Policy Institute, argue that biotechnology could help prop up unsustainable forms of agriculture, diverting attention and limited funding resources away from more desirable research targets.

'Modern agriculture,' he has argued, 'is high-pedigree agriculture; it is a pampered system that is tended and maintained by technology and driven to perform at peak levels. In that sense our agricultural system might be compared to a thoroughbred race horse. It is a system built increasingly on hybrid crops and livestock, heavy inputs of fertilizer, antibiotics, water, and pesticides, a system that is capital, energy, and technology intensive. It is, in short, a demanding, high-strung system.'

Harnessed to such a system, even a potentially benign technology may be distorted to produce the wrong results. Even if biotechnology is solely harnessed to desirable ends, which seems unlikely, there are still what Dr Ernst von Weizsäcker, director of the Institute for European Environmental Policy, has called the 'dangers of success'. While a single automobile or a single drum of dioxin might not produce irreversible environmental damage, he has pointed out, the introduction of a million autos or a million drums of dioxin inevitably brings problems.

Biotechnology, too, could make certain forms of development so successful that they impose unacceptable pressures on agriculturally marginal habitats such as wetlands or rainforests. Australian environmentalists, meanwhile, have expressed alarm that 'super-sheep', produced by genetically engineering sheep to produce more growth hormone, could aggravate the overgrazing and erosion of the country's ecologically sensitive rangelands. 'Soil conservation is crucial if Australia is to maintain its agricultural output,' noted Dr Geoffrey Mosley, director of the Australian Conservation Foundation, 'and the prospect of heavier sheep raises concern about soil erosion. Overgrazing exposes the soil and makes it vulnerable to compaction, and that, in some cases, can impede germination and regeneration.'

However, while those who attack the biotechnology industry for fear that it will cause massive ecological damage are just as likely to be right as were the nuns of Sterkrade, the prospects of a green sunrise are higher this time than they were at the dawn of the Industrial Revolution. For one thing, today's emerging technologies are typically considerably cleaner and more resource-efficient than those they will replace. For another, they will be developed and deployed in a climate in which environmental concerns are increasingly important. This time around, if environmental excellence becomes a standard yardstick against which business success is measured, there should be a good chance that we can have both industry and fish, while leaving the option of doing our laundry on the riverbank open.

Chapter 9

IN EXCELLENT COMPANY

What makes an excellent company? The green agenda
was not discussed by the authors of *In Search of
Excellence*, but many 'excellent' US companies have
also pursued environmental excellence. The same is
true of a growing number of European companies. So
how do such companies view the future and how are
they trying to ensure that their plans get the
green light?

'To work to your utmost, make money, win fame, beat the competition—I realized just how great those things are.' That was the way Yoshihisa Tabuchi described the pleasures of being a capitalist to the *Wall Street Journal* a few days before taking over as president of Japan's leading securities house, Nomura. But pleasures can sour. Financiers and industrialists who become so absorbed with the pleasures of doing business that they forget to keep an eye on the wider implications of their activities can, in the words of Cape Industries finance director David Llewellyn, find themselves plunged into a 'dark night of the soul'.

Like Manville, the American asbestos company which was forced to adopt a $1 billion re-organization to cope with the claims of existing and expected future asbestos-related disease victims, Cape has been struggling to rise from the ashes of the asbestos business. Like Dow Chemical, it has been finding that a company's image can be critical if it wants to shift from selling bulk commodities to marketing consumer products. This is where the name on the label really begins to matter.

Admittedly, there have been some remarkable examples of phoenix-like corporate recoveries following major disasters. Even the Three Mile Island nuclear power station had brought some of its reactors back on stream six years after the partial meltdown of one of its reactors led to the evacuation of more than 150,000 Pennsylvania residents.

Meanwhile, increasing numbers of companies believe that major disasters are an integral part of modern business and are setting up, commando-style 'SWAT' crisis management teams which can swing into action once a crisis starts to break. A survey of chief executives carried out by one American company revealed that nine out of every ten subscribed to the view that 'a crisis in business is as inevitable as death and taxes.' Crises come in many different forms, of course, but only 50 per cent of the companies contacted had any sort of crisis management plan.

To fill the gap, new crisis management businesses are springing up. Public relations and legal firms are offering to handle the crisis management needs of corporate clients for a fee. The problem which such communications companies have to wrestle with is that their clients too often underestimate the potential significance of a particular issue or problem. There had been advance warnings of the Three Mile Island, Love Canal and Bhopal disasters, for example, but the companies involved chose to ignore them. The conclusion, as Harvard business school professor Stephen A. Greyser warned *Business Week*, must be that: 'Communications can only take you so far if subsequent investigation shows you screwed up.'

Excellent pursuits

One company which has invested a considerable amount of time in crisis management is Dow Chemical Canada. Following the derailment of a toxic chemical rail-tanker in 1979, which forced the evacuation of 250,000 residents, Dow Canada prepared information kits on the hazards associated with its chemicals and trained its executives in interview techniques, so that they could respond coherently to the media's probing even in the wake of a disaster.

When a further spill affected the water supply of several Canadian towns in 1982, Dow Canada was prepared. The company's emergency response team was soon on the spot and set up a press centre. Equally important, however, Dow recruited an independent expert, the regional public health officer, to talk to the media about the hazards associated with those particular chemicals and the ways in which the clean-up should proceed.

The result was that Dow earned praise for its handling of what might otherwise have been a very tricky incident. Perhaps we should expect no less from Dow Chemical, which featured in Peters and Waterman's book *In Search of Excellence* as one of their excellent companies. But perhaps, too, we should expect more, including fewer such accidents.

A key characteristic of the excellent companies highlighted by Peters and Waterman was that they have been highly innovative and, we were told, 'innovative companies are especially adroit at continually responding to change of any sort in their environments.' Now the term 'business environment' means something very different to the industrialist or to financiers such as Yoshihisa Tabuchi, revolving around trade policies, interest rates and labour relations, for example. Indeed, Peters and Waterman had little, if anything, to say about environmental issues proper. Even so, the green agenda is an increasingly important component of the international business environment and it is possible to assess some of their excellent companies against a number of environmental yardsticks to see how far the 'greening' process has gone.

Many of them, Dow included, have been responsible for major environmental problems. Lee Iacocca's main competitor, General Motors, turned up as an 'excellent' company, for example, but was soon in the headlines following air pollution around one of its plants in Detroit. The problem began when GM unknowingly burned somewhere between 50,000 and 200,000 gallons of liquid wastes which were contaminated with highly toxic chemicals. GM, in fact, had bought 500,000 gallons of liquid waste from a Canadian disposal company as boiler fuel.

GM may well have demonstrated 'excellence' in handling the community and media relations side of the ensuing scare, but surely an *excellent* company would have ensured that those wastes were thoroughly tested before being burned?

Such mistakes can help sensitize other companies to the potential dangers, of course. Indeed many companies which currently achieve environmental excellence do so because they themselves have previously encountered major problems. Du Pont, another of Peters and Waterman's excellent companies and the most admired of America's chemical companies according to surveys published by the American business magazine, *Fortune*, is a case in point.

Founded in 1802 to manufacture explosives, Du Pont soon hit trouble. An explosion in 1818 killed 40 employees. The company's founder, Eleuthère Irenée du Pont, assumed responsibility for the establishment and enforcement of safe practices. In the early days of capitalism, this might have been simply a ruse to keep the whole area under wraps, but in Du Pont this early commitment by top management gave considerable momentum to the whole question of employee safety. Later, this spilled over into the related areas of occupational health and environmental protection.

Many other companies, including most of those picked by Peters and Waterman, have appointed environmental specialists and advisers to ensure that they are kept abreast of the latest developments in environmental legislation, science and technology, but the problem is that such responsibilities have often been institutionalized at the wrong level. If a chief executive or managing director can shrug off such responsibilities onto someone else much lower down the management hierarchy, the purposes of environmental excellence are unlikely to be well served.

Indeed, the environmental staff of some of those excellent companies have been trying to give their activities a much higher internal profile. Take Essochem Europe, part of 'excellent' American oil company Exxon, as an example. 'There cannot be many companies which introduce their environmental and health and safety policies to employees on their first day of work,' noted *ENDS Report* editor Marek Mayer. 'Yet every newcomer to Esso Chemical is handed a booklet on "Business Ethics and Responsible Behaviour", spelling out the personal contribution he or she is expected to make to ensure that the firm's reputation in these and other fields is beyond reproach. It is a telling sign of the times—and of enlightened management—that policies for environment and health and safety feature in the booklet alongside those covering the more traditional corporate concerns of business ethics, conflicts of interest, competition law, and political contributions.'

But, as the booklet itself noted, 'exhortation and good intentions are not enough,' so the company has made considerable efforts to ensure that the group's broad policies are translated into effective day-to-day management practices. In the toxic chemicals field, for example, the company has defined a policy and produced guidelines which stress that if the risks associated with particular chemicals cannot be adequately controlled, 'the manufacture or use of such materials should cease until the requirements of this policy are satisfied.' Equally, if Essochem finds that its products are being used in an unsafe way by a customer, it will warn the user and provide additional safety advice. If the user persists, the company may refuse to sell him any more of the product.

Despite such policies and guidelines, however, the company decided that it needed to take further steps to ensure that its operations were environmentally acceptable. 'If things go wrong in environmental affairs, the effects on a company's hard-won reputation can be pretty devastating,' as Essochem Europe environmental health adviser, Ron Hewstone, put it, 'hence our attempt to further raise the profile of the environmental affairs function in management's eyes with a new series of management systems surveys.'

Survey teams visit associated companies and run a fine-toothed comb through their activities. Private interviews are carried out with all grades of personnel. At manufacturing sites, for example, those interviewed will include the site manager, plant managers, environmental affairs and safety specialists, the site physician and a number of shop-floor employees chosen at random. At marketing and headquarters sites, those covered generally include the chief executive, the environmental affairs, public affairs, marketing and distribution managers, other key staff members and some hourly-paid employees.

The final report is circulated to top management, once those whose operations are described have had an opportunity to comment on the report and remedy any immediate problems. Not surprisingly, perhaps, these surveys have stirred up a considerable amount of interest in environmental issues. Indeed, as Ron Hewstone himself commented, the environmental function 'has gained manpower at a time when other activities have been cut back, convincing me that management must believe in it.' By the time of the Sandoz accident, in fact, Essochem Europe (now part of Exxon Chemical International) was sufficiently confident of its approach to conclude that no new steps were necessary to avoid such an incident.

Cleaning up

One of the key factors which drive such environmental excellence is what Peters and Waterman called 'positive reinforcement'. In simple terms, excellent companies do not simply rely on punishments to encourage sound environmental performance: they also rely on rewards for important jobs done well.

Positive reinforcement, Peters and Waterman noted, 'has an intriguing zen-like property. It nudges good things onto the agenda instead of ripping things off the agenda. Life in business is fundamentally a matter of attention—how we spend our time. Thus management's most significant output is getting others to shift attention in desirable directions. The 'nudge it on the agenda' approach leads to a natural diffusion process. The positively reinforced behavior slowly comes to occupy a larger share of time and attention.'

Without a shadow of a doubt, the most impressive example of this approach has been the Pollution Prevention Pays (or 3P) Program at Minnesota Mining and Manufacturing (or 3M). 3M was listed by Peters and Waterman as an excellent company, although they made no mention of the 3P Program. This, to quote the company, 'gives individuals or groups of individuals who contribute innovative pollution prevention ideas and accomplishments an opportunity to gain recognition for their efforts.' Dr Joe Ling, the former 3M vice president responsible for launching the 3P Program has warned that 3M is a unique company, committed to developing a constant succession of new innovative products, making it difficult for many other companies to follow in its excellent footsteps. Innovation is crucial for 3M, which aims to make at least 25 per cent of its annual sales from products introduced within the previous five years.

Fortune's corporate image surveys list 3M as one of the three most admired US companies for innovation, the wise use of assets and for community and environmental responsibility. But the potential impact of the company's basic approach on industry's staff morale and environmental performance deserves much wider recognition.

If you want to improve your environmental performance without bankrupting yourself in the process, 3M believes, you need carefully defined targets, detailed plans to follow and a concerted team effort by the right people, who should have a clear responsibility for meeting the targets. The key to 3M's success was summarized in a formula it adopted in the mid-1970s: 'Pollutants (waste materials) + knowledge (technology) = potential resources'.

Instead of simply adding on pollution control equipment at the end of a manufacturing process, 3M has stressed the prevention of pollution at source. The 3P Program has focused on the elimination of pollution through product reformulation, process modification, the redesign of equipment and the recovery of waste materials for re-use. It also lays a good deal of responsibility on the individual employee to identify actual or potential pollution problems and rewards creative solutions for solving them.

Any such idea, the company stresses, should *make or save money*. By 1983, for example, a total of 52 projects had been accepted for 3M's programme in the United Kingdom, bringing savings over six years of more than £2.25 million. Altogether, those projects eliminated 3,150 tonnes of air pollutants, 830 tonnes of sludges and solid wastes and 34 million gallons of contaminated water. Worldwide, nearly 1,000 3P projects had made or saved £77 million.

Not surprisingly, some industrialists have challenged the accounting methods used to produce such figures. The claim, embodied in the title of Dr Michael Royston's influential book, *Pollution Prevention Pays*, that environmental protection is a profitable activity has been challenged by Dr John Lawrence, director of ICI's Brixham Laboratory. Brixham carries out environmental research for ICI, a company which has long pursued environmental excellence, and for outside clients. What concerned Dr Lawrence was the fact that the EEC Environment Directorate was beginning to sell stringent new legislation on the basis that it would boost Europe's economy.

The notion that tough pollution control standards can improve the financial performance of individual companies and, indeed, of entire economies was too much for Dr Lawrence to accept. 'If either or both of these is accurate, then we must be grateful,' he admitted, 'for where is the disadvantage? But if they are inaccurate,' he warned, 'then they are dangerous because they will either harm companies or harm economies by encouraging the misapplication of resources.'

Examples of 'clean technologies', he suggested, show that where good management finds ways to reduce costs, particularly by introducing new technologies, there is often a bonus result in terms of waste reduction. 'Since an attempt to find technology that will reduce costs will often look at the raw material yield this is not very surprising,' he argued, 'because higher yield often means less waste. Where there is no new technology one wonders why the changes had not been implemented earlier. The answer is probably that it took the pressure to reduce pollution to provide the stimulus to look for cost savings.'

If industry is charged a good deal of money for the privilege of discharging its effluents to the environment, then investment in pollution control equipment and cleaner production technologies will obviously make a great deal more economic sense than if the environment were to be a free commodity. Sometimes the savings can be very considerable. Cider-makers H. P. Bulmer, for example, used biotechnology to devise an effluent treatment plant able to clean up hot, acidic wastes from their pectin plant. The total capital cost for the plant was £24,000, while the savings in its first year of operation alone were estimated to have been £30,000.

However, in many cases, environmental controls result in lost profits, lost jobs and plant closures. A recent survey of 4,000 US chemical companies, for example, estimated that if they adopted the best practicable technology it would cost $139 million, cutting profitability by about nine per cent, causing four plant closures and destroying 251 jobs. If, on the other hand, these companies were forced to go for the ultimate, in the form of best available technology, the cost would be around $677 million, profits would be cut by a third, 20 plants would be forced to close and nearly 10,000 jobs would be lost.

In today's world, however, gross pollution is no longer tolerated and even vanishingly small amounts of certain pollutants are found to have some effect on human health or environmental quality. 'The truth is that for far too long industry has succeeded in transferring a substantial proportion of its real costs to the community as a whole,' stressed Tom Burke, director of Britain's Green Alliance. 'It is only the inevitable consequence of the efficient working of the marketplace that society should develop mechanisms for transferring them back. There are no free lunches in the environment.'

Companies or countries that invest in environmental protection in the belief that they will *automatically* make or save money may be in for a shock, but there are many other reasons for pursuing environmental excellence. For one thing, the regulatory framework within which industry operates is making environmental incompetence increasingly expensive. Apart from anything else, it is becoming increasingly difficult for companies to get insurance for their activities.

'Our premiums for product and general liability and worker compensation have gone up 200 per cent in the last year,' noted the risk manager at Manville, the troubled American asbestos company. 'But it's not only high costs that are the problem: trying to find cover at all is increasingly difficult.' Following the Bhopal disaster, Dow Chemicals' massive Agent Orange settlement with Vietnam veterans and other similar insurance disasters, many companies are finding that insurance is becoming prohibitively expensive. Industry's past failures are leading to higher costs for all.

In these circumstances, no company can now afford to leave the environmental agenda to some time-expired manager sitting in an office out on the corporate periphery. The sense of mission in this area has to come from the very top of the company and it has to be constantly reinforced.

Certainly there must be people whose job it is to alert senior executives of impending problems, but they must be highly respected in their own right, with adequate resources to ensure that they can develop a real feel for what is going on in the environmental field. Excellent companies will also give their employees confidence that if they report emerging problems or misdemeanours they will not suffer as a result. Handing out a booklet on business ethics to new employees is a good start, but giving them the sense that their views on their company's environmental performance are also welcome may be rather more difficult.

One of the worst examples of what can happen to someone who speaks out against malpractice was Stanley Adams, who leaked information on unfair trading practices at his employer Hoffmann-La Roche to the EEC's competition directorate. Despite the fact that he had asked that his identity should not be revealed, it was; and his life was devastated as a result. Now some companies, particularly those which are trying to rebuild their credibility following the exposure of past malpractice, are trying to ensure that there are channels in future through which employees can make their views known without losing their career prospects.

General Dynamics, for example, was accused of overcharging the US government for more than a decade on defence contracts. Now it has a new ethics programme, backed by a 'squeal clause' which protects, and may even reward, employees who blow the whistle on colleagues who violate the company's ethical guidelines.

Business ethics can have a tremendous impact on companies in today's world. For instance, take the case of Rio Tinto-Zinc (RTZ), one of the world's most powerful corporations, but long harassed by anti-apartheid, anti-nuclear and pro-environment protest groups. Traditionally, big mining companies have taken what can only be called a robust approach to such protests, but RTZ increasingly recognizes that the issues cannot be ducked. When protesters turned up at the company's annual meeting in London during 1985, for example, RTZ chairman Sir Alistair Frame patiently answered questions for several hours and then offered to meet the protesters later to discuss the issues they wanted to raise.

The greening of Glaxo

If any one characteristic marked out the companies highlighted by *In Search of Excellence*, it was their 'quality obsession'. Whether they made computers, hamburgers or caterpillar tractors, these companies were, and still are, obsessed with quality and obsessed with service. Peters and Waterman were interested solely in the performance of *America's* best-run companies, but the same characteristics can be found in companies around the world.

However, one of the dangers which they warned against was the 'gimmick trap'. The current gimmick, they suggested, was the quality circle, an approach which enables management to tap the experience and ingenuity of the company's workforce to improve the quality of its operations and output. 'There is absolutely nothing wrong with the idea,' they noted, 'as the Japanese have forcefully reminded us,' but managers who go looking for a quick fix for complex problems are likely to be disappointed.

Quality control has a great deal in common with pollution control, in fact, and quality assurance with pollution prevention. Consider recent experience at Glaxo, one of Britain's most profitable and fastest growing companies. As the company becomes increasingly international in its operations and marketing, so it is having to bring its quality assurance standards up to the level prevailing in the most quality-conscious corners of the world.

Indeed Glaxo's new generation of quality assurance policies set some ambitious goals, calling for 'the manufacture of products which *consistently* meet the demands of high quality *in every way*.' If you talk to Dr Alex Sinclair, Glaxo's international quality assurance director, the links between his brief and that pursued by corporate environmentalists soon become clear. As with any rapidly growing field of business activity, the drive for product quality has spawned endless debate and a flood of new buzz-words. 'Total quality, quality assurance, quality assessment, quality circles: these are just some of the phrases you hear,' said Dr Sinclair. But the vital distinction between quality control and quality assurance is that the former is something companies have adopted largely in response to legislation, whereas the latter, like environmental assessment procedures, is designed to 'push this concern for quality back upstream to the point where the company first begins to consider how a new product might be developed and presented.'

Quality assurance is a much broader concept than quality control. 'Experience shows that fundamental product quality problems are rare,' Dr Sinclair noted, 'whereas product quality defects are due to lapses in our operations and their control. These operational factors can occur at all levels and in all functions, any one of which can contribute ultimately to a product quality problem. As a consequence, quality assurance embraces the design, development, production, marketing and distribution of a product, together with all the associated interactions between such functions as purchasing, packaging and materials management.'

Inevitably, some will see this as simply another case of professional empire-building. Not so, said Dr Sinclair. 'Product quality is like a house. The house will only stand up if all the bricks are present and put together correctly. Neglect one and you have a faulty house. Obviously some bricks are more critical than others, but the analogy serves to illustrate the involvement of everyone.'

Clearly, the pursuit of environmental quality is a very similar challenge. So how has a pharmaceutical company like Glaxo, whose main product lines are environmentally uncontroversial, responded to the environmental challenge? In fact it recognized the challenge very early on. Even before the watershed Stockholm Conference on the Human Environment in 1972, Glaxo's then technical director, Arthur Lockwood, asked an interested employee, Arthur James, to take responsibility for environmental protection. 'He said that he didn't know what the term really meant,' James recalled 13 years later, 'but he asked me to find out and to report to him regularly.'

No company which spends over £4 million a week on capital projects, as Glaxo does, can expect to avoid environmental controversies entirely, whatever business it is in. Glaxochem, for example, which is responsible for manufacturing the chemicals that Glaxo's pharmaceutical operations need, produces effluents and emissions which would cause problems if not properly managed. In fact the company introduced its environmental policy in the late 1970s, a policy which was interesting because it stressed that whether executives were overseeing the construction of new facilities in Scotland or Singapore, they should aim to comply with the *spirit*, not just the letter, of local environmental legislation.

This is a critical distinction for any company concerned to ensure that it achieves and maintains a reputation for environmental excellence. Today, this facet of a company's reputation can be the deciding factor determining whether or not it gets the green light for environmentally sensitive projects.

But this somewhat open-ended brief can prove surprisingly taxing for hard-pressed senior managers. 'It's all been a bit of a jigsaw,' explained Dr Jim Harvey, factory manager at Glaxo's Annan production site in Scotland. 'You can see some bits fairly obviously, then other bits come together over the years.' The Annan plant spends around £450,000 a year on environmental protection and as the newest Glaxochem plant, it embodies many of the latest environmental technologies, including energy and water conservation systems. Indeed, in some respects Annan was probably over-designed. But, as safety adviser Dr Bob Beresford stressed, 'you can't just think of the legislation of the day when you design a plant. You must think 10 to 15 years ahead.'

Clearly, such thinking has got to be integrated with the group's overall business strategy. Probably the most significant element of Glaxo's current strategy is its drive into international markets. 'We are already a highly international company, even by the standards of our industry,' noted the group's chairman, Paul Girolami. 'But it is my belief that we will become even more so, indeed this is a "must" if our ambitions for the future are to be realized.' To succeed, such companies have to have their fingers on the environmental pulse worldwide.

Setting up a pharmaceutical production plant in Singapore, for example, is no easy option. 'Glaxo does not go overseas to avoid environmental legislation,' explained John Brennand, managing director of Glaxo Production and Engineering Services, and previously managing director of Glaxochem's Singapore operation. 'Singapore was keen to have the plant,' he recalled, 'but not at the expense of its environment. And, just to illustrate the sort of pressures we operated under, at that time the pollution control unit reported direct to Prime Minister Lee Kuan Yew.'

Clearly, trained people are needed to keep the board and senior management posted on the developing 'green' agenda. So far, however, Glaxo has shied away from the idea of having a central environmental unit in the belief, as John Brennand put it, that this would enable line managers to 'shuffle off responsibility for environmental protection.' But the company is changing and its environmental set-up will need to keep pace.

The green agenda, which is made up of a growing number of interrelated issues, is now an inescapable fact of business life. 'Environmental issues now take up 50 per cent of my time,' said John Allsop, safety adviser at Glaxochem's Montrose plant in Scotland. 'And I don't think this is just a temporary blip. The environmental pressure, in my view, is unlikely to return to the lower level of earlier days. Increasingly, for example, we are adopting a "cradle to grave" approach to the management of potentially hazardous materials.'

But, noted Ron Dodsworth, who replaced Arthur James as Glaxo's environment adviser when the latter retired, while 'health and safety considerations tend to be built into line management thinking, environmental thinking is less so—probably because we haven't had many real problems. This means that our job often involves stirring people's imaginations. Line managers, and I know this from my own experience, are so busy getting products out of the gate that they haven't got time to stand back and think: *What if?*'

Process designers have to be prompted down the lateral thinking path in the same way. 'One of our goals,' as Dodsworth explained, 'is to design out problematic process materials or wastes. We don't do this just for environmental reasons. But we have managed to drop some fairly unpleasant materials. One that leaps to mind was phosgene, which we dropped in the late 1970s. It's a marvellous reagent, but a horrible substance. We had devoted a great deal of effort to safety systems designed to ensure that there was no risk to the community, but when the opportunity came to design out this reagent we took it like a shot.'

Many of the most impressive achievements one comes across when touring Glaxo's facilities simultaneously protect the environment and save money. At Glaxo's Ulverston site in Cumbria, for example, Dr Tony Sherrard pointed out that the factory's solvent recovery plant recycles materials which might otherwise cause air and water pollution and in the process cuts the company's solvent bill by £20 million a year. Energy conservation is another vital area of activity. The combined energy bill for Glaxochem and Glaxo Pharmaceuticals may be running at over £12 million a year, but it would have been well over £16 million without energy efficiency projects, which cost a total of £2 million. Conservation, in short, can pay handsome dividends.

In the longer term, in fact, the main problem faced by Glaxo may be one bred of success. How, for example, do you continue to motivate people to tighten standards and improve operating procedures if the environmental pressure relaxes as a company builds up a record for environmental excellence?

'There's no room for complacency,' warned Arthur James. 'The group is bringing in new generations of chemical engineers and other people who may need environmental training. At the same time, we are constantly looking for new products, new reagents, new processes. We have got to be sure that they are environmentally sound—and you can't assume that just because a process has always been safe that it will continue to be safe. The aim must be to keep people on their toes.'

The view from Big Blue

If any one company sums up what Peters and Waterman meant when they talked about excellence, however, it is probably IBM. This giant company, which in 1984 employed nearly 400,000 people in 100 countries, also regularly scores top points in *Fortune*'s surveys of corporate performance in terms of its long-term investment value, its use of corporate assets and its ability to attract, develop, and keep talented people. Once again, IBM's environmental performance was not even mentioned by the authors of *In Search of Excellence*, but there is a good deal that can be said on the question.

IBM's environmental policy dates from 1971, was revised in 1973, is commendably short and to the point and is worth quoting from. 'IBM will reduce to a minimum the ecological impact of all of its activities,' it noted. 'Management in IBM is expected to be continuously on guard against adversely affecting the environment and to seek ways to conserve natural resources.' More specifically, the policy continues, IBM will aim to meet or exceed all applicable government regulation in any location; to establish stringent standards of its own where government regulations do not exist; attempt to use non-polluting technologies and to improve the energy efficiency of products and processes; to cut the need for waste treatment by recovering and re-using air, water and materials; and, where the company's skills and resources are relevant, to assist governments to develop solutions to pressing environmental problems.

When environmental consultant Brian Johnson was asked by Britain's Centre for Economic and Environmental Development (CEED) to assess IBM UK's environmental sensitivity, he emerged impressed. 'Not only is the company record outstanding as a manufacturing corporation committed to clean industry of low environmental impact,' he concluded, but its 'perception of quality, initially applied to maintain IBM's position in a highly competitive field, is naturally extended to include quality in environmental performance generally.'

Like many other sunrise industries, information technology is intrinsically a great deal more environment-friendly than the 'smokestack' technologies which are now beginning to drop out of the industrial profile of many leading industrial economies. Indeed, Johnson argued, in comparison to the situation in 'materials crunching' industries, the natural resources component of the *Limits to Growth* thesis 'is something of a non-issue' as far as IBM is concerned. That said, however, IBM 'clearly has an interest, for cost reasons, in minimizing the volume of resource throughout, be it of silica, metals, resins, the chemicals used as solvent and cleansing agents, or the oil-based feedstocks used to produce plastics.'

As far as pollution goes, sunrise companies are far from blameless, as the groundwater pollution caused by such Silicon Valley companies as Fairchild Camera and Instrument and Intel has shown. But when new regulations followed, IBM was able to show that its own groundwater protection programme was already in compliance with the new standards. 'IBM had in fact discovered groundwater contamination at several of its plants in the United States during the mid-1970s,' explained Johnson, 'mostly at levels ranging from a few parts per billion up to 10 parts per million. In some cases, expensive remedial measures had been required, as at the company's plant in Boulder, Colorado, where a three-year investment programme costing over $4 million was launched in 1981.'

The company's policy of adopting worldwide environmental standards based on the highest purity or emission control standards applied anywhere has paid real dividends. 'Because we have made detailed undertakings to minimize pollution,' Steve Horsfall, IBM UK's hazardous materials co-ordinator told the *ENDS Report*, 'it makes increasing sense to look for inherently less polluting or material recovery processes rather than to adopt conventional— and more costly—abatement techniques.'

IBM's computers are already helping other companies increase the resource-efficiency of their processes. In its own facilities, Johnson noted, 'IBM uses its computers to monitor buildings' energy consumption, with programmes to turn on and off lighting, heating and air conditioning so as to conserve resources and obtain optimum value from their use.'

If there is one thing about IBM's business strategy which jars with environmentalists, however, it is the company's goal of maintaining high compound rates of growth. Johnson asked whether this goal was really sustainable indefinitely. The reply he was given by IBM UK's chief executive officer, Tony Cleaver, was that, 'while it is recognized that indefinite compound interest growth is obviously an impossibility for any organism or institution, the potential of the information technology industry as a whole is so great, and as yet so little realised, that it is premature for a part of that industry to start, at this stage, planning for the end of its growth phase.' In Cleaver's view, IBM UK can readily achieve growth rates of at least 10 per cent annually into the late 1990s, well outside the time horizon used by the company's planners.

'We recognise that the technology of our industry, information technology, cannot replace the natural ecosystems that are so badly threatened,' Cleaver noted, 'but we do believe that technology, properly used, can be a key ingredient in managing the resources of this planet more sensibly and *that*, at the end of the day, is what sustainable development is all about.'

Bridges to the future

Overall, if there is a single message which *The Green Capitalists* should convey, it is that the goals of environmentalists and the more thoughtful industrialists are beginning to converge rapidly. The important need today is to build bridges between these two constituencies, to explore the potential for working together towards a more sustainable future.

The need now is for concerned business leaders to get involved in the environmental debate, rather than waiting for environmentalists to beat their door down. 'Business leaders need to become political surfers,' advised Joseph T. Nolan, vice president for public affairs at Monsanto, 'swimming into the public policy ocean prepared to catch the big wave.'

He also suggested that 'instead of ignoring or denouncing what activists are up to, business leaders should study them as object lessons in issue management—and learn to ask probing questions about them. What do activist proponents of change really want to bring about? What societal trends or organizing strategies are likely to help or hinder them in their pursuit? What if they succeed? How would that affect my company's products, or markets, or finances?'

Meanwhile, leading companies around the world are paying so-called 'creativity consultants' to teach them how to be less rigid, more creative in their thinking. IBM, Exxon and Apple Computer, for example, pay considerable sums for the advice of such people as Dr Edward de Bono, who coined the phrase 'lateral thinking'. In Silicon Valley, too, they listen to people like Roger van Oech, who *Business Week* described as 'the *enfant terrible* of the creativity crusade'. His approach has been to offer tips on how to overcome the most common obstacles to creative thought. If these fail, he administers a metaphorical 'whack on the side of the head'.

Cheaper by far, and probably at least as effective in stimulating innovative thought, would be a meeting with some of today's leading environmentalists and environmental entrepreneurs. Companies should also pay much more attention to some of the messages that are coming up from inside their own ranks. A new generation of directors, managers and workers is moving up and it views the world very differently from the generation it is replacing.

'It used to be believed that as we became more affluent we would all become the same,' noted Peter Schwartz, then head of Shell International's business environment group. 'Back in the 1950s and early 1960s there was a lot of discussion about conformity as a problem. The exact opposite has happened. As we became richer, and the choices became wider, we became more different from each other. What we have found is that we have tended to become a more diverse world, despite the homogenizing influence of technology, communications and economic development.'

This fact is extremely important, because it means that consensus is that much harder to reach. Coupled with the growing complexity and volatility of the world we live in, it means business needs to adopt a dramatically different approach in dealing with the green agenda. If one assumes that there are forces working for growth in an economy and forces working against growth, introducing 'friction' into the system, there are three main options facing the major industrial societies. These are summed up in Shell as the conflict, compromise and synergy scenarios.

If we all pursue our own narrow interests, we end up with the high-friction, conflict scenario. 'In such a situation the various forces at work in the system will act in a counter-productive way,' Schwartz warned. 'They will tend to be working against each other—unions against management, business against government, environmentalists against others, and so on. We would not reach our maximum potential. This in turn would lead to very poor economic growth, extended recessions and ultimately decreasing diversity as everyone is driven down the economic ladder together.'

In the compromise scenario, on the other hand, all sides agree not to demand total solutions. 'Nobody is dealing with fundamental problems,' Schwartz stressed, 'but everyone is trying to patch the system together as they go along. Such a scenario would lead to a constrained growth path. It would be cyclical, weak and the divisions in society would continue to widen.'

The third scenario, based on *synergy*, could produce very different results. 'Synergy,' Schwartz noted, 'means the coherence of forces working together. A synergy scenario takes our diversity into account. In other words, we stop pretending that we can solve everybody's problems with the same set of solutions. We accept the fact of decentralization of institutions as fundamental to the reality of a world of diversity and we stop trying to impose universal solutions on organizations both within and among countries. A new generation of less resource-intensive technologies,' he predicted, 'could make possible a new era of growth.'

Similar ideas are surfacing around the world, as some environmentalists talk of 'green growth' and industrialists and politicians try to find ways of blending economic and environmental objectives. 'You have to prepare revolutions slowly,' was the way Baden Wurttenemberg Prime Minister Lothar Spaeth explained his approach to building a German equivalent of Silicon Valley in the Black Forest. 'Resources must be used to dissolve the artificial conflict between economy and ecology, young and old, capital and labour.'

Environmentalists might point to the damage done to the Black Forest by 'acid rain' as evidence that such conflicts are real, if undesirable. But a growing number of those in the green movement recognize that they have got to start working with industry to develop more sustainable forms of development.

Environmental fund-raising organizations, for example, are working up new approaches for helping companies tap into the green marketplace. The World Wide Fund for Nature has worked with such companies as Fiat, Kleenex and Kodak to boost their sales. When Kleenex developed its 'Wildlife Tissues', sales leaped 76 per cent. Fiat, meanwhile, offered £1 for every telephone call in support of its campaign to protect Madagascar's wildlife. More to the point, at least from Fiat's point of view, the promotion attracted an extra 90,000 people through the company's showrooms. In some campaigns, like Shell's Better Britain Campaign and the company's link-up with Britain's Channel 4 TV's *The Longest Running Show on Earth*, the idea, as Hazel Barbour of Shell explained, has been 'to get over to people not normally interested in conservation the message that they could do something.'

However, it is one thing to get Fiat to back a wildlife appeal or to persuade Volvo to help fund the Rare Breeds Survival Trust, but a more important long-term challenge is to convince industrialists that charitable donations are only part of their responsibilities to the future. Where companies draw on such fundamental natural resources as the planet's biological diversity, they must increasingly become actively involved in their conservation and sustainable development.

An interesting step in this direction came when the US seeds and plant biotechnology company Pioneer Hi-Bred International announced a $1.5 million grant to support research on germplasm stored in Latin American seedbanks. Meanwhile, in Cameroun, West Africa, companies like Unilever have been helping to develop sustainable development techniques for large areas of protected rainforest. Such alliances are likely to become increasingly important and increasingly productive, identifying new opportunities for industry while helping ensure the long-term survival of key environmental resources.

A fair amount of nonsense has been talked about the commercial potential of the planet's biological diversity, but the biotechnology revolution makes it very much more likely that the genetic resources found in threatened ecosystems can be exploited without destroying those ecosystems in the process. Scientists at Australia's Institute for Marine Science (AIMS), for example, have been looking for new chemicals, drugs and food products along the continent's coral reefs. The first commercial product they have come up with is a 'sunscreen', a compound which is produced by corals near the surface of the ocean to protect them from ultraviolet light. ICI bought the rights to the compound, synthesized it and is looking into the possibility of selling it to stop sunburn and to protect its own mainstream paint and plastic products.

Commerce and conservation have often been at odds in the past, but a new breed of entrepreneur is beginning to emerge in the field of sustainable development. 'To be effective,' as Dr John Meadley, chief executive of Rural Investment Overseas (RIO) and (at the time) of Bioresources, put it, 'the call for conservation must be concerned with the economic well-being of those directly or indirectly affected. That is why we are looking at the sustainable use of natural resources within an economic and commercial framework.'

Among the projects RIO has been working on to demonstrate the acceptable face of the private sector in Third World development is a programme designed to cut deadly aflatoxin contamination of Thailand's maize crop. Following decolonization, many Third World countries continued to need the private sector, but Dr Meadley recalls that they typically 'employed individuals and companies as servants, rather than as partners. Our aim has been to show that the private sector has a considerable contribution to make to the sustainable development of the Third World's natural resources—in a partnership role.'

The Body Shop International has been one of the most astoundingly successful examples of green enterprise. 'One of the rules of a successful company,' says Anita Roddick, the company's founder and managing director, 'is to find out what your original features are and shout them from the rooftops, because they're the ones that count. State and restate them and state them yet again.' Apart from sheer enthusiasm, the most striking feature of The Body Shop's corporate culture has been its focus on such issues as conservation, animal experiments, youth employment and Third World development.

Like all good business ideas, at the *Financial Times* noted, 'the initial concept was so simple that you now wonder why nobody had previously thought of it. Anita Roddick looked at cosmetic products and realised that a large part of their cost was incurred in producing expensive disposal wrappings and containers. In addition, the products themselves were almost entirely man-made and synthetic, at a time when beauty conscious women were becoming aware of the animal experimentation lobby, and of the move back to nature in foods and health products. Producing natural products in cheap refillable containers made both commercial and ecological sense.'

The company's ecological principles were not simply grafted onto the business. 'Although some people may think that we are recent converts,' Roddick commented, 'the reality is that these concerns were always there. They are coming to the fore because we are the flavour of the month, but The Body Shop dates from 1976 and we were already featuring Greenpeace's anti-whaling campaign in 1977.'

As far as the Third World is concerned, The Body Shop buys

raw materials from developing countries on an increasing scale. 'At the moment we buy through agents,' explained Nicola Lyon, the company's head of environmental projects, 'but we are looking at ways in which we might increasingly buy direct from farmers' co-operatives. We are keen that people know that we are in the market for interesting products, which might even be by-products of something that is already being grown.'

While travelling through China, Roddick came across an oil that the Chinese have traditionally used in cooking. Like jojoba, the shrub which has helped wean the cosmetics industry away from the use of sperm whale oil, this cooking oil is produced by a plant which might help in desert reclamation programmes. So she sent a sample to the University of Pennsylvania, to see whether the oil might have potential in the cosmetics field. Businesses like The Body Shop, in fact, are beginning to play a key role not only in marketing environmentally acceptable products, but also in promoting the transition to more sustainable forms of development.

Ever since the Industrial Revolution, far-sighted industrialists have recognized that unbridled capitalism could destroy itself by seeking to maximize short-term profits. Such long-term thinking has often been discouraged by the intense day-to-day, month-to-month problems of survival in the thick of the worldwide recession. But, with increasing frequency, leading industrialists are admitting that they have responsibilities to people other than their share-holders, employees and customers. Some are explicitly beginning to include future generations among the 'stake holders' in their businesses.

Often such industrialists speak out because they can see emerging threats to, and opportunities for, their own businesses. When the European Community reached a compromise agreement on ways of controlling auto exhaust pollution, following bitter political in-fighting, Mercedes manufacturer, Daimler-Benz, strongly attacked the agreement. Not, like British Leyland, because it feared the new standards would add an estimated £1,000 to the price of the average family car, but because it genuinely believed that the new standards were 'environmentally unsatisfactory'.

The company's sales director, Hans-Jurgen Hinrichs, predicted that clean cars would come to dominate the new car market in the very near future and he warned that Europe had missed an important chance to steal a march on its American and Japanese competitors.

Losing less fast?

In the wake of disasters such as that at Bhopal it is scarcely surprising that the media tend to paint capitalism as a force for evil. But Henry Ford, one of the fathers of the global mass production economy, once suggested that 'what we call evil is simply ignorance bumping its head in the dark.' Evil exists, as this century has sickeningly demonstrated. But too many of the disasters, too much of the destruction, which industry has inflicted on the environment has resulted from corporate heads colliding with unsuspected obstacles in the dark of their own ignorance.

The time has come for a much more intelligent approach. As earlier chapters have illustrated, a ferment of new ideas is bubbling up in private sector companies around the world. The underlying principle of the synergy strategies is to work with new partners on previously intractable problems, combining existing elements to come up with workable solutions.

Perhaps symbolically, as these final paragraphs were tapped into the word processor, the phone rang. On the other end of the line was Bechtel, another of the excellent companies featured in *In Search of Excellence*. Along with Boeing and Fluor, Bechtel, whose corporate motto is 'A Fine Feel for the Doable', was described as one of 'the undoubted project management stars'. Such companies, Peters and Waterman noted, 'both take pride in the quality and reliability of their services, and then charge a lot for both.' Interestingly, too, they noted that Bechtel 'urges that every project manager spend fully 20 per cent of his time experimenting with new technologies.'

The call was from a Bechtel engineer interested in a project we were carrying out for the Nature Conservancy Council and British Petroleum (BP), effectively building bridges between Britain's on-shore oil and gas industry and environmental interests. But we got on to the subject of the increasingly stringent environmental conditions now being placed on such contractors by their government or industrial clients. Increasingly, companies like Bechtel are specifically asked whether they have the environmental expertise to build a given project in an acceptable fashion. Environmental excellence, he noted, is now a key factor ensuring that a project is 'doable'.

The danger of drawing up a list of 'excellent' companies is illustrated by the fact that just two years after *In Search of Excellence* was published, *Business Week* noted that 14 out of the original 43 'excellent' companies were doing distinctly less well. Thomas Peters retorted that: 'There's no real reason to have ever expected that all of these companies would have done well forever and ever. If you're big, you've got the seeds of your own destruction in there.' The excellent companies, Peters and Waterman suggested, had seemed to be big corporations that were 'losing less fast'.

Any civilization also contains the seeds of its own destruction. Our own possesses weapons which could kill over half the world's population and precipitate a nuclear winter which would go a long way towards finishing the job. But if we are to achieve environmental excellence, we cannot afford simply to 'lose less fast', although even that would be welcome at the moment in many parts of the world.

If we, our children and our children's children are to enjoy a sustainable future in the world which we have borrowed, we must do the doable and work together to develop ways in which we can begin to do the currently undoable. We face a tremendous challenge, but at least it is one which will give capitalists like the Japanese financier, Yoshihisa Tabuchi, a real chance to do their utmost, win fame, beat their environmentally incompetent opposition and make money in the process.

A key part of our problem, however, is the science of economics. 'Conventional economics,' as futurist Hazel Henderson once put it, 'is a form of brain damage.' What she meant was that economists suffer from a worryingly limited form of selective vision, which often ignores or downplays natural cycles, human values and the need for social responsibility. Henderson, along with European counterparts working in such organisations as The Other Economic Summit (TOES), is working towards a new economics. Fritz Schumacher spoke of an 'economics as if people mattered'. What we need today is an economics as if people *and* their planet mattered. The necessary concepts and intellectual frameworks are hardly going to be invented overnight, but there is no reason to believe that the challenge is any greater than splitting the atom or landing a man on the

Moon. In the long run, it will almost certainly prove to have been a better investment of scarce time and resources.

Interestingly, having been a laggard in environmental affairs throughout much of the 1970s and 1980s, Britain is now giving some signs of regaining its pioneering spirit. On the financial side, for example, we have seen the launch of the Merlin Ecology Fund, which only invests in companies that are pursuing environmental excellence in their operations and, in a growing number of cases, are developing products with the Green Consumer in mind. Merlin's early success has helped put much-needed pressure on the City to look rather more carefully at the environmental performance of some of the companies it invests in.

But what should ordinary manufacturing or retailing companies be doing in the meantime? Chapter 10 outlines a number of guiding principles which a growing number of companies are adopting to ensure that their activities, technologies and products are environmentally acceptable.

Chapter 10

TEN STEPS TO ENVIRONMENTAL EXCELLENCE

The key to environmental excellence is to identify
priority targets and get people moving towards them,
however slowly they may start. Ten guiding principles
are outlined below which should help most
companies achieve environmental excellence in a
growing number of their businesses. By doing so,
they can enhance their corporate image, promote sales
of their products or services, identify impending
problems and pinpoint potential future market
opportunities.

Excellent companies are committed to people: their employees,
their customers and those who are affected, in one way or another,
by their operations. The difficulty they face in the environmental
field, however, is in identifying everyone who is likely to be affected
by their operations. Instead of concentrating exclusively on the area
within the factory fence, or even on the communities living immediately around their manufacturing sites, such companies also now
recognize that their operations may have implications for people
who they may never meet, either because they are geographically
remote or, in some cases, because they are not yet born.

The Green Capitalists has concentrated on the manufacturing industry, rather than on agriculture or the investment community. This
is not because farmers and investors do not have an impact on the
environment: they most certainly do. Indeed, sustainable agriculture and other forms of sustainable development are only likely to
emerge if investors can be persuaded that it is in their long-term
interest to support them. An enormous amount of work still needs

to be done if we are to have any hope of seeing the emergence of a new breed of 'green financiers' and 'green investors'.

Obviously, the companies described in earlier chapters cannot hope single-handedly to achieve the necessary shift in the world-view of those who work in the City of London or on Wall Street, the Paris Bourse or the Tokyo Stock Exchange. But industrialists can have a profound influence by ensuring that their development proposals are environmentally acceptable and sustainable *before* they are submitted to potential investors. The investment community relies on entrepreneurs and industrial managements to tell it what is likely to be required for a business venture to proceed and succeed.

But how should a given company set about achieving environmental excellence? There is no guaranteed route, but all of the ten steps outlined below have been followed by almost every one of the environmentally excellent companies mentioned in previous chapters. Sir Peter Parker, chairman of Rockware and of the British Institute of Management, first came up with the idea of using a checklist approach and suggested many of the individual steps. As he put it, 'there is an urgent need to simplify management ideas and action on this 360 degree challenge of the environment.' These ten steps are not the complete answer as far as environmental excellence is concerned, but they do represent a framework within which excellence can be pursued with a real hope of success.

1 Develop and publish an environmental policy

The first step is to produce a company environment policy. There is no standard format for such policies, with many of them being very short documents, but such a policy, adopted by the company's Board, effectively legitimizes all the subsequent steps.

'All industrial activity has an impact on the environment,' ICI's environmental policy begins. 'It is the policy of ICI to manage its activities so as to ensure that they are acceptable to the community and to reduce adverse effects to a practicable minimum. This policy recognizes that the environment is able to absorb certain man-made effects, and is thus a resource to be used as well as one to be conserved.' The policy goes on to discuss the way in which ICI deals with the environmental aspects of its existing and new activities, its processes and its products. One interesting sentence notes that the Group will: 'Take positive steps to conserve resources, with particular regard for those which are scarce and non renewable.'

IBM's policy, as we have seen (page 217), states that 'IBM will reduce to a minimum the ecological impact of all its activities. Management in IBM is expected to be continuously on guard against adversely affecting the environment and to seek ways to conserve natural resources.' The company also goes a long way towards ensuring environmental excellence by insisting that its various businesses match their environmental standards with the toughest prevailing anywhere in the world.

At BP, meanwhile, the Group's policy states that: 'It is a primary and continuing policy of the BP Group that in the conduct of its activities it will endeavour to protect the health and safety of its employees, customers and others who may be affected by these activities and endeavour to limit adverse effects on the physical environment in which its activities are carried out.' Each BP company then prepares its own policy, objectives and guidelines, appropriate to its own businesses.

2 Prepare an action programme

A policy statement is a vital first step, but if it is to be implemented it needs to be spelled out in the form of a number of much more specific objectives for all company personnel, with guidelines on how these objectives should be met. At BP, for example, there are eight overall objectives:

i to set standards which will at least meet the relevant statutory requirements for health and safety, product safety and environmental matters, as these may affect its own employees, customers, contractors and their employees and the public at large;

ii to review and, where appropriate, develop these standards in the light of changes in technology, industry practices and trends in legislation, and to sponsor research and development to improve the rationale for the setting of standards;

iii to co-operate with the appropriate authorities and technical organizations on the formulation of standards and the means of compliance;

iv   to ensure that the potential health and safety factors and environmental effects are assessed for all new products, projects, activities and acquisitions;

v   to ensure that all employees are properly informed of their responsibilities for health, safety and environmental matters and discharge them effectively and are encouraged to participate in the prevention of accidents;

vi   to ensure that contractors working under the operational control of a BP Company are informed of its relevant standards, and that appropriate procedures exist for monitoring compliance without detracting from the legal responsibilities of the contractors;

vii   to ensure that mechanisms are established and are used for consultation with employees on such matters; and

viii   to ensure that these objectives are being fulfilled through the auditing of the Group's activities.

The purpose of an action programme is to determine where the immediate priorities for action lie and to ensure that the appropriate targets are clearly identified and the responsibilities for achieving them are given to people who have the power, initiative and resources to succeed in the task.

Where they do not already exist, environmental impact assessment procedures should be instituted to ensure that new projects, processes and products do not damage the environment in unsuspected ways.

3   Organization and staffing

Most excellent companies which operate in environmentally sensitive businesses ensure that the responsibility for the environmental agenda is vested in top management. For example, the responsibility for determining BP's policies on health, safety and environmental matters lies with the Board, advised by the Group Health, Safety and Environment Committee.

Any company aiming for environmental excellence will need to identify a 'champion' for health, safety and environment, typically a Main Board Director. He or she will need the advice and support of a sufficient number of appropriately trained people, with access to all of the company's operations. But the responsibility for ensuring that individual plants or processes are environmentally acceptable must be pushed down to individual line managers. Their suitability for higher positions in the company should be explicitly assessed, as is now the practice in a growing number of companies, on the basis of their success in meeting health, safety and environmental targets, as well as other job- or task-related criteria.

4 Allocate adequate resources

If such environmental policies are to be translated into effective action, those responsible must be given adequate resources. As the 3M experience shows (see page 208), such expenditures need not necessarily be a net drain on the company's resources. The key point, however, is that money spent in pursuit of environmental objectives should be subject to the same accounting procedures as the rest of a company's activities. Some of the benefits, particularly in the public relations and corporate image fields, may be hard to quantify, but the Board and shareholders must be assured that the environmental budget is being professionally managed.

5 Invest in environmental science and technology

Whether one thinks of acid rain or the impending choice between catalytic converters and 'lean-burn' engines for the cars of the future, sound environmental decision-making depends on the availability of sound scientific research. Industry must help ensure that the environmental debate is well-informed and that the necessary data bases exist to ensure that pressing questions about the potential environmental implications of particular decisions or activities can be assessed within a reasonable time-scale. A key development in this respect is the co-operation between the World Resources Institute (WRI) and the International Institute for Environment and Development (IIED) on the production of an annual series of *World Resources* reports on trends in the international environment.

New, environmentally acceptable technologies can be developed and deployed in an economically efficient manner if industry works closely with environmental interests and the regulatory agencies. The key objective must be to ensure that technology is designed from scratch to be cleaner, quieter or more energy-efficient, rather than having to be modified once in use. 3M's Pollution Prevention Pays Programme illustrates how product reformulation, process modification, equipment redesign and the recovery of wastes for re-use can help cut pollution and energy wastage dramatically. The example of Rolls-Royce (see page 140) shows how complex the process of technology development can be, with different environmental factors often needing to be traded off. But companies which fail to keep their technologies up to scratch environmentally risk going out of business.

6 Educate and train

People are much more likely to respond to company objectives and action plans if they know exactly what is expected of them and how they should respond. Company policy should be spelled out fully and effectively, while progress with the environmental action programme should be regularly reviewed. 'I take the line that people in our companies are not just employees, not just trade unionists,' noted Sir Peter Parker: 'they are citizens at work, so the message of environmental quality must matter to them. At work, we are all environmentalists now.'

The important thing is to get people launched on the path towards environmental excellence, even if the early steps are fairly small. As the authors of *In Search of Excellence* noted in a different context, 'what's called "foot-in-the-door" research demonstrates the importance of incrementally acting our way into major commitment. For instance, in one experiment, in Palo Alto, California, most subjects who initially agreed to put a *tiny* sign in their front window supporting a cause (traffic safety) subsequently agreed to display a billboard in their front yard, which required letting outsiders dig sizable holes in the lawn. On the other hand, those not asked to take the first small step turned down the larger one in ninety-five cases out of a hundred.'

The implications are clear, as Peters and Waterman pointed out. 'Only if you get people *acting*, even in small ways, the way you want them to, will they come to believe in what they're doing. Moreover, the process of enlistment is enhanced by explicit *management* of the after-the-act labeling process—in other words, publicly and ceaselessly lauding the small wins along the way. "Doing things" (lots of experiments, tries) leads to rapid and effective learning, adaptation, diffusion, and commitment; it is the hallmark of the well-run company.'

7 Monitor, audit and report

Once the appropriate management systems are in place, their performance should be assessed regularly. This will involve a number of separate activities. The state of the environment will need to be monitored, to check that the company's controls are effective. But there will also be a need to check on the extent to which impacts which were predicted in the initial environmental impact assessment work have been borne out in practice, to ensure that the base of environmental science on which the company's procedures have been erected is sound.

As the Essochem Europe example (see page 206) showed, regular audits and surveys can help assess the extent of management involvement in, and support for, a company's environmental policy and action programme. The sort of questions Essochem Europe asks include the following:

i   In the planning of environmental conservation activities:
    —Are all functions included?
    —Who co-ordinates such activities? How is the plan stewarded?
    —How are priority conflicts resolved?

ii   With regard to legal requirements and developing legislation:
    —Are laws available and understood?
    —How is responsibility allocated?
    —How is compliance audited internally?
    —How is information obtained on developing legislation?
    —How does the organization try to influence legislators?

iii   In ensuring compliance:
    —What monitoring programmes are conducted?
    —Are records required by the authorities?
    —What actions are taken following non-compliance episodes?

—Are legal and company standards well defined and understood?

—What changes in standards are anticipated?

iv   To maintain good relations with the public:

—Are there systems for recording, investigating and responding to complaints?

—Is there an effective emergency plan for accidental spills or emissions. When was it last tested? What was the result?

—What actions have been taken to inform the local community of your environmental conservation initiatives?

v   In the area of training:

—What training has the environmental conservation co-ordinator received? Is it enough?

—Are there formal training programmes for operators, mechanical staff, technicians and contractors on the environmental policy and requirements?

vi   In the area of potential environmental hazards:

—Are the hazards associated with all chemicals and processes known and communicated to the appropriate people?

—How is the information updated? How often?

—Are protective measures widely known?

—Does the organization have discussions and exercises with local authorities in handling environmental emergencies?

—What waste disposal techniques are adopted? What are the relevant regulations? How are the dumps monitored?

vii   Where there are gaps or inadequacies in the available technology:

—How are they assessed?

—How are they followed up?

viii   What specific objectives exist in the area of developing 'clean technology'? What steps are under way to eliminate the use of undesirable chemicals and toxic materials?

ix   What work is under way on specific problems related to the need to eliminate or reduce the toxicity of plant and process effluents?

8 Monitor the evolution of the green agenda

The environmental agenda is constantly evolving. Any company which assumes the adequacy of information which it picked up two years ago, or even three months ago, may be in for an unpleasant surprise. As in any other area of business, the regular gathering and assessment of information is the intelligent approach. Excellent companies also keep up to date on international developments which may influence the environmental agenda in other countries in which they operate. Key publications here are the *ENDS Report*, published monthly by Environmental Data Services, based in London, and the *State of the World* reports, published annually by the Worldwatch Institute, based in Washington, D.C.

9 Contribute to environmental programmes

There are a tremendous range of projects and programmes under way in the environmental field which need help from industry, whether it is in the form of money, help in kind or seconded staff. The return on voluntary, charitable contributions to conservation organizations can be very high indeed, provided the corporate sponsor selects a well-run charity or other organization. Some companies, such as BP, are helping to train the staff of environmental charities and other non-governmental organizations in business management techniques. Internationally, too, industry should support programmes which make available environmental experts to countries which might not otherwise be able to afford them. Some of these experts should be drawn from industry itself.

10 Help build bridges between the various interests

One of the most critical needs in today's business environment, as Chapter 7 explained, is to build bridges between business, government and environmental interests. 'There is a growing realization among business and environmental leaders that confrontation isn't helpful in achieving their ends,' explained Monsanto chairman, Louis Fernandez. 'It is a time of transition and the climate is ripe for initiatives to be taken by industrialists and by responsible environmental leaders.'

Any company which has worked its way through the previous nine steps will have found such bridges beginning to form almost automatically. The key to environmental excellence is the recognition that such activities need not be a drain on the company's resources. Rather, they can help in training key personnel to operate effectively in today's world, in providing advance warning of impending pressures on core businesses and in identifying the business opportunities of tomorrow.

POSTSCRIPT TO 1989 EDITION

As the 1980s draw to their end, one thing is clear: the 1990s will be the Green Decade. The speed at which the environment has become a central commercial issue has left many businesses unsure of their response. Even in such a fast-moving field, however, it is still possible to make a number of predictions about the likely shape of things to come. For example:

* The environment will hit the top of the political agenda, spurring tighter standards and new laws.

* Consumer concern and commitment to choosing products that 'don't cost the earth' will grow.

* Demand for environment-friendly products will expand dramatically, initially in the developed nations but later in the Third World.

* Poor environmental performance will cost some companies market share at home and abroad, while others will exploit new opportunities and win new markets.

The environment, in short, is in the process of becoming a major new competitive arena for business. Understanding the impact of the relevant issues, and responding to the resulting opportunities and threats, will become an important source of competitive advantage. The impact will be felt in terms of corporate image, manufacturing strategy, product specification, design, marketing and promotional strategies, not just in manufacturing industry but also across industries as diverse as retailing, leisure and agriculture.

In fact these extraordinary changes have already had a major impact on our own work. When *The Green Capitalists* was first published, my colleagues and I at SustainAbility were working on a range of corporate consultancy projects. These were mainly defensive in nature, with the main purpose of helping companies to develop environmental policies, training procedures and internal and external communications programmes. Today, by contrast, we are helping business to switch to a much more pro-active, market-oriented stance.

SustainAbility has now linked up with two much larger companies—Brand New Product Development (part of the Michael Peters Group) and PA Technology—to offer a unique 'Green Consumer Marketing Service'. The sort of questions we are helping companies to answer include the following:

* With so many issues in the air, which should I take seriously?

* Our competitors have started to talk about the environmental performance of their products. Should we?

* How quickly should I react?

* What are consumers' real concerns?

* Is there ever a 'right' answer anyway—don't the goalposts keep shifting?

* Isn't there a danger of appearing to be jumping on the bandwagon?

* Every dark cloud has its silver lining. Can we develop a 'green' version of our product?

* Are there any problem areas that have not yet emerged?

In attempting to 'green' capitalism, we have embarked on a process of enormous dimensions, whose outcome is as yet unclear. But the evidence to date suggests that market economies can respond very rapidly indeed if the relevant environmental issues are translated into effective market signals. Tom Burke expands on this theme in his end-piece, which starts on page 243.

The task of greening world markets is one of the key challenges for the 1990s. And since no-one has a monopoly on the 'right answers', we would be delighted to hear from others working in this rapidly growing field. SustainAbility's address can be found on page 254.

IV

OUTLOOK

Into the 21st Century

Chapter 11

GREENER GROWTH

Tom Burke

Excellence is not independent of context. It is no accident that many of the world's most excellent companies are found in the United States and Japan. These are both in their very different ways enterprise cultures in which excellence is fostered and rewarded.

In Britain, we live in an anti-industrial culture. This is a strange plight for an industrial nation. The antipathy to industry that is so marked a feature of our society has its origins deep in the bones of British history. But its manifestations are very contemporary.

The best and the brightest of our graduates predominantly choose the professions, the City, academic life or the voluntary sector in preference to industry. Investment in education and training is amongst the lowest in the OECD region and there is little connection between industrial needs and educational priorities. Few national, and even fewer local, public officials spend any of their working lives in industry.

The industrial world for most people in Britain is a *terra incognita* peopled by the left-wing shop stewards of tabloid mythology fighting a permanent war of attrition with the hard-nosed, hard-headed executives of the popular novel. As industrial decline has removed any experience of the realities of industrial life further from the lives of most people so these gulfs of understanding have grown.

Industrial leaders have repeatedly warned that Britain's economic survival depends on rolling back anti-industrial attitudes and creating a national climate of opinion much more supportive of industry. 1986 was designated Industry Year in an effort to launch just such a process. Although one of the most successful of the many 'years' that punctuate each decade, no-one is under any illusions that anything more than a start has been made.

The image of industry as environmental vandal was already well established in the 18th Century. Blake's 'dark satanic mills' are locked deep into our collective consciousness. The next century and a half of industrial development reinforced this perception as the rushing tide of economic growth brought its environmental consequences into more intimate contact with the broad mass of the population.

Today, poor environmental performance by industry simply reinforces and legitimizes anti-industrial attitudes. As workers in frontline industries such as the nuclear industry or the chemical industry have found, it is difficult to feel motivated and positive about your job when your own family wishes you were doing something else. Every time a company allows chemicals to leak into a river, it confirms the beliefs of those opposing any industrial development anywhere that they are right. For those choosing careers, the sight of Greenpeace members saving the planet's seas in small boats is a more compelling role model than the picture of a grey-suited corporate executive assuring a television audience yet again that there is absolutely no risk at all in his company's activities —well, only a vanishingly small risk.

We have created a vicious spiral of decline in Britain, whereby anti-industrial attitudes contribute to poor economic performance. This in its turn means that British companies in both public and private sectors cannot invest in the training and technology necessary to improve their environmental performance. Failure to improve environmental standards leads in its turn to a strengthening of anti-industrial attitudes which further weakens economic performance and round we go again.

The pursuit of environmental excellence thus has a broader purpose than simply maximizing an individual company's own performance. In the public mind industry is one seamless whole. Just as the successes of one or two companies—the Jaguars or ICIs —cast a glow over the whole of British industry, so too do the failures. All of British industry suffers when British Nuclear Fuels is prosecuted for mishandling radioactive waste. It also suffers when Union Carbide releases poisonous chemicals in India or Sandoz deposits dangerous chemicals in the Rhine.

Every company has a stake in encouraging environmental excellence in every other company. Creating a cultural context in which industrial excellence is fostered rather than diminished demands that we roll back anti-industrial attitudes. Improved environmental performance is central to this endeavour. The very visibility of environmental problems, in both the literal and the editorial sense, makes it so.

There are now alert and informed groups in every community ready to seize on failures and, albeit less frequently, to praise successes. The media appetite for environmental stories with their inherent David and Goliath structure is insatiable. (Environmental stories are practically always about individuals or small groups taking on big government or big industry. No one ever remembers who David and Goliath were fighting for or what they were fighting about and no-one is ever on Goliath's side.) No effort to roll back anti-industrial attitudes can hope to succeed unless industry's impact on the environment is seen to diminish.

Improved environmental performance is not, of course, a sufficient condition for the transformation of our anti-industrial culture. But it is a necessary condition. Failure on the environment will both mask and interfere with other changes that are taking place. But the very visibility of the environment can be turned to advantage. Success in reducing industry's environmental impact, because it will be seen, will reinforce other efforts to change attitudes.

The collective challenge facing Britain's industrial managers is to reverse the spiral of decline which confirms the low status of industrial endeavour in this country. What needs to be built is a virtuous cycle whereby improved environmental performance helps to roll back anti-industrial attitudes and thus to encourage better economic performance and so permit more investment in environmental improvement.

There is a growing recognition that the health of both the environment and the economy are interdependent. Maintaining and improving our environment requires investment in many forms: in infrastructure such as the water and sewerage systems; in energy conservation; in public transport; in cleaner, quieter, more resource efficient technologies. But to invest we must earn and in order to earn, industry must succeed.

This is a relatively new perception. Since the environmental debate began in the late sixties there has been a tendency—deeply felt on both sides of the argument—to view industry and the environment as mutually antagonistic. The one could only succeed if the other failed in a classic zero-sum game. The result has been an undeclared war of attrition between the heavy battalions of the big corporations and the green guerillas of the environment movement.

As with most wars, everyone has been losing. The environmentalists have scored some notable one-off victories—ending the import of whale and seal products to the EEC, for instance, or halting the Swedish nuclear power programme. But for each species that is saved several more become endangered and nuclear power stations continue to be built in Russia, France and other countries. Industry too has had its victories—the Third London Airport or oil drilling on Furzey Island. But the price of each victory in terms of delay and the insistent leaking away of public goodwill grows higher every time.

Environmentalists, convinced from brutal experience of the virtues of forward defence, have been tempted to fight every development in order to establish a principle or a precedent or just to keep the thin edge of the wedge as far away as possible. Industrialists have fought every new regulation as if it were the coils of Laocoon threatening to strangle their business completely. Each has tended to see any initiative by the other in the worst possible light.

Through all this the truth that some developments bring positive environmental gains—the Channel Tunnel for example, or the revitalization of London's docklands—and that not all legislation has the effect it intends is obscured. Just as is the equally significant truth that some developments have few if any real benefits and do wholly unnecessary damage to the environment—any one of a dozen dams in the Third World for example, or many of the agricultural drainage projects in Britain so liberally financed from the public purse throughout the seventies. And, as we saw earlier, where would Rolls-Royce be without the opportunities created by tough noise control legislation?

This mutual hostility is a product of the growth mania of the fifties and sixties to which the environment movement was a vigorous reaction. It is now hard in our post oil-price-hike world to recall the heady days when economic growth was considered endless, bringing with it a solution to all the world's ills. We now know that economies can shrink as well as expand and that not all growth is good. But in the late sixties when Rachel Carson was writing *Silent*

Spring, the book which launched the environmental revolution, growth was seen as always and universally good.

And industry was seen as the motor of growth. The logic was compelling. Unbridled growth was responsible for both the rising tide of pollution threatening to engulf us all and for the massive environmental damage contingent upon the pursuit of new supplies of ever scarcer natural resources. If industry was the motor of growth and the only way to preserve the environment was to halt growth, then industry was the enemy and must be defeated.

Industry reciprocated this stance with vigour. Environmental concern was a sentimental barrier to progress erected largely by those who were doing very nicely thank you. Fears about the impacts of new technologies were simply spasms of latter day Luddism by those too lazy or too timid to understand their potential. Environmental pressure was seen by industrial opinion as a constraint on the economic growth essential to human well-being to be overwhelmed where it could not be out-manoeuvred. If environmentalists were anti growth then they were the enemy and must be defeated.

This is less of a caricature than is comfortable. What both positions had in common was a false assumption. They shared, albeit from different perspectives, the belief that the environment and the economy were at either end of a see-saw on which it was only possible for the environment to be protected at the expense of the economy or for the economy to thrive at the expense of the environment. Throughout the seventies the 'growth' versus 'no-growth' debate raged in newspapers, magazines, television studios and public meeting rooms.

It was only as the onset of global recession demoted growth from the heroic status it had assumed in the eyes of politicians—they are quick to recognize the futility of pursuing the no longer deliverable —and the focus of environmental concern shifted from non-renewable to renewable (mineral to biological) resources that wiser counsels prevailed. As crisis turned to catastrophe in the African drylands it was soon apparent that economic and ecological failure were intimately engaged to each other. In the industrial North it was equally apparent that every call for economic regeneration began with pleas to invest in environmental improvements—energy conservation programmes, housing rehabilitation schemes, new public transport projects.

The recognition of the interdependence of the environment and the economy is now formally enshrined in the communiqué from the Bonn Seven Nations Summit of 1985. The argument has now shifted. It is no longer seen as simply a choice between 'growth' or 'no growth', but the much more difficult task of discriminating that growth which is sustainable in the ecological as well as the economic sense from that which is not. Sustainable growth, or 'green growth' to distinguish this use of the term from the more orthodox economists' use of 'sustainable' to mean simply 'endless', reconciles economic and environmental imperatives.

We can now begin to map out the kinds of investments, in both public and private sectors, that would generate both environmental and economic benefits. The principal elements making up a determined drive for green growth are already clear. They are no longer just the pipedreams of environmentalists. In a major speech in 1984, Dr David Owen, leader of the SDP and a most unlikely member of the 'brown bread and sandals brigade', urged the Alliance to go for green growth and outlined his view of what that might entail.

In the public sector there is an undoubted need for greater investment in the water and sewage system. A decaying sewage system will destroy three decades of effort to clean up our rivers. Unrepaired water supply pipes lead to the loss of between a quarter and a third of all the water collected in reservoirs thus increasing the need for new water storage capacity. The environmental benefits of making these investments are obvious. So, too, are the economic benefits of stimulating an under-used construction industry with high job creation potential. Investment in domestic insulation not only brings rapid social benefits, particularly to the poor and elderly, but it reduces the cost of social service and health provision and creates employment in precisely the areas and labour market sectors where they are most needed. By reducing energy demand it contributes to solving the problems of acid rain, carbon dioxide build-up and radioactive waste.

Similar stories can be told for public sector investment in rail electrification, road maintenance, bus services, housing rehabilitation, derelict land reclamation and waste recycling. In all these areas economic growth is accompanied by improvements in environmental quality. Nowhere would this be more beneficial than in the shift of agricultural investment away from its current over-emphasis on the high-input, high-output approach that has produced the absurdity of current surpluses to a lower-input, lower-output style of farming. Farm incomes could be sustained, land kept in production and the costs of producing, storing and disposing of surpluses reduced at the same time as pollution loads are reduced and wildlife habitats restored.

In the private sector, the range of green growth investments is, as is shown throughout this book, even wider. Developments in ceramics and carbon-based composites allow the replacement of scarce metals for structural uses with lighter materials made from abundant raw materials. Fibre optics can similarly replace metals of inferior performance in dozens of applications. As the transformation to a carbon and silicon based economy occurs, the environmental impacts of the extractive industries are reduced at the same time as high value added goods, with all their economic advantages, are produced. Johnson-Matthey and Davy are among the leading British companies that have already profited from their share of the burgeoning pollution abatement industry. The cutting edge of the future is increasingly composed of products which are knowledge rich rather than resource-intensive.

The drive for green growth offers an enterprise in which environmentalists and industrialists can join together wholeheartedly. This will not eliminate all the conflicts between industry and the environment, especially on a small and overcrowded island such as ours, where land use is the dominant environmental issue. But it may help to confine conflict to those areas where it is unavoidable. There is no fundamental reason why cooperation and competition cannot go hand in hand, provided the boundaries are clearly drawn between the protagonists and the respect for and tolerance of the others' point of view is mutual.

It would be foolish to pretend that this will be an easy task. The basis for the antagonism that existed throughout most of the past two decades may no longer exist, but the legacy remains. Positions once adopted are not lightly dropped, nor attitudes once established easily changed. But in the creation of a new endeavour, the pursuit of green growth, it will be possible to count successes to first balance and then to outweigh the failures.

Nor is it simply a question of changing perceptions. Behaviour too is in transition. The very success of the consumer society is breeding new opportunities. As quantitative consumption needs have become increasingly satisfied for a majority of those in the industrial world, so a new emphasis on qualitative consumption has begun to emerge. We are now witnessing the arrival of the 'green consumer'.

This should surprise no-one. The same primary human motivations that drove the consumer boom of the four decades since the war remain. For many people, real disposable income is at an all-time high. The goods of mass consumption are now so cheap as to be available to all bar the very poor. When everyone has a car, television, video machine, hi-fi, dishwasher or personal computer of roughly equivalent performance, some other way must be found to express differences of wealth and personality.

If mass availability, and the simple absence of enough disposable time, constrain quantity as an expression of choice, so a premium falls ever more heavily on quality consumption. It is the market place, for instance, that is filling the vacuum left by the National Health Service in the provision of preventative health care. Organically grown vegetables sell at a premium in Tesco's and Sainsbury's as consumers seek to purchase better health by avoiding chemical additives. Sainsbury's have even taken to advertising themselves as being a health food store! This transformation of the orthodox image of the supermarket as purveyor of the blandest, most denatured foodstuffs is simply a response to consumer preferences. London is now burgeoning with clinics offering every conceivable kind of alternative medicine and therapy, from acupuncture to foot massage, as growing numbers of people spend more of their higher incomes on the search for health and well being. One of the fastest growing of all markets currently is the fitness market as the connection between health and fitness has become better known.

A similar pattern is discernible in holidays where there is a growing market for wilderness vacations of all kinds and a rejection of mass resorts in favour of more individually tailored packages through mechanisms such as timeshare. In clothing the premium is on natural fibres, in cosmetics, on natural products. The theme running through all these developments is an equation of 'natural' with 'better'. Customers are now increasingly concerned in their purchasing habits with how a product is made as well as how it performs. Choice is being expressed further up the production process as consumers reject those goods whose production is perceived to be socially or environmentally damaging. The vast explosion in voluntary organizations of all kinds is yet another expression of the pursuit of quality consumption. The massive public response to appeals from bodies such as Band Aid or Greenpeace reflects the wish by consumers to purchase a better quality of life and a willingness to pay for it.

Capital markets may also be on the point of changing in a similar way. It is rarely realized that industry and finance are separate institutions with different—and occasionally conflicting—priorities. The chronic short termism of the City is a constant refrain of British industry's explanations of why it does not do as well as its competitors. Many of the investments necessary for the pursuit of environmental excellence are inhibited by the preoccupation of the financial institutions with quarterly or half yearly returns. Industrialists, increasingly under pressure from both their customers and the general public, may well understand the necessity of responding to the demand for higher environmental standards, but find it hard to persuade their financial masters, who remain loftily isolated from all external pressures.

The return of the personal shareholder may breach this ivory tower. It is not so much Prime Minister Margaret Thatcher's ideological commitment to popular capitalism that is stimulating this prospect, though she will undoubtedly claim credit for it, as the simple logic of our massive post-war investment in the owner-occupation of houses. The parents of the baby boomers, those born between 1945 and 1960, led the charge into home-ownership. Their children have all grown up and most of them have now also acquired houses. Meanwhile the value of the parental houses has risen dramatically. As their parents die, the baby boomers, already well settled and into early middle age, will receive a substantial capital gain for which they will have no immediately pressing use. We are entering an era not just of high real disposable income, but of high disposable capital.

Competition among the financial institutions to manage these funds will be fierce. It is unlikely that all the customers for financial services will not wish to express in their investment choices the same kind of preferences that they are making in their consumption patterns. Thus a significant proportion of those funds will be looking for a home that is compatible with the broader values of the baby boomer generation. We have already seen the first signs of this opening market in the emergence of ethical investment funds. There is no reason to suppose that the striking inventiveness of the financial institutions will not respond to these opportunities as swiftly and efficiently as they have done to others. Thus we can hope to see in the coming decade the growth of a variety of green funds committed to supporting environmental excellence.

Perhaps what we are seeing is the emergence of a new age capitalism, appropriate to a new millennium, in which the boundary between corporate and human values is beginning to dissolve. It is now clear from the results who won the nineteenth-century argument about capital and labour. Socialism, as an economic theory, though not as a moral crusade, is dead. The argument now is about what kind of capitalism we want. In this book we have explored one dimension, the green dimension, of the kind of capitalism we must have if there is to be a planet worth having for our children to inherit.

SOME USEFUL ADDRESSES

A tremendous number of organizations are now active in the environmental field. The addresses of some of those mentioned in the text are given below. If you need further information on any of these organizations, write to them. For further details on any of the other organizations mentioned in *The Green Capitalists*, contact John Elkington at SustainAbility Ltd (see below). SustainAbility has produced two related publications: the *Green Pages Yearbook and Directory* by John Elkington, Tom Burke and Julia Hailes (Routledge and Kegan Paul, 1988) and *The Green Consumer Guide* by John Elkington and Julia Hailes (Victor Gollancz, 1988). Other useful addresses include:

Centre for Economic and Environmental Development (CEED)
712 Upper Belgrave Street, London SW1 or on 01-245 6440.

Earthscan
3 Endsleigh Street, London WC1H 0DD or on 01-388 2117.

Environmental Data Services (ENDS) Ltd
The Finsbury Business Centre, 40 Bowling Green Lane, London EC1R 0NE or on 01-278 4745.

Friends of the Earth
26–28 Underwood Street, London NW1 7SQ or on 01-490 1555.

The Green Alliance
60 Chandos Place, London WC2N 4HG or on 01-836 0341.

Greenpeace
36 Graham Street, London N1 8LL or on 01-251 3020.

International Institute for Environment and Development (IIED)

3 Endsleigh Street, London WC1H 0DD or on 01-388 2117. In the USA, IIED is at 1717 Massachusetts Avenue NW, Washington DC 20036 or on (202) 462 0900.

International Union for Conservation of Nature and Natural Resources (IUCN)

Avenue du Mont-Blanc, Ch-1196 Gland, Switzerland, or on 022-64-71-81.

Royal Society of Arts

8 John Adam Street, London WC2N 6EZ or on 01-930 5115.

SustainAbility Ltd

49 Princes Place, London W11 4QA or on 01-243 1277. For details of the Green Consumer Marketing Service, contact John Elkington or Dorothy Mackenzie, Green Consumer Marketing, Brand New Product Development Ltd, 49 Princes Place, London W11 4QA or on 01-221 7011/2828.

UNEP Industry & Environment Office

Tour Mirabeau, 39–43 Quai André Citroën, 75739 Paris, France or (from England) on 010 331 45 78 4310.

World Bank

1818 H Street NW, Washington DC 20433, USA or on (202) 477 1234.

World Resources Institute (WRI)

1735 New York Avenue NW, Washington DC 20006, USA or on (202) 638 6300.

Worldwatch Institute

1776 Massachusetts Avenue NW, Washington DC 20036, USA or on (202) 452 1999.

World Wide Fund for Nature (WWF)—UK

Panda House, Weyside Park, Godalming, Surrey GU7 1XR or on 0483 426444.

RECOMMENDED READING

In supplying a bibliography for a book like *The Green Capitalists* one is either tempted to provide references for every source used, and run the risk that no-one will ever refer to them, or to provide no follow-up suggestions at all. In this case, what follows is a highly personal listing of some key books which may be of interest to readers who find that the current book has left them wanting to know more.

First, because it is often mentioned in the text, there is *In Search of Excellence: Lessons from America's Best-Run Companies*, by Thomas J. Peters and Robert H. Waterman, Jr (Harper & Row, 1982). This has been an immensely influential book, spawning several sequels and many imitators – but it is worth pointing out again that environment is nowhere mentioned in the book. One of the most influential books in this respect was Michael Royston's *Pollution Prevention Pays* (Pergamon Press, 1979).

The report of the World Commission on Environment and Development, *Our Common Future* (Oxford University Press, 1987), is essential reading, particularly the industrial section (pp. 206–234). This draws on a wide range of referenced sources, including work that we have been doing for the World Resources Institute (WRI) in Washington, D.C., on the environmental implications and applications of some of the emerging technologies (e.g. biotechnology, satellite remote sensing, information technology and waste treatment systems). The first report, *Double Dividends: U.S. Biotechnology and the Third World* was published late in 1986.

WRI (see page 254) has also published a number of more general books on the role of industry in sustainable development, including a number of excellent titles by Charles Pearson. A good start here would be *Multinational Corporations, Environment, and the Third World*, edited by Charles Pearson and published by Duke University Press in 1987.

WRI has collaborated with the International Institute for Environment and Development (IIED: see page 253) to produce the annual *World Resources* series. The series, published by Basic Books, is subtitled 'An Assessment of the Resource Base that Supports the Global Economy'. Not a book most people would read from cover to cover, but an important reference source.

Equally useful have been the enormous number of publications produced by the Worldwatch Institute (see page 254). Particularly useful are the annual *State of the World* reports, published by W. W. Norton & Co. Inc, which monitor 'Progress Toward a Sustainable Society'. A helpful overview of Worldwatch's work was provided by *Building a Sustainable Society* (W. W. Norton, 1981), by Lester Brown.

If the economic dimensions of the ground covered by *The Green Capitalists* are of interest, try *The Living Economy: A New Economics in the Making*, edited by Paul Ekins (Routledge and Kegan Paul, 1986).

Of more general interest, perhaps, is a book which the present authors contributed to, *Gaia: An Atlas of Planet Management* (Pan Books, 1985). And for those with an interest in where all this activity sprang from, Max Nicholson's latest book, *The New Environmental Age* (Cambridge University Press, 1987), is a must.

Finally, anyone with a real need to keep up with what is happening at the industry-environment interface should subscribe to the pathfinding *ENDS Report*, published by Environmental Data Services (see page 253). If, on the other hand, you want a route map of where some of the new commercial opportunities are likely to open up in this area, *Green Pages* (compiled by the present authors and published by Routledge & Kegan Paul in 1988) could be the answer. And if 'green consumerism' and the growth of markets for 'environment-friendly' products and services are of interest, read *The Green Consumer Guide*, by John Elkington and Julia Hailes, published by Victor Gollancz Ltd in 1988.

INDEX